D0855882

Anaïs Nin Reader

Works of Anaïs Nin

Fiction

Ladders to Fire (*Swallow*)
Children of the Albatross (*Swallow*)
The Four-Chambered Heart (*Swallow*)
A Spy in the House of Love (*Swallow*)
Seduction of the Minotaur (*Swallow*)
Collages (*Swallow*)
Winter of Artifice (*Swallow*)
Under a Glass Bell (*Swallow*)
House of Incest (*Swallow*)

Non-fiction

D. H. Lawrence: An Unprofessional Study (*Swallow*)
The Novel of the Future (*Macmillan*)

The Diary of Anaïs Nin

Volume One 1931-1934 (*Harcourt/Swallow*)
Volume Two 1934-1939 (*Harcourt/Swallow*)
Volume Three 1939-1944 (*Harcourt*)
Volume Four 1944-1947 (*Harcourt*)

Anaïs Nin Reader

edited by

Philip K. Jason

introduction by

Anna Balakian

THE SWALLOW PRESS INC.
CHICAGO

Printed in the United States of America

First Edition
First Printing

Published by
The Swallow Press Incorporated
1139 South Wabash Avenue
Chicago, Illinois 60605

This book is printed on 100% recycled paper.

ISBN (CLOTHBOUND EDITION) 0-8040-0595-8
ISBN (PAPERBOUND EDITION) 0-8040-0596-6
LIBRARY OF CONGRESS CARD CATALOG NUMBER 72-91913

"The Poetic Reality of Anaïs Nin" by Anna Balakian was written for and first presented at a Magic Circles weekend celebration for Anaïs Nin in April 1972.

Contents

Anaïs Nin Reader

Foreword

> When a revolutionary spirit confronts his contemporaries, the violence of his contempt for banalities, for the dead weight of worn out traditions, for dead symbols as D.H. Lawrence called them, causes antagonism and resistance. Fear paralyzes understanding.
>
> Anaïs Nin, Preface to *Antonin Artaud: Man of Vision* by Bettina Knapp

Although Anaïs Nin has been a published writer for four decades, her work has been given serious critical attention only in recent years. One reason for the recognition of Nin's work having been so long delayed is its unconventional nature. The art of Anaïs Nin cuts across traditional literary categories. She combines poetic lyricism with an extended fable, blurring the distinction between poetry and prose. Her writings are presented to us both as separate, self-contained compositions and as part of a continuous work-in-progress; moreover, they hover in that contemporary no-man's-land between autobiography and fiction. Finally, she is a truly international writer whose work belongs to no one national literature.

Still, other factors played a part in the long underground career of Anaïs Nin's art. Significant among these was the belief, in part instigated by Nin herself, that her fictions were pallid reflections of her diaries.

Anaïs Nin began writing a detailed, private diary as a child. As an adult, she continued the diary; she also began to draw upon it for her fiction. Diary, stories, and novels existed side by side. The relationship between them was legendary, but not really known. The few privileged readers of the diaries in manuscript had kept us aware of them and had proclaimed, in advance, their importance. It was clear that her work had a continuous quality, in some ways similar to that of Miller and Beckett. There were recurrent types of situations, recurrent patterns of imagery, and continuing characters. In some of Miss Nin's creations, the narrator was explicitly a diarist.

The question that teased the curious reader for many years was "how great is the dependence of the fiction on the diary?" When the diaries began to be published in 1966, their popularity provided Miss Nin with a greater reading audience than she had ever had before. Instead of displacing the fiction, the diaries brought it new attention and esteem. The interdependence of Nin's diary and her fiction has been a fruitful one from which two essentially different renderings of experience have resulted. Her low-key radicalism, for so long either overshadowed by the work of more aggressively public writers or just plain misunderstood, began to be perceived as part of a significant modern tradition, a tradition with few representatives writing in the English language.

In 1942, Anaïs Nin had to set up her own hand press in Greenwich Village so that she could share her art with others. By the late 1940s a few of her works had been published by a major house, but they did not sell well enough to be kept in print. In 1961 Alan Swallow decided to reissue Nin's earlier work and to bring out her new fiction. Swallow's paperback editions introduced a new generation of readers to works that had been almost impossible to obtain for a decade. Then, in 1966, began the long-awaited publication of the diaries. By 1968, Miss Nin's own critical study, *The Novel of the Future,* was available, and in that same year Oliver Evans' *Anaïs Nin,* the first book-length study of her fiction, appeared. Early in 1970, the steadily increasing interest in Nin's life and art gave rise to a quarterly newsletter, *Under the Sign Pisces: Anaïs Nin and Her Circle.* Most recently, a comprehensive survey of all of Miss Nin's writings, *The Mirror and the Garden: Realism and Reality in the Writings of Anaïs Nin* (1971) by Evelyn J. Hinz, has been published.

The poetical novel, the novel of personal experience, the novel of psychological reality—each of these gained critical and popular acceptance in the United States during the 1950s and 1960s, as did various idiosyncratic combinations of these types. However, Anaïs Nin's growing popularity cannot be attributed solely to the public acceptance of other writers. The unique flavor of her work is finally more important than whatever critical labels may be placed upon it. One feature that differentiates her work from that of other poetic novelists is an old-fashioned dedication to ideas. Since Anaïs Nin's art develops from a theory of personality and psychological health, her fiction is not modishly noncommittal. Having first discovered how she is to be read, readers are more and more impressed by what she has to say.

Since Anaïs Nin considers the truths of the inner life to be the ultimate realities, her work is partly a rebellion against the "realist" tradition in fiction. Surface details are sparse, and they are never merely documentary, but are imagistic echoes of an emotional drama as well. The reader who needs to know what time it is, the pattern of the silverware, or how much dust has gathered on the wallpaper will be disappointed. Her art has little interest in what is most perishable. The designs she is after are the designs of human personality. The reader is invited to share the anxieties of Nin's characters, yet remains capable of detached evaluation. What a character only sees, the reader comes to understand as part of that character's pattern of perception.

The distinctions between realism and reality, between fact and truth, permeate all of Miss Nin's work: diary, fiction, and criticism. Writing about the diary in his essay, "Portrait of Anaïs Nin as Bodhisattva" (*Studies in the Twentieth Century,* Fall 1968), Wayne McEvilly described the uniqueness of Anaïs Nin's art most effectively:

> While many writers see what is before their eyes, Anaïs Nin looks into the heart of what confronts her, dissolving barriers, allowing us to participate, through the alchemy of her words, in the depths of the things which surround us and in whose shallows most lives are spent.

In making the following selections, I have attempted to represent the range of Miss Nin's art and interests as well as the contours of her career. A few pieces have been excerpted, but most of what appears here can be read as discrete units. The most important Nin characters are here, and so are many of her essential themes. Although I have separated the fiction from the non-fiction (including a passage from the diary), the reader may decided to pay strict attention to chronology and move back and forth between the critical ideas, the life in process, and the stories and novels that emerge as a crystallization of the artist's purposes and the woman's experiences.

The prose-poem *House of Incest* has a strong affinity with the productions of the French Symbolist movement. The relationship between Sabina and the narrator is presented as a misguided search for fulfillment. The narrator's controlling intelligence is beguiled by the instinctive and destructive night-world of Sabina. Ostensibly an external conflict of feminine prototypes, the relationship becomes incestuous in that the narrator's "love" is directed toward a figure who finally represents another, more submerged, part of herself. The House of Incest, then, is an extended conceit on the prison of self-love. The first of many failed attempts by Nin's characters to reconcile internal conflicts, *House of Incest* is marked by a lush orcestration of images, an unusually evocative auditory magic, and a surrealistic dream quality.

The unnamed narrator of *House of Incest* may be identified with the protagonist of "Winter of Artifice" and with Djuna of "The Voice" and the novels. In "Winter of Artifice" the theme of narcissism is continued in terms of the relationship between father and daughter. Destructively depending on distorted visions of each other, the characters are torn between continuing an empty charade which allows for a superficial security or accepting the reality of their mutual shortcomings. The "Djuna" character can finally no longer pretend to have found the father of her childhood imagination; neither can she pretend to be the "double" to whom he directs his crippled love.

All of Miss Nin's fictional pieces may be thought of as charting the ebbs and flows of the disturbed self moving toward psychic integration. In the story "Houseboat," the protagonist takes refuge from the chaotic world of external reality into the world of dreams. Since this movement is not so much a matter of choice as of psychological necessity, it is not evaluated on traditional moral grounds. "Ragtime" is a brief, impressionistic jewel. The ragpicker is a kind of alchemist who can put the remnants of old objects to new uses. The narrator who invents him and follows him in his wanderings is ironically added to the bag of materials to be recycled. This twist underscores the fable's affirmation that the process of mutability has spiritual as well as material levels. In the celebrated story, "Birth," we are given a most realistic dramatization of this same truth: the experience of this movement is not so much a matter of choice as of psychological study, "Hejda" is one of a number of Nin's narratives that explores as a secondary theme the conflict of cultures. Readers interested in the women's liberation movement may find still another layer of significance.

In selecting from the five novels that make up *Cities of the Interior,* I have been forced to be less than representative because of space limitations. Rather than give bits and pieces from each, I have decided to present a major sub-section from *Children of the Albatross,* an early novel, and the opening passages from *Seduction of the Minotaur,* the last. Certain differences in style will be obvious, especially the greater integration of the inner story with the surface of the external world in the later piece.

"The Sealed Room" section of *Children of the Albatross* is a tightly controlled narrative focusing on Djuna's relationship with a group of young men, adolescents, to whom she is an enchanting mother figure. Evelyn Hinz has suggested that Djuna's experiences "reveal the triple need in woman for the child, the father, and the lover, and the necessity for keeping these roles unconfused." Father and lover are confused in "Winter of Artifice," child and lover in "The Sealed Room." Djuna sympathizes with the problems that the youths have with ineffective, authoritarian parents, and feels the need to give them understanding, encouragement, and dignity. In providing sanctuary for these young men, particularly Paul, Djuna comes to realize that she has not overcome her own childhood injuries, and that her maternal giving is not completely selfless. Living in a closed, safe, and largely illusory world is again seen as a necessity rather than a fault, but the "sealed room" can only be a temporary haven. In the second section of *Children of the Albatross,* "The Cafe," Djuna moves into a world of larger social context.

All of Nin's major female figures make this outward journey. Lillian, who is most prominent in the first and last of the *Cities* novels, is considered by Oliver Evans to be the central figure of the series. He calls her "a woman of unbounded, restless vitality and voracious appetites." *Ladders to Fire,* the first novel of *Cities,* explores the failure of her marriage to Larry and her futile attempts to find herself in affairs with other men (and with Sabina). In *Seduction of the Minotaur,* Lillian has taken a job in a resort town in Mexico. In new surroundings she feels an illusionary freedom and sense of renewal. Still, this step towards greater self-dependence, though a faltering one, is better than no action at all. As the novel proceeds, Lillian perceives that her new experiences curiously mirror those of her past; that is, she sees more clearly her own part in earlier misfortunes. With this added perspective, the anticipated progress towards greater stability begins. Her journey homeward is hallmarked by a cautious optimism.

Since Miss Nin's third major character, Sabina, has not been represented in these selections from the novels, I have included the previously uncollected story, "Sabina." This piece condenses some of the intricacies of *A Spy in the House of Love* (the fourth novel of *Cities*), continues the development of that character, and provides for interesting comparisons with the Sabina of *House of Incest.*

At the beginning of these remarks I observed that there is a continuous quality to Miss Nin's work. The Nin canon, particularly the *Cities of the Interior* sequence, can be viewed as an organic whole. The overall impression is similar to a mosaic. Yet each piece has an integrity of its own. *Collages,* Anaïs Nin's most recent fiction work, is a microcosm of the structural method that one can perceive organizing the whole body of her writing. In *Collages* many settings, characters, and stories are held together by recurring themes, the presence of Renate as a fairly consistent point of view, and the central intelligence of the narrator whose acts of juxtaposition involve risks that we are invited to share. More than any of Miss Nin's previous works, *Collages* has abundant wit. Moreover, Miss Nin seems to direct a good deal of that wit at herself. Described by Sharon Spencer as a "mobile construct" (*Space, Time and Structure in the Modern Novel,* 1971), *Collages* doubles back on itself to remind us that beginnings and ends are arbitrary focal points that have little to do with Nin's view of art or life.

Miss Nin's critical prose takes second place to her fiction both in achievement and general interest. It is a criticism written from the writer's perspective, and her observations are often most enlightening about her own work. *D. H. Lawrence: An Unprofessional Study* was

Anaïs Nin's first book. It is most useful as an early statement of her own position as an aspiring artist rather than as an exposition on Lawrence. Lawrence's influence on Nin's fiction is a qualified one, but any Nin student will benefit from determining the direction in which Nin's reading of Lawrence headed her. Writers have generally had more praise for the Lawrence study than have critics. In fact, the manuscript of this work led to the first meeting between Anaïs Nin and Henry Miller.

For many years Anaïs Nin's place in popular literary history was only that of friend and confidante to Henry Miller. One of a number of people who watched *Tropic of Cancer* take shape, she found herself aiding in bringing about its publication. Her understanding of the landmark significance of *Cancer* is conveyed in her Preface, which is still the best short appreciation of that work.

Anaïs Nin communicated her early enthusiasm for Otto Rank's psychological work to Miller as well as to other friends. In Rank's exploration of the artistic personality and in such studies as *Don Juan. Une Etude Sur le Double,* she found confirmation of her own intuitions. The essence of Rank's teaching, as it applies to the creative personality, is presented in Nin's "Review of Rank's *Art and Artist.*" Since Nin's relationship with Rank included being a patient, a student, and an assistant, the student of Nin's writing must eventually become a student of Rank as well.

"The Id of Dostoevsky" is a review of Edward Wasiolek's translation of the notebooks for *Crime and Punishment.* Nin's comments on the creative process, especially on the interaction between life and art, between autobiography and fiction, provide insights into the nature of her own works. We are once again reminded of the European traditions with which Nin is most congenial and of Henry Miller's early comparison of Nin's diaries to "the raw pith of some post-Dostoevskian novel" (*The Cosmological Eye,* 1939).

The selections from *The Novel of the Future* describe in satisfying detail Nin's own theory and practice in developing a mutually beneficial relationship between autobiography and art. Still, the greatest discoveries are not to be found in Miss Nin's explanations, useful as they are, but in the reader's own journey through Nin's life and art.

No single excerpt from Anaïs Nin's diary can fairly suggest the intricate, interlacing patterns of a consciousness in deliberate and delicate search of itself that that work as a whole conveys. The short passage presented here is an exceptionally self-contained part of that patterning. One of Nin's basic image-motifs, that of the labyrinth, is carried out most effectively in this story of a trip to Morocco. Associated with the labyrinth image is a poetic treatment of the psychology of veiling; here are basic insights that are developed in many of Nin's characterizations, including that of Hejda. The detail of the Arabic women's use of kohl dust for eye makeup is turned to advantage in Miss Nin's portrait of the mysterious and exotic Sabina in *A Spy in the House of Love.*

The diary, primarily significant as a literary seismograph of psychic pilgrimage, is also valuable, then, as a sourcebook for Miss Nin's fictive art. A careful study of the diary and the fiction together reveals the distillations, selections, transmutations, and elaborations of the creative process. In the diary we have not only the story of the making of an artistic personality, but also the personal experiences which are later blended with imagination and shaped to take on a life of their own.

PHILIP K. JASON

◈ This symbol is used to indicate excisions in original Nin material made for the purpose of this *Reader*.

Chronology

1903	Born in Neuilly, France.
1932	*D. H. Lawrence: An Unprofessional Study* (Paris)
1934	"Preface" to Miller's *Tropic of Cancer.*
1936	*House of Incest* (Paris).
1937-39	Associated with *The Booster* and *Delta,* publications of the Villa Seurat circle.
1939	*Winter of Artifice* (Paris); relocates in New York's Greenwich Village.
1942	Establishes Gemor Press; reissues *Winter of Artifice* (New York).
1944	*Under a Glass Bell* (New York: Gemor Press).
1945	*Winter of Artifice, revised* (New York: Gemor Press). *This Hunger* (New York: Gemor Press); sections of this book incorporated into later volumes.
1946	*Realism and Reality* (New York); *Ladders to Fire* (New York: E. P. Dutton).
1947	*On Writing* (New York); reissues *House of Incest* (New York: Gemor Press); *Children of the Albatross* (New York: E. P. Dutton).
1948	*Under a Glass Bell* & *Winter of Artifice* in one volume (New York: E. P. Dutton).
1950	*The Four-Chambered Heart* (New York: Duell, Sloan and Pearce).
1954	*A Spy in the House of Love* (New York: British Book Center).

1958 *Solar Barque* (Ann Arbor).

1959 *Ladders to Fire, Children of the Albatross, The Four-Chambered Heart, A Spy in the House of Love,* and *Solar Barque* collected in one volume as *Cities of the Interior* (New York).

1961 Nin's fiction reissued by Alan Swallow (Denver); *Seduction of the Minotaur* (Denver: Swallow).

1964 *D. H. Lawrence: An Unprofessional Study* reissued (Denver: Swallow); *Collages* (Denver: Swallow).

1966 *The Diary of Anais Nin, 1931-1934* (New York: Swallow and Harcourt, Brace & Jovanovich).

1967 *The Diary of Anais Nin, 1934-1939* (New York: Harcourt, Brace & Jovanovich).

1968 *The Novel of the Future* (New York: MacMillan).

1969 *The Diary of Anais Nin, 1939-1944* (New York: Harcourt, Brace & Jovanovich).

1971 *The Diary of Anais Nin, 1944-1947* (New York: Harcourt, Brace & Jovanovich).

Introduction

THE POETIC REALITY OF ANAÏS NIN

In terms of contemporary definitions of reality, dream, the human psyche, and its communication through the mythology of signs and symbols, Anaïs Nin's work looms as a constellation of first magnitude. Since these elements have assumed greater priorities in the composition of the novel now than when she began to write, our receptivity to her work is more direct and propitious than it was at the moment of the work's genesis.

Literary criticism does not occur in a vacuum; unless it is purely impressionistic, it can best speak of the unknown in its relation to the known, which means that Anaïs Nin's work appearing in the 1930s and 1940s was immediately associated with the pattern of the successful novel of the time. But in *Cities of the Interior,* she was challenging both the realistic and the psychological novel so ably practiced at the time by the giants of American and European literature. To her, as she explains in the *Novel of the Future,* they contained a common element which equated them: they both oversimplified the human psyche and reduced it through rational analyses. "Too much lucidity," she says, "creates a desert."

But the "desert" of the European novel between the two world wars, and even afterward, was a fruitful one. Particularly as the European novel developed among American writers who dominated the literary scene, it distinguished itself primarily in terms of three basic features: sociological realism, psychological realism, psychological rationalism, and the inception of demotic language into the literary context. On all three counts Anaïs Nin's writing proved unrelated to it. The great books of our era have, from the point of view of sociology, brought into crystallization the American mores, the ethnic separations, urban poverty, archetypal middle class heroes, regional deviations, and the strata of the multifaceted realities of such groups as the social elite. When they have delved into the psychological factors that motivate the hero or antihero, they have had a distinctly and rather superficially Freudian approach. The interior monologue and the autopsychoanalysis that dominated so many novels were indeed reductive devices that resolved problems in terms of a priori value structure such as sin, guilt, complex, frustration, obsession—elements suggesting the impoverishing or deteriorating qualities of the human personality. The built-in and recognized notion of reality presupposed a structure of norms; conflicts of the fictional reality were unfurled in terms of these so-called normal values; the notion of the tragic or the absurd resolution of conflicts was dependent on ingrained, collective determination of what is normal and what is abnormal, what is true and untrue, what is fidelity and adultery, what is innocence and what is evil. The fictional archetypes either disintegrated in the process of confrontation with the code or they transcended it; but even rebellion was defined in terms of the concerted notion of conformity. Nothing is abnormal unless you first propose the dimensions of the normal; nothing is irrational unless you have consensus as to what is rational, nothing is unreal unless you agree on the tenets of the real.

The armor with which American realism covered itself was the development of a demotic language. Previously, even in realistic literature when all else was a transcription of vital statistics, the use of language created a distinct separation between journalistic communication and the language of literary text. Gradually the literary uniqueness of language disappeared and the gap between oral and written language closed, making this transfer one of the most characteristic features of our current literary form.

In the midst of this current toward absorbing the fictional world of the literary artists into the mainstream of phenomenal experience, literature in America gradually lost its ontological character: it was no longer a reality in itself but the written, documentary of events.

Relating the work of Anaïs Nin to this literary orientation is like relating the plays of Yeats to the London stage of his time. If Yeats did not document the mores of his time, that was simply not the intention of his work. His was a poetic and universal reality. So is Anaïs Nin's. She does observe the mores and the places of their framework, but her observation is gauged on a level where time and region are not determinants of judgment and truth. Her work contains none of the dimensions of that reality defined by her generation of novelists: it reveals no group dynamics because Anaïs Nin's world is peopled by individuals; it contains no linear psychological consistency because in the revelations of human personality there are enigmas and half-opened windows but no generalizations to guide us. If the rest of the world measured, mathematically speaking, according to base ten, her computations of reality had an entirely different base. She arrives at reality through inductive observation and experience; she projects the human psyche not through reductive, analytical procedures, but through a series of revelations, showing not deviations from a norm, but a fluidity of progression from one form to another. Her work has no trace of demotic speech. The language she uses belongs to no school or time or placé, but it builds up its own code; words have their special meanings, and symbols which are culled from the common body of mythology take on particular significances in the code of her reality.

The first problem that comes up in discussing Anaïs Nin's work is the relationship of the diary to the creative writing. In the case of a diarist such as André Gide, the procedure is easy. The memoirs record facts, give outright confessions, which the critic studies to determine the creative transformation of materials into fictional reality. Knowledge of Gide in the journals furnishes clarity of comprehension of the man, and leads to the kind of method recommended by the 19th century patron of critics, Sainte-Beuve: to understand the work through the study of the man, for the relation of the work to the man is as the fruit to the tree. Following this precept it would indeed be nice and easy to suggest that Anaïs Nin is a fountainhead of sensibilities and perceptions overflowing into two parallel streams: one the diary, the other the continuous novel. It would be so convenient to propose that one stream represents reality, the other fiction. But the psyche of Anaïs Nin does not project into written language in such a convenient manner. The diary has creative perspective, the creative writing is drenched in lived experience. In fact, the diary and the creative work are like two communicating vessels, and the division is an imaginary one; they feed each other constantly, the diary feeds the imagination with encounter and experience, the creative process invades the diary with its iridescence, transforming the perceptions of the author in regard to her sensory data and emotional reactions to events. Moreover, at times one has the feeling that the diary has a literary structure as much and even more than the novels; if it reflects a life, it reveals, at least in the parts that have been published, *chosen* moments, *chosen* events, highlights rather than composites of personalities; the climate that the author breathes in the diary and that her characters breathe in the loose-fitting pattern of the novels is the same.

To grasp Anaïs Nin's notion of reality, therefore, I feel that it should be viewed as a composite of the two forms through which the author chose to express herself; and most important, it has to be considered in its evolutionary character, just as we discover that her characters do not reveal their truth in one portrait sitting, but as their picture is taken in successive stages, as they travel from one City of the Interior to the next.

If the work of Anaïs Nin is not compatible with the general guidelines of fiction, it is much more intimately related to two currents in European poetry and contains within its progression the special conflict of philosophy and style that occurred in the passage from Symbolism to Surrealism. Although Anaïs Nin chose to express herself through the forms of the diary and the novel, the quality of her communication and the pitch of her literary voice were much more in harmony with the poetic evolution of European poetry than with the American novel.

Certainly the heritage conveyed to her by her musician father was a symbolist one, that of the later symbolists of the turn of the century: Yeats, Oscar Wilde, Válery, T.S. Eliot, Debussy and Fauré. Her early work is penetrated by many of the elements of a *fin de siècle* philosophy and its delicacy of communication through suggestion rather than outright description. The large influence of music on human sensibilities, the rarefaction of the concrete, physical attributes of the exterior world, a language vague and evocative, emulating the non-conceptual communication which we generally associate with musical expression, are pronounced characteristics of her writing.

The symbolist psyche was one of self-containment, introverted self-contemplation, preoccupation with inscapes. The symbolist eye sucked the material substance of the surrounding and turned it into idealized, formless, fluid images all bearing the imprint of the writer's own psyche. The language of the symbolist was a purification of all functional connotations; it created, as Mallarmé stated, the flower that is absent from all bouquets, i.e. the flower *as essence.*

As one reads Anaïs Nin's early writings, which as she says contain "the seed of all my work," such as the pieces that constitute *House of Incest, Under a Glass Bell,* and parts of *Winter of Artifice,* the birth of the symbols that will eventually run throughout her work have their initial appearances: the glass, the mirror, the water are images that envelope. They cover, protect, separate, imprison.

The mirror is misty: "vision like human breath blinding a mirror," she says (*House of Incest,* 22 [34]).* The atmosphere is pervaded with smoke, and low ceilings threaten us. One is reminded of Baudelaire's imagery from *Spleen et Idéal* when Anaïs Nin conveys the same obsessive image of oppression in terms of "a vast lead roof which covers the world like the lid of a soup pan." There is greyness in the air, and narrow horizons obstruct the heroine's vistas. She is "at war with sun and light," "her smile is closed," her abodes remind one of Mallarmé's *Herodiade*: she inhabits cellars and belfries, she is as a princess in Byzantium—the mythological concept of Byzantium with which the symbolists identified, a place of beauty and impending downfall.

The famous labyrinth symbol that will also run through the entire work of Anaïs Nin is at first not a channel of liberation but the movement of a non-voyage into constricted places, the refuge places where dream protects the sensitive creature from reality.

* All quotations are from current editions. Page numbers enclosed in brackets indicate where a cited passage can be found in this *Reader.*

> To destroy reality. I will help you: it is I who will invent lies for you and with them we will traverse the world. But behind our lies I am dropping Ariadne's golden thread—for the greatest of all joys is to be able to retrace one's lies, to return to the source and sleep one night a year washed of all superstructures. (*House of Incest*, p. 26 [37])

The dream in this first stage of Anaïs Nin's work is not a source of illumination but a submergence. It is closely associated with the kind of love which is ingrown: that for father, sister, members of the same sex, all related to the cult of Narcissism, or self-contemplation and self-love.

The route through which she moves is, as she calls it in the beginning, "the route of the dream." But the dream has to be protected from the pervasive character of external reality. In this sense the first world of Anaïs Nin resembles that of symbolist heroines like Mélisande, Herodiade, Deirdre; it is a distinct evasion of the brutality of exterior reality, effacing that reality to put in its place unrealizable loves, blurred, misty visions, subterranean tunnels constantly confronted by impasses, negative images of attritions and wastelands similar to T. S. Eliot's scenery in the first four lines of *The Waste Land* or of Stefan George's *Algabal*: garden of decapitated trees, dead meteors, dried semen, sceneries in which nature's power of metamorphosis and transmutation has failed. Even the image of the sea and the ship, which are in general liberating images, convey in the early work of Anaïs Nin just the opposite impact. The sea is associated with curtain, veil, blanket. As she says at the beginning of *House of Incest*:

> My first vision of earth was water veiled. I am of the race of men and women who see all things through this curtain of the sea. (p. 15 [33])

The isle of non-reality and non-existence toward which she voyages is precisely the lost continent of Atlantis where the poetic vision of Anaïs Nin mingles with the lost sounds, lost colors, soundless music—in a state where there is no cold, no heat, no hunger, no weeping. Fishes and flowers have the countenances and contours of unreality and artifice. Even in her use of present participles she creates an atmosphere of weightlessness reminiscent of Mallarmé's *Coup de dés.*

Anaïs Nin's first fiction book, *House of Incest,* conceived under the sign of dissolution, transforms even the most common symbol of movement and displacement, the ship into a shipwreck, a skeleton of a ship, choked in its own sails, sails which become ripped apart in a later image. The language spoken is "the language of nerves:"

> The shadow of death running after each word so that they wither before she has finished uttering them. (p. 48)

The mirror image is a purely Narcissist one in these early writings. It reflects the self-image and the self-love even in the guise of a brother, a sister, or a woman likeness. "Our love of each other is like one long shadow kissing without hope of reality" (*House of Incest,* p. 48).

But if we have piled up the evidence to bring into focus the archetypal image of the Symbolist hero or heroine, we must adjust our lens. The interesting phrase in the last quotation is "without hope," which in the act of desperation implies a desire for release and carries a built-in indictment of a condition. As in a musical composition, there is a point where the music turns, modulates from one key to another; so in *House of Incest* there occurs a turning point, after which the ethereal beauty of the world of illusion carries an element of self-censure, brought to its climax in *Under a Glass Bell* and *Winter of Artifice.* "Without hope" becomes an anguished drive for self-demystification and liberation. The narrator and her alter ego, Jeanne, reach a position of confrontation and disparity. The narrator is led to innermost haunts of the House of Incest, into a room without window, where the beat of time is lost and where everything takes on the static posture of finality; but the narrator refuses to accept the situation, for the descriptions have a built-in vocabulary of criticism:

> The collision between their resemblances, shedding the odor of tamarisk and sand, of rotted shells and dying sea-weeds, their love like the ink of squids, a banquet of poisons. (*House of Incest,* p. 52 [39])

Through the image of a "modern Christ" who dreamed of having his skin peeled off so that he would be receptive to all the impacts of sensory reality, the wish is spoken:

> If only we could all escape from this house of incest, where we only love ourselves in the other, if only I could save you all from yourselves, said the modern Christ. (*House of Incest,* p. 70 [42])

There are two other images in the closing sequences of *House of Incest* that prefigure the conversion: the tunnel that leads out of the house opens up into broad daylight, and a dancer dances away from those who are trapped in the House of Incest, "dancing towards daylight." So it is on the word "daylight" that *House of Incest* ends, just as Rimbaud's *Une Saison en enfer,* with which it has been compared, ends in dawn and with the rejection of night, moving toward freedom.

In the next volume, *Under a Glass Bell,* the title story is a portrait of Jeanne in which the narrator can take a more objective stance and cast an ironic look of censure. Jeanne speaks in a confessional tone; she walks into a house in which mirrors cover the walls and ceilings. The picture is striking and terrifying:

> Jeanne walked into the house and entered the room of mirrors. Ceilings of mirrors, floors of mirrors, windows of quicksilver opening on windows of quicksilver. The air was made of gelatine. Around her hair there was a saffron aureole and her skin was a sea shell, an egg shell. There was a lunar wax light on the rim of her shoulder. Woman imprisoned in the stillness of mirrors washed only by jellied colors.... On her breast grew flowers of dust and no wind came from earth to disturb them. (p. 40)

The narrator's own confession about her dream-trapped condition and the labyrinth which the diary has become appear in the story, "The Labyrinth." We are first given several other images of labyrinth from nature's own pattern: soft turning canals of ears, honeycomb of ivory-white cells, leaf pattern of intricate flowers, network of streets like seashells. After the motif is established, we proceed to the metaphor of the diary:

> Serpentines of walls without doorways, desires without issues... I was lost in the labyrinth of my confessions, among the veiled faces of my acts unveiled only in the diary. I heard the evening prayer, the cry of solitude recurring every night... The white orifice of the endless cave opened. On the rim of it stood a girl eleven years old carrying the diary in a little basket. (*Under a Glass Bell,* pp. 66-67)

In other words, it is interesting to note that at the beginning the diary is a means of refuge which, in retrospect, the author views with a certain degree of self-censure manifest in words such as "lost," "solitude," "veil," and "mutilation." Even as in the novels, the purpose of the diary as it reaches the level of publication will be changed from refuge to release, as Anaïs Nin reaches a change of posture.

"The All-Seeing," another story from *Under a Glass Bell,* seems to be a transitional piece. We are introduced to another labyrinthian character; but this time there is in him the resonance of reality even as the sound of the waves inside a seashell. It is a story of the inadequacy of dream conceived as detachment from reality. And in this short piece we have premonitions of a new concept of the dream as a resolution of the dichotomy between dream and reality. The conciliation of the notion of opposites:

> Two people who love the dream above all else would soon vanish altogether. One of them must be on earth to hold the other down. And the pain of being held down by the earth, that is what our love for others will be. (p. 76)

The narrator, described by Jean, seems like a prisoner about to be liberated, whose love of other prisoners is the only obstacle in the way of the open door.

Winter of Artifice is a crossroad. As the father image fades, the narrator gravitates toward the summer solstice. She realizes that the music of the father is still-life meditation. Music becomes rhythm, vibration, the spiral leading to reality. If we compare the synchronization of the novels with the diary we find that at this time the author comes in contact with Jungian psychology, and in "The Voice" we see psychiatry as a releasing agent. The dream's position is transformed. The Jungian device leaves its impact as the author accepts the motto: "from the dream outward." Henceforth the images of descent into consciousness and dream, the spirals of downward movement are replaced by a ladder intentioned for climbing upward even if there is the danger of fire at the top. The censure of a total kind of introspection is more explicit: "Bring me one who knows that the dream without exit, without explosion, without awakening, is the passageway to the world of the dead" (*Ladders,* p. 151).

Now it is interesting to observe that although in the most fertile era of the surrealists Anaïs Nin was writing in a symbolist vein, the one surrealist she was closest to was Antonin Artaud, the very one who, in terms of philosophy and physiognomy, was the farthest removed from the surrealists. He could join the surrealist world only through laudanum. Pierre, as he is called in Anaïs Nin's story, "Je Suis Le Plus Malade des Surréalistes," is a creature who "draws everything inward," a brother of Jeanne, and of Jean, and of all the other refugees from reality. His anguish had little to do with the visionary reality of the surrealists. There are allusions to several contacts with André Breton's cénacle in the diary, but they are not of an intimate nature. If Anaïs Nin identifies with surrealism in her evolution from dreaming inward to dreaming outward, and in her eventual philosophy of love as a dynamic release from the cult of self, of the luminosity of human character, and of so many other characteristics that can be identified with essential surrealism, it seems to me that it is not simply through direct influence that she reaches this luminosity and the identification of art as knowledge and revelation, but rather by being in contact with the same sources as the surrealists and by developing in the same direction as André Breton. The kind of psychoanalysis to which Anaïs Nin was introduced appears to be the same as that to which Breton was exposed at the Faculty of Medicine in Paris, based on the teachings of Pierre Janet. The distinction between Janet and Freud is precisely the distinction between psychiatry as applied in most modern novels, and the one manifest in Anaïs Nin's observation of real life and created personalities, and as it is defined in Breton's surrealist manifestoes: i.e., the exploration of the depth of consciousness as a power for release and domination of reality, and as a channel for the liberation of the imagination for everyman. The teachings of Janet had a tremendous influence on Breton. They showed him that the observation of the subconscious need not necessarily be motivated by the desire to correct deviations from the norm, as in pathological cases: the study of the unconscious was meant better to comprehend the vistas of consciousness itself, to break the barriers of reality, to bring about a new grasp of sexuality, not in terms of neurosis but of its catalytic expansion of the sense of being and the comprehension of the metamorphoses of personality. In *Seduction of the Minotaur* the probe is likened to an archeological expedition: "geological depths where lay hidden the imprisoned self" (p. 95).

The art and life experience of Anaïs Nin are not derivative of Breton's, but parallel, concurrent, synchronic. In trying to rejuvenate art by expanding the field of consciousness, they arrived at the same global definitions of love, liberty, and poetry.

"From the dream outward"; it is the same image that Breton gives in his *Les Vases Communicants*: the dream feeds reality and actualizes desire. This is the theme of all Breton's poems. To be a poet is to create this constant stream between the dream and what we experience when we are awake. Over this stream is the bridge by means of which the subjective world and the objective are in constant conjugation, indivisible. Soon, as Breton said, there is no object, only subject. Lillian in *Seduction of the Minotaur* associates her feeling with the Talmudic words: "We do not see things as they are, we see them as we are" (p. 124).

But the subjective vision no longer produces a hothouse plant; it is projected into the outer world, there to combine with other beings, to make the inert object unique.

The role of the novelist in this neosurrealist context becomes modified. The enigma of human personality is not resolved or reduced, but rather conveyed. There is no lucid comprehension at the end of a story, but a synthesis of all the parts that have been viewed whether in quick succession or in collage, in juxtaposition or in superposition like the metaphors of a poem. The projected personality in the novel is a composite whole made up of the disparate entities that constitute a human psyche. When there is incomprehension between characters it is because they are clinging to one photograph of themselves or each other instead of realizing the possible replacements. In explaining the alienation of Larry and Lillian in *Seduction of the Minotaur,* the narrator says:

> The passageway of their communication with each other had shrunk. They had singled out their first image of each other, to live forever, regardless of change or growth. They had set it upon their desks, and within their hearts, a photograph of Larry as he had first appeared behind the garden gate, mute and hungry, and a photograph of Lillian in distress because her faith in herself had been killed by her parents. (p. 102)

In *The Four-Chambered Heart,* Djuna's self-analysis leads to the same kind of realization: "The trap was the static pause in growth, the arrested self caught in its own web of obstinacy and obsession" (p. 179).

"I is another," said Rimbaud, from whom the surrealists derived so many of their attitudes. In breaking the mirror that reflected constantly and hauntingly the single image, as we noticed in the early writings, Anaïs Nin learned from open contact with many others, from the richness of her associations, the variety implicit in the universal psyche, As we glide through her parade of recurring characters in and out of the diary and in and out of the continuous novel, we may indeed be disappointed if we are looking for a totality of characterization. Totality means static completion. The characters of Anaïs Nin are in flux, in movement, in the process of becoming. They have, therefore, the flowing forms of Dali watches, or suggest power, rather than contour. One can indeed liken her characters to the word portrait that Breton gives of woman in *L'Union Libre.* The relationship between characters no longer creates the effect of equating each other, dissolving each other, but rather enriching each other. This is how the relationship between Lillian and Sabina is explained in *Ladders to Fire*:

> They both wanted to exchange bodies, exchange faces. There was in both of them the dark strain of wanting to become the other, to deny what they were, to transcend their actual selves. (p. 124)

What is the role that love plays in these later works? It is no longer self-adoration, but a vitalizing force, projected toward the other and combining that quality that some have called "pity," but which may be better identified with "charity," caritas, in its etymological sense of total love, a word again so close to Rimbaud, a longing for the innocence of love, the generosity and gratuity of love, the semblance of the sacred communion. It is implicit in Breton's love poetry, in his relationship with his last wife, Elisa, in *Arcane 17*; it is a running motif in volumes three and four of the diary and in *A Spy in the House of Love,* and already suggested in *Ladders to Fire*:

> Not to possess each other but to become each other, not to take but to imbibe, absorb, change themselves" (p. 125).

As the dream is projected into outer reality, the notions of time and place undergo the same type of mutation as in surrealist writing. Chronology disappears because like Breton she is not about to give us an account of the empty moments of her life, or of the life of her characters. The critic Frank Kermode in his book, *Sense of an Ending,* has well analyzed the mutation of the time factor in the experimental novel. He aptly distinguishes between the *kairos* of time, that is, the dynamic moments that one can distinguish from the measured ones or *chronos.* It is always *kairos* in the diary and in the novels of Anaïs Nin, unless she is showing the inertia of the other kind of time. There is, moreover, through the choice of highlighted events, an immediacy in the encounters of Anaïs Nin, whether in the diary or in the novels, which make the present tense the dominant moment of action; in fact, in contrast to Proust, who like the symbolists was an introspective artist, memory is cast aside by Anaïs Nin when it interferes with the full enjoyment of the present time. Hers is a Bergsonian time duration in which past, present and future mingle selectively.

As for places, they are always illuminated in the later works, i.e., after her vision has emerged from the House of Incest. In some of Anaïs Nin's descriptions there is an emblematic persistence of the Chirico mystery of denuded streets, but as she pours the dream out into the familiar landmarks in her environment, whether in Paris or in New York, it takes on the glow of adventure or an unexpectedly explosive vitality. "She devoured the noises of the street... she was only the finger of a whole bigger body, a body hungry, thirsty, avid" (*Ladders to Fire*, p. 88).

The symbols of darkness and of misty, cloudy skies disappear and are replaced by a search for luminosity just as in Breton's poetry. Breton once said that man's greatest curse was his opacity. A good part of Anaïs Nin's work is this journey from opacity to light. On the way she discovers phosphorescence, which becomes a dominant motif both in the diary and in the novels; in fact, her attraction to people or the attraction of her characters to each other depends a great deal on the degree of phosphorescence that radiates from them. The albatross image in her work does not have the emblematic character of Baudelaire's albatross. In Baudelaire's poem the albatross represented the mighty poet, clumsy in ordinary life activities as he is brought down to earth, just as the mariners bring the mighty albatross down to their deck; Anaïs Nin is attracted to the albatross because it has a phosphorescent glow. She explains it beautifully in the fourth volume of the diary in connection with her lack of rapport with Edmund Wilson:

> Wilson, if he ever tastes of me, will be eating a substance not good for him, some phosphorescent matter which illuminates the soul and does not answer to lust. Impossible, for we are children of the albatross, and our luminosity is a poison! (p. 84)

All the way through her many encounters she searches for the children of the albatross, those humans, mostly young, who still preserve the luminous center of their essence. It is the sign of their inner dream: "each one threw upon the other the spotlight of his inner dream," she says in *Children of the Albatross* (p. 37 [142]). In *Ladders to Fire* she describes another character as having eyes which left phosphorescent streaks.

The labyrinth occupies in Anaïs Nin's work as important a place as in that of many contemporary writers such as Breton, Beckett, Alain Robbe-Grillet, Octavio Paz, Luis Borges, and others. To look at some of these others first, the same mythological emblem serves many purposes. In the symbolist frame of reference it signifies refuge and barrier, conveying the feeling of being trapped. In the non-anthropocentric world of Beckett and Alain Robbe-Grillet, it is the symbol of confusion and drifting. For Breton and for Octavio Paz it symbolizes man's conquest of obstacles in his effort toward liberation and the liberation of the spirit.

In Anaïs Nin's writing, the labyrinth is ambivalent and undergoes a change of function. It is representative of the human personality. At first it is constricted; it is an emblem of fear and frustration not only in terms of the human being's passage through it, but of his fear of what he will find at the end of it. In *Seduction of the Minotaur* we find in the beginning that Lillian came to Golconda to flee from the labyrinth:

> There were tears in Lillian's eyes, for having made friends immediately not with a new, a beautiful, a drugging place, but with a man intent on penetrating the mysteries of the human labyrinth from which she was a fugitive. (p. 19 [195])

But as in the case of Voltaire's Candide who visited Eldorado, she soon finds out that gold and bliss and serenity can become boring if they are a constant; at least that is the opinion of another visitor, Michael, who has stayed around Golconda for some time: "The gaiety and liveliness of Golconda hurts me, like too much light in your eyes" (*Seduction*, p. 67). Lillian takes up once more her battle with the labyrinth and at the end of the passages of darkness she is illuminated by the revelation of its true meaning. Her own image looms, suggesting in the moment of self-knowledge that indeed we have to fear only fear itself:

> She had come face to face with it, the Minotaur resembled someone she knew. It was not a monster. It was a reflection upon a mirror, a masked woman, Lillian herself, the hidden masked part of herself unknown to her, who had ruled her acts. She extended her hand toward this tyrant who could no longer harm her. It lay upon the mirror of the plane's round portholes, traveling through the clouds, a fleeting face, her own, clear and definable only when darkness came. (p. 111)

At the beginning of *Seduction of the Minotaur* the ship that we had seen earlier in a state of wreck and destruction is whole again but still incapable of movement. This incapacity is brilliantly conveyed in the metaphor of a ship trying to move through an inappropriate medium, i.e., land. It is the image of desperate dislocation:

> Lillian's recurrent dream of a ship that could not reach the water, that sailed laboriously, pushed by her with great effort, through city streets, had determined her course toward the sea, as if she would give this ship, once and for all, its proper sea bed. (p. 5 [183])

The obsessive image of the ship-dream recurs again a little later in even more gripping form:

> The dream of a boat, sometimes large and sometimes small, but invariably caught in a waterless place, in a street, in the jungle, in the desert. When it was large it was in the city streets and the deck reached to the upper windows of the houses. She was in this boat and aware that it could not float unless it were pushed, so she would get down from it and seek to push it along so that it might move and the street was immense and she never accomplished her aim. Whether she pushed it along cobblestones or over asphalt, it moved very little, and no matter how much she strained she always felt she would never reach the sea. When the boat was small the pushing was less difficult; nevertheless she never reached the lake or river or the sea in which it could said. Once the boat was stuck between rocks, another time on a mud bank. (*Seduction,* p. 23 [198])

It can be observed that whereas in earlier books the sea was a covering, a mist producing envelope, here it eventually becomes the emblem of liberation. The passage through Golconda becomes indeed a liberating experience for Lillian because finally the ship begins to move as it reaches the element through which it can function:

> Today she was fully aware that the dream of pushing the boat through waterless streets was ended. In Golconda she had attained a flowing life, a flowing journey. It was not

> only the presence of water, but the natives' flowing rhythm; they never became caught in the past, or stagnated while waiting for the future. Like children, they lived completely in the present. (*Seduction*, p. 23 [198]

Actually the dream-ship splits into two, the one representing the heavy, static position of the persistence of memory; the other the floating one on the route to discovery. The ship is metamorphosed into a solar barque: "magnetized by sun and water, gyrating and flowing, without strain or effort" (*Seduction*, p. 24 [199]).

Finally, it must be noted that the notion of liberty in Anaïs Nin, as in Breton, is cast on a transcendental rather than social level. In the personal lives of both Breton and Nïn one can observe a total absence of elitism. There is a spirit of comradeship, fraternity, and charity not of words but of deeds. Anaïs Nin's whole diary is eloquent evidence of this, as were the works and conduct of Breton.

Although Breton had joined the French communist party for a few months in the early part of his life, he quickly recoiled from the leveling process of the human spirit, which he observed in terms of that ideology. His notion of liberty had a personal basis. He thought that woman should assume a new role as a liberator and guardian of the free human spirit. "The crisis is so acute that I personally find no solution; the time must have come to make way for the ideas of woman, instead of those of man, whose failure is consummate today" (*Arcane 17*).

If there is a unifying motif in all that Anaïs Nin has written it is precisely the theme of liberation. All exercises in search, whether inward or outward, are motivated by the drive toward freedom; freedom from heritage, freedom from binding memories, freedom from growth-stunting inhibitions, freedom from ill-conceived unions.

If music is the initial ally of Anaïs Nin's writing, art replaces it little by little as the objective correlative. In *Seduction of the Minotaur* there is the emblem of a free and open canvas

> ... with elements left out allowing each spectator the freedom to fill in the spaces for himself. The missing elements of the half-empty canvas were important because they were the only spaces in which human imagination could draw

> its own inferences, its own architecture from its private myths, its streets and personages from a private world." p. 61)

In a later volume, *Collages,* she talks mostly of painters: the woman artist, Renate, who has also a hobby of opening the cages of emprisoned animals, and Varda, he of the "landscapes of joy," who replaces the father image of the earlier works.

"He was the alchemist searching only for what he could transmute into gold" (*Collages,* p. 60 [239]). It could have been a portrait of André Breton who in old age talked more and more about the philosopher's stone and focused his activities on the search for the magnetic and unifying elements of the universe.

The landscapes of Varda create a climate far removed from that of *House of Incest.* It is an atmosphere permeated with light, not light of the moon but of the sun:

> In his landscapes of joy, women became staminated flowers, and flowers women. They were as fragrant as if he had painted them with thyme, saffron and curry. They were translucent and airy, carrying their Arabian Night's cities like nebulous scarves around their lucite necks. (*Collages,* p. 59 [238])

Although earlier in her work Anaïs Nin had sought the quality of phosphorescence in the young, she found the most luminosity in the older Varda. Actually, Varda becomes the archetype of the artist whose language and visions transcend those of youth and those provoked in the non-artist by hallucinatory drugs like LSD. Varda had the power contained in all the words that begin with the prefix "trans:"

> What I wanted to teach you is contained in one page of the dictionary. It is all the words beginning with *trans*: transfigure, transport, transcend, translucent, transgression, transform, transmit, transmute, transpire, and all the trans-Siberian voyages. (*Collages,* pp. 65-66 [244])

The parable that follows is the implementation of the motto we had noted earlier: "from the dream outward." It is the simple story of a blind man whose only knowledge of reality came to him from the descriptions that his daughter made of it. When miraculously his blindness is cured, he discovers how far removed reality was from the image that his daughter had conveyed to him. But, says Anaïs Nin, he did not die of shock. Instead he told his daughter: "It is true that the world you described does not exist, but as you built that image so carefully in my mind and I can still see it so vividly, we can now set about to build it just as you made me see it" (*Collages*, p. 66 [244]).

So, the eventual impact of the work of Anaïs Nin is very close to that of André Breton: the search for luminosity through the cult and realization of the dream, through the effort to preserve the phosphorescent child image of ourselves, through the expanding consciousness that love in all its forms creates, through art which is a more sensitive instrument than a seismograph, recording the artist's passage from the mudbanks of sterile relationships to emergence into the regions of light.

If the myth of the labyrinth suggests the confusion of modern man's mind and his progression through human contacts and contingent events, identified in Anaïs Nin's work with the very human and vulnerable personality of the artist, the myth of the philosopher's stone is identified here also with the image of the artist, but an artist who has become almost transhuman: the myth of the philosopher's stone becomes the victory over the labyrinth, the power of creation, inherent in the human context, but passively dormant in most people. The artist is he who can put the latent power into motion and transmit the power of seeing which is native but unexploited in most humans.

There is a marvelous juxtaposition possible between *Seduction of the Minotaur* and *Collages*. *Seduction* presents a landscape of gold, exterior to the viewer, which becomes monotonous and inert for those who merely pass through it. In *Collages* the golden landscapes are produced from within, and therefore their impact is dynamic and contagious. Golconda is, metaphorically speaking, the divinity of nature; in *Collages* we are confronted with the divinity of man. In the final pages of *Collages* Anaïs Nin's parable of the writer who meets the incarnation of one of his characters brings into focus the universal truth of the relationship essential between the outer world and the artist's inner one:

> We are indispensable to each other. I to your work and you to my life. Without me spending your words you may not be incited to mint new ones. I am the spendthrift and you the coiner. We cannot live completely apart. (p. 116 [251])

There is in the work of Anaïs Nin a progression and an evolution discernible in the changing patterns of her mythological motifs. If I traced her works' passage from the orbit of symbolism to that of surrealism, it does not mean that is the only curb possible to draw in her multifaceted writings. As T. S. Eliot said: "You cannot value the artist alone; you must set him in contrast and comparison among the dead. I mean this as a principle of esthetic, not merely historical criticism."

The essential quality of her writing is that it possesses, like the best creative works of our time in all the branches of the arts, that magnetic quality which provokes in each serious viewer or reader the power to partake, to relate, to become, by breaking down the barrier between the artist and his public.

ANNA BALAKIAN

FICTION

from *House of Incest*

The morning I got up to begin this book I coughed. Something was coming out of my throat: it was strangling me. I broke the thread which held it and yanked it out. I went back to bed and said: I have just spat out my heart.

There is an instrument called the quena, made of human bones. It owes its origin to the worship of an Indian for his mistress. When she died he made a flute out of her bones. The quena has a more penetrating, more haunting sound than the ordinary flute.

Those who write know the process. I thought of it as I was spitting out my heart.

Only I do not wait for my love to die.

My first vision of earth was water veiled. I am of the race of men and women who see all things through this curtain of sea, and my eyes are the color of water.

I looked with chameleon eyes upon the changing face of the world, looked with anonymous vision upon my uncompleted self.

The night surrounded me, a photograph unglued from its frame. The lining of a coat ripped open like the two shells of an oyster. The day and night unglued, and I falling in between not knowing on which layer I was resting, whether it was the cold grey upper leaf of dawn, or the dark layer of night.

From *House of Incest* (Swallow, 1958), pp. 1, 15, 18-28, 51-56, 62-72.

Sabina's face was suspended in the darkness of the garden. From the eyes a simoon wind shrivelled the leaves and turned the earth over; all things which had run a vertical course now turned in circles, round the face, around HER face. She stared with such an ancient stare, heavy luxuriant centuries flickering in deep processions. From her nacreous skin, perfumes spiralled like incense. Every gesture she made quickened the rhythm of the blood and aroused a beat chant like the beat of the heart of the desert, a chant which was the sound of her feet treading down into the imprint of her face.

A voice that had traversed the centuries, so heavy it broke what it touched, so heavy I feared it would ring in me with eternal resonance; a voice rusty with the sound of curses and the hoarse cries that issue from the delta in the last paroxysm of orgasm.

Her black cape hung like black hair from her shoulders, half-draped, half-floating around her body. The web of her dress moving always a moment before she moved, as if aware of her impulses, and stirring long after she was still, like waves ebbing back to the sea. Her sleeves dropped like a sigh and the hem of her dress danced round her feet.

The steel necklace on her throat flashed like summer lightning and the sound of the steel was like the clashing of swords... Le pas d'acier... The steel of New York's skeleton buried in granite, buried standing up. Le pas d'acier... notes hammered on the steel-stringed guitars of the gypsies, on the steel arms of chairs dulled with her breath; steel mail curtains falling like the flail of hail, steel bars and steel barrage cracking. Her necklace thrown around the world's neck, unmeltable. She carried it like a trophy wrung of groaning machinery, to match the inhuman rhythm of her march.

The leaf fall of her words, the stained glass hues of her moods, the rust in her voice, the smoke in her mouth, her breath on my vision like human breath blinding a mirror.

Talk—half-talk, phrases that had no need to be finished, abstractions, Chinese bells played on with cotton-tipped sticks, mock orange blossoms painted on porcelain. The muffled, close, half-talk of soft-fleshed women. The men she had embraced, and the women, all washing against the resonance of my memory. Sound within sound, scene within scene, woman within woman—like acid revealing an invisible script. One woman within another eternally, in a far-reaching procession, shattering my mind into fragments, into quarter-tones which no orchestral baton can ever make whole again.

The luminous mask of her face, waxy, immobile, with eyes like sentinels. Watching my sybaritic walk, and I the sibilance of her tongue. Deep into each other we turned our harlot eyes. She was an idol in Byzance, an idol dancing with legs parted; and I wrote with pollen and honey. The soft secret yielding of woman I carved into men's brains with copper words; her image I tattooed in their eyes. They were consumed by the fever of their entrails, the indissoluble poison of legends. If the torrent failed to engulf them, or did they extricate themselves, I haunted their memory with the tale they wished to forget. All that was swift and malevolent in woman might be ruthlessly destroyed, but who would destroy the illusion on which I laid her to sleep each night? We lived in Byzance, Sabina and I, until our hearts bled from the precious stones on our foreheads, our bodies tired of the weight of brocades, our nostrils burned with the smoke of perfumes; and when we had passed into other centuries they enclosed us in copper frames. Men recognized her always: the same effulgent face, the same rust voice. And she and I, we recognized each other; I her face and she my legend.

Around my pulse she put a flat steel bracelet and my pulse beat as she willed, losing its human cadence, thumping like a savage in orgiastic frenzy. The lamentations of flutes, the double chant of wind through our slender bones, the cracking of our bones distantly remembered when on beds of down the worship we inspired turned to lust.

As we walked along, rockets burst from the street lamps; we swallowed the asphalt road with a jungle roar and the houses with their closed eyes and geranium eyelashes; swallowed the telegraph poles trembling with messages; swallowed stray cats, trees, hills, hedges, Sabina's labyrinthian smile on the keyhole. The door moaning, opening. Her smile closed. A nightingale disleafing melliferous honeysuckle. Honey-suckled. Fluted fingers. The house opened its green gate mouth and swallowed us. The bed was floating.

The record was scratched, the crooning broken. The peices cut our feet. It was dawn and she was lost. I put back the houses on the road, aligned the telegraph poles along the river and the stray cats jumping across the road. I put back the hills. The road came out of my mouth like a velvet ribbon—it lay there serpentine. The houses opened their eyes. The keyhole had an ironic curve, like a question mark. The woman's mouth.

I was carrying her fetiches, her marionettes, her fortune teller's cards worn at the corners like the edge of a wave. The windows of the city were stained and splintered with rainlight and the blood she drew from me with each lie, each deception. Beneath the skin of her cheeks I saw ashes: would she die before we had joined in perfidious union? The eyes, the hands, the senses that only women have.

There is no mockery between women. One lies down at peace as on one's own breast.

Sabina was no longer embracing men and women. Within the fever of her restlessness the world was losing its human shape. She was losing the human power to fit body to body in human completeness. She was delimiting the horizons, sinking into planets without axis, losing her polarity and the divine knowledge of integration, of fusion. She was spreading herself like the night over the universe and found no god to lie with. The other half belonged to the sun, and she was at war with the sun and light. She would tolerate no bars of light on open books, no orchestration of ideas knitted by a single theme; she would not be covered by the sun, and half the universe belonged to him; she was turning her serpent back to that alone which might overshadow her own stature giving her the joy of fecundation.

Come away with me, Sabina, come to my island. Come to my island of red peppers sizzling over slow braseros, Moorish earthen jars catching the gold water, palm trees, wild cats fighting, at dawn a donkey sobbing, feet on coral reefs and sea-anemones, the body covered with long seaweeds, Melisande's hair hanging over the balcony at the Opera Comique, inexorable diamond sunlight, heavy nerveless hours in the violaceous shadows, ash-colored rocks and olive trees, lemon trees with lemons hung like lanterns at a garden party, bamboo shoots forever trembling, soft-sounding espadrilles, pomegranate spurting blood, a flute-like Moorish chant, long and insistent, of the ploughmen, trilling, swearing, trilling and cursing, dropping perspiration on the earth with the seeds.

Your beauty drowns me, drowns the core of me. When your beauty burns me I dissolve as I never dissolved before man. From all men I was different, and myself, but I see in you that part of me which is you. I feel you in me; I feel my own voice becoming heavier, as if I were drinking you in, every delicate thread of resemblance being soldered by fire and one no longer detects the fissure.

Your lies are not lies, Sabina. They are arrows flung out of your orbit by the strength of your fantasy. To nourish illusion. To destroy reality. I will help you: it is I who will invent lies for you and with them we will traverse the world. But behind our lies I am dropping Ariadne's golden thread—for the greatest of all joys is to bc able to retrace one's lies, to return to the source and sleep one night a year washed of all superstructures.

Sabina, you made your impression upon the world. I passed through it like a ghost. Does anyone notice the owl in the tree at night, the bat which strikes the window pane while others are talking, the eyes which reflect like water and drink like blotting paper, the pity which flickers quietly like candlelight, the understanding on which people lay themselves to sleep?

DOES ANYONE KNOW WHO I AM?

Even my voice came from other worlds. I was embalmed in my own secret vertigoes. I was suspended over the world, seeing what road I could tread without treading down even clay or grass. My step was a sentient step; the mere crepitation of gravel could arrest my walk.

When I saw you, Sabina, I chose my body.

I will let you carry me into the fecundity of destruction. I choose a body then, a face, a voice. I become you. And you become me. Silence the sensational course of your body and you will see in me, intact, your own fears, your own pities. You will see love which was excluded from the passions given you, and I will see the passions excluded from love. Step out of your role and rest yourself on the core of your true desires. Cease for a moment your violent deviations. Relinquish the furious indomitable strain.

I will take them up.

Cease trembling and shaking and gasping and cursing and find again your core which I am. Rest from twistedness, distortion, deformations. For an hour you will be me; that is, the other half of yourself. The half you lost. What you burnt, broke, and tore is still in my hands: I am the keeper of fragile things and I have kept of you what is indissoluble.

Even the world and the sun cannot show their two faces at once.

So now we are inextricably woven. I have gathered together all the fragments. I return them to you. You have run with the wind, scattering and dissolving. I have run behind you, like your own shadow, gathering what you have sown in deep coffers.

I AM THE OTHER FACE OF YOU

Our faces are soldered together by soft hair, soldered together, showing two profiles of the same soul. Even when I passed through a room like a breath, I made others uneasy and they knew I had passed.

I was the white flame of your breath, your simoon breath shrivelling the world. I borrowed your visibility and it was through you I made my imprint on the world. I praised my own flame in you.

THIS IS THE BOOK YOU WROTE

AND YOU ARE THE WOMAN

I AM

She led me into the house of incest. It was the only house which was not included in the twelve houses of the zodiac. It could neither be reached by the route of the milky way, nor by the glass ship through whose transparent bottom one could follow the outline of the lost continents, nor by following the arrows pointing the direction of the wind, nor by following the voice of the mountain echoes.

The rooms were chained together by steps—no room was on a level with another—and all the steps were deeply worn. There were windows between the rooms, little spying-eyed windows, so that one might talk in the dark from room to room, without seeing the other's face. The rooms were filled with the rhythmic heaving of the sea coming from many sea-shells. The windows gave out on a static sea, where immobile fishes had been glued to painted backgrounds. Everything had been made to stand still in the house of incest, because they all had such a fear of movement and warmth, such a fear that all love and all life should flow out of reach and be lost!

Everything had been made to stand still, and everything was rotting away. The sun had been nailed in the roof of the sky and the moon beaten deep into its Oriental niche.

In the house of incest there was a room which could not be found, a room without window, the fortress of their love, a room without window where the mind and blood coalesced in a union without orgasm and rootless like those of fishes. The promiscuity of glances, of phrases, like sparks marrying in space. The collision between their resemblances, shedding the odor of tamarisk and sand, of rooted shells and dying sea-weeds, their love like the ink of squids, a banquet of poisons.

Stumbling from room to room I came into the room of paintings, and there sat Lot with his hand upon his daughter's breast while the city burned behind them, cracking open and falling into the sea. There where he sat with his daughter the Oriental rug was red and stiff, but the turmoil which shook them showed through the rocks splitting around them, through the earth yawning beneath their feet, through the trees flaming up like torches, through the sky smoking and smouldering red, all cracking with the joy and terror of their love. Joy of the father's hand upon the daughter's breast, the joy of the fear racking her. Her costume tightly pressed around her so that her breasts heave and swell under his fingers, while the city is rent by lightning, and spits under the teeth of fire, great blocks of a gaping ripped city sinking with the horror of obscenity, and falling into the sea with the hiss of the eternally damned. No cry of horror from Lot and his daughter but from the city in flames, from an unquenchable desire of father and daughter, of brother and sister, mother and son.

I looked upon a clock to find the truth. The hours were passing like ivory chess figures, striking piano notes, and the minutes raced on wires mounted like tin soldiers. Hours like tall ebony women with gongs between their legs, tolling continuously so that I could not count them. I heard the tolling of my heart-beats; I heard the footsteps of my dreams, and the beat of time was lost among them like the face of truth.

I came upon a forest of decapitated trees, women carved out of bamboo, flesh slatted like that of slaves in joyless slavery, faces cut in two by the sculptor's knife, showing two sides forever separate, eternally two-faced, and it was I who had to shift about to behold the entire woman. Truncated undecagon figures, eleven sides, eleven angles, in veined and vulnerable woods, fragments of bodies, bodies armless and headless. The torso of a tube-rose, the knee of Achilles, tubercles and excrescences, the foot of a mummy in rotted wood, the veined docile wood carved into human contortions. The forest must weep and bend like the shoulders of men, dead figures inside of live trees. A forest animated now with intellectual faces, intellectual contortions. Trees become man and woman, two-faced, nostalgic for the shivering of leaves. Trees reclining, woods shining, and the forest trembling with rebellion so bitter I heard its wailing within its deep forest consciousness. Wailing the loss of its leaves and the failure of transmutation.

Further a forest of white plaster, white plaster eggs. Large white eggs on silver disks, an elegy to birth, each egg a promise, each half-shaped nascence of man or woman or animal not yet precise. Womb and seed and egg, the moist beginning being worshipped rather than its flowering. The eggs so white, so still, gave birth to hope without breaking, but the cut-down tree lying there produced a green live branch that laughed at the sculptor.

I walked into my own book, seeking peace.

It was night, and I made a careless movement inside the dream; I turned too brusquely the corner and I bruised myself against my madness. It was this seeing too much, this seeing of a tragedy in the quiver of an eyelid, constructing a crime in the next room, the men and women who had loved before me on the same hotel bed.

I carry white sponges of knowledge on strings of nerves.

As I move within my book I am cut by pointed glass and broken bottles in which there is still the odor of sperm and perfume.

More pages added to the book but pages like a prisoner's walking back and forth over the space alloted him. What is it allotted me to say? Only the truth disguised in a fairytale, and this is the fairytale behind which all the truths are staring as behind grilled mosque windows. With veils. The moment I step into the cavern of my lies I drop into darkness, and see a mask which stares at me like the glance of a cross-eyed man; yet I am wrapped in lies which do not penetrate my soul, as if the lies I tell were like costumes.

LIES CREATE SOLITUDE

I walked out of my book into the paralytic's room.

He sat there among many objects under glass as in a museum. He had collected a box of paint which he never painted with, a thousand books with pages uncut, and they were covered with dust. His Spanish cape hung on the shoulders of a mannequin, his guitar lay with strings snapped like long disordered hair. He sat before a note book of blank pages, saying: I swallow my own words. I chew and chew everything until it deteriorates. Every thought or impulse I have is chewed into nothingness. I want to capture all my thoughts at once, but they run in all directions. If I could do this I would be capturing the nimblest of minds, like a shoal of minnows. I would reveal innocence and duplicity, generosity and calculation, fear and cowardice and courage. I want to tell the whole truth, but I cannot tell the whole truth because I would have to write four pages at once, like four long columns simultaneously, four pages to the present one, and so I do not write at all. I would have to write backwards, retrace my steps constantly to catch the echoes and the overtones.

His skin was transparent like that of a newborn child, and his eyes green like moss. He bowed to Sabina, to Jeanne, and to me: meet the modern Christ, who is crucified by his own nerves, for all our neurotic sins!

The modern Christ was wiping the perspiration which dripped over his face, as if he were sitting there in the agony of a secret torture. Paincarved features. Eyes too open, as if dilated by scenes of horror. Heavy-lidded, with a world-heavy fatigue. Sitting on his chair as if there were ghosts standing beside him. A smile like an insult. Lips edged and withered by the black scum of drugs. A body taut like wire.

In our writings we are brothers, I said. The speed of our vertigoes is the same. We arrived at the same place at the same moment, which is not so with other people's thoughts. The language of nerves which we both use makes us brothers in writing.

The modern Christ said: I was born without a skin. I dreamed once that I stood naked in a garden and that it was carefully and neatly peeled, like a fruit. Not an inch of skin left on my body. It was all gently pulled off, all of it, and then I was told to walk, to live, to run. I walked slowly at first, and the garden was very soft, and I felt the softness of the garden so acutely, not on the surface of my body, but all through it, the soft warm air and the perfumes penetrated me like needles through every open bleeding pore. All the pores open and breathing the softness, the warmth, and the smells. The whole body invaded, penetrated, responding, every tiny cell and pore active and breathing and trembling and enjoying. I shrieked with pain. I ran. And as I ran the wind lashed me, and then the voices of people like whips on me. Being touched! Do you know what it is to be touched by a human being!

He wiped his face with his handkerchief.

The paralytic sat still in the corner of the room.

You are fortunate, he said, you are fortunate to feel so much; I wish I could feel all that. You are at least alive to pain, whereas I....

Then he turned his face away, and just before he turned away I saw the veins on his forehead swelling, swelling with the effort he made, the inner effort which neither his tongue nor his body, nor his thoughts would obey.

If only we could all escape from this house of incest, where we only love ourselves in the other, if only I could save you all from yourselves, said the modern Christ.

But none of us could bear to pass through the tunnel which led from the house into the world on the other side of the walls, where there were leaves on the trees, where water ran beside the paths, where there was daylight and joy. We could not believe that the tunnel would open on daylight: we feared to be trapped into darkness again; we feared to return whence we had come, from darkness and night. The tunnel would narrow and taper down as we walked; it would close around us, and close tighter and tighter around us and stifle us. It would grow heavy and narrow and suffocate us as we walked.

Yet we knew that beyond the house of incest there was daylight, and none of us could walk towards it.

We all looked now at the dancer who stood at the center of the room dancing the dance of the woman without arms. She danced as if she were deaf and could not follow the rhythm of the music. She danced as if she could not hear the sound of her castanets. Her dancing was isolated and separated from music and from us and from the room and from life. The castanets sounded like the steps of a ghost.

She danced, laughing and sighing and breathing all for herself. She danced her fears, stopping in the center of every dance to listen to reproaches that we could not hear, or bowing to applause that we did not make. She was listening to a music we could not hear, moved by hallucinations we could not see.

My arms were taken away from me, she sang. I was punished for clinging. I clung. I clutched all those I loved; I clutched at the lovely moments of life; my hands closed upon every full hour. My arms were always tight and craving to embrace. I wanted to embrace and hold the light, the wind, the sun, the night, the whole world. I wanted to caress, to heal, to rock, to lull, to surround, to encompass. And I strained and I held so much that they broke; they broke away from me. Everything eluded me then. I was condemned not to hold.

Trembling and shaking she stood looking at her arms now stretched before her again.

She looked at her hands tightly closed and opened them slowly, opened them completely like Christ; she opened them in a gesture of abandon and giving; she relinquished and forgave, opening her arms and her hands, permitting all things to flow away and beyond her.

I could not bear the passing of things. All flowing, all passing, all movement choked me with anguish.

And she danced; she danced with the music and with the rhythm of earth's circles: she turned with the earth turning, like a disk, turning all faces to light and to darkness evenly, dancing towards daylight.

from *Winter of Artifice*

WINTER OF ARTIFICE

She is waiting for him. She was waiting for him for twenty years. He is coming today.

This glass bowl with the glass fish and the glass ship—it has been the sea for her and the ship which carried her away from him after he had abandoned her. Why has she loved ships so deeply, why has she always wanted to sail away from this world? Why has she always dreamed of flight, of departure?

Today this past from which she has struggled so long to escape strikes her like a whip. But today she can bear the lash of it because he is coming and she knows that the circle of empty waiting will close.

How well she remembers their home near the sea, the villa which was in ruins. She was nine years old. She arrived there with her mother and two brothers. Her father was standing behind a window, watching. His face was pale, he did not seem glad to see them. She felt that he did not want them, that he did not want her. His anger seemed to be directed against all of them, but it touched her more acutely, as if it were directed entirely against her. They were not wanted, why she did not understand. Her mother said to him: It will be good for your daughter here. There was no smile on his face. He did not seem to notice that she was wasted by fever, that she was hungry for a smile.

There was never a smile on his face except when there were visitors, except when there was music and talk. When they were alone in the

From *Winter of Artifice* (Swallow, 1945, 1946, 1948), pp. 55-119.

house there was always war: great explosions of anger, hatred, revolt. War. War at meals, war over their heads when her brothers and she were left in bed at night, war in the room under their feet when they were playing. War. War....

In the closed study, or in the parlor, there was always a mysterious activity. Music, rehearsals, visitors, laughter. She saw her father in movement, always alert, tense, either passionately gay or passionately angry. When the door opened her father appeared, luminous, incandescent. A vital passage, even when he passed from one room to another. A gust of wind. A mystery. Not a reality like her mother with her healthy red checks, her appetite, her frank natural laughter.

Never any serenity, never any time for caresses, for softness, Tension always. A life ripped by dissension. Even while they were playing, the dark fury of their perpetual warring hung over them like threats and curses and recriminations. Never a moment of complete joy. Aware always of the battles that were about to explode.

One day there was a scene of such violence that she was terrified. An immense, irrational terror overwhelmed her. Her mother was goading her father to such anger that she thought he would kill her. Her father's face was blue-white. She began to scream. She screamed until they became alarmed. For a few days there was an interval of quiet. A truce. A pretense of peace.

The walls of her father's library were covered with books. Often she stole into the library and she read the books which she found there, books which she did not understand. Within her there was a well of secret thoughts which she could not express, which perhaps she might have formulated if someone had leaned over them with tenderness. The one person who might have aided her terrified her. Her father's eyes were always cold, critical, unbelieving. He would not believe the drawings she showed him were hers. He thought she had traced them. He did not believe that she had written the poems that were handed to him. He thought she had copied them. He flew into a rage because he could not find the books from which he had imagined she had copied her poems and drawings.

He doubted everything about her, even her illnesses. In the train once, going to Berlin where he was to give a concert, she had such an earache that she began to weep. If you don't stop crying and go to sleep, he said, I'll beat you. She stuffed her head under the pillow so that he would not hear her sobs. She sobbed all the way to Berlin. When they got there they discovered that she had an abscess in her ear.

Another time he was taken down with an attack of appendicitis. Her mother was tending him, fussing over him, running about anxiously. He lay there very pale in the big bed. She came from the street where she had been playing and told her mother that she was in pain. Immediately her father said: Don't pay any attention to her, she is just acting. She is just imitating me. But she did have an attack of appendicitis. She had to be taken to the hospital and operated on. Her father, on the other hand, had recovered. He was in bed only three days.

Such cruelty! She asked herself,—was he really cruel, or was it mere selfishness? Was he just a big child who could not bear to have a rival, even in the person of his own daughter? She did not know. She was waiting for him now. She wanted to tell him everything. She wanted to hear what he had to say. She wanted to hear him say that he loved her. She did not know why she loved him so much. She could not believe that he meant to be so cruel. She loved him.

Because he was so critical, so severe, so suspicious of her, she became secretive and lying. She would never say what she really thought. She was afraid of him. She lied like an Arab. She lied to elude his stern glances, his cold, menacing blue eyes. She invented another world, a world of make-believe, of illusion, of games, of comedies. She tyrannized over her two brothers, she taught them games, she amused them, acted for them, enchanted them. She was a spitfire and they loved her. They never deserted her, even for a moment. They were simple, honest, frank. She complicated everything, even the games they played.

In Berlin, when she was five years old, she ran away. There was a seven-year-old boy waiting for her around the corner. His name was Heinrich.

She was a pale and sickly child. The doctor in Berlin had said: She must live in her native climate. Take her back. But there was no money for that. Her youngest brother had just been born. There was no money in the house, except for books and music, for a fur-lined coat, for the cologne water which her father had to sprinkle over his handkerchiefs, for the silk shirts which he demanded when he went on his concert tours.

At the villa near the sea she lay in bed and wept all night without knowing why. But there was a garden attached to the villa. A beautiful garden in which one could get lost. She sat by the big Gothic window studded with colored stones and looked out through a prismatic-colored stone in the center of the window; she sat there for hours at a stretch gazing upon this mysterious other world. Colors. Deformations. Trees that are ruby-colored. Orange skies. She felt that there were other worlds, that one might escape from this one which was so full of misery. She thought a great deal about this other world.

About her father there was an aureole of fragrance, of immaculateness, of elegance. His clothes were never wrinkled; he wore clean linen every day and the fur collar on his coat was wonderful to caress. Her mother was busy, bustling, maternal. Her mother was never elegant.

Since he often left them to go on concert tours they were so used to her father's departures that they barely ceased playing to embrace him. She remembered now the day he was leaving to go on tour. He was standing at the door, elegant, aristocratic. He looked the same as always. Suddenly moved by an acute premonition, she threw herself on him and clung to him passionately. "Don't go, Father! Don't leave me!" she begged. She had to be torn away. She wept so violently that her father was startled. Even now she could feel again the effort her mother made to loosen her clutch. She could still see the hesitancy in her father's face. She begged and implored him to stay. She clung to him, desperately, her fingers knotted in his clothes. She remembered the effort he made to wrench himself loose and how he walked swiftly off without once looking back. She remembered too that her mother was surprised by her despair. She couldn't understand what had possessed her to behave as she did.

Since that day she had not seen her father. Twenty years have passed. He is coming today.

* * *

They entered New York harbor, her mother, her two brothers and she, in the midst of a violent thunderstorm. The Spaniards aboard the ship were terrified; some of them were kneeling in prayer. They had reason to be terrified,—the bow of the ship had been struck by lightning. She busied herself making a last-minute entry in her diary, which she had begun when they left Barcelona.

It was a monologue, or dialogue, dedicated to him, inspired by the superabundance of thoughts and feelings caused by the pain of leaving him. With the sea between them she felt that at least she might be able to reveal to him with absolute sincerity the great love she bore him, as well as her sadness and her yearning.

They arrived in New York with huge wicker baskets, a cage full of birds a violin case and no money. She carried her diary in a basket. She was timid, withdrawn.

She caught only fleeting patches of this new reality surrounding her. At the pier there were aunts and cousins awaiting them. The Negro porters threw themselves on their belongings. She remembers vividly how she clung to her brother's violin case. She wanted everybody to know that she was an artist.

Entering the subway she observed immediately what a strange place New York was,—the staircases move up and down by themselves. And in the train hundreds of mouths chewing, masticating. Her little brother asked: "Are Americans ruminants?"

She was eleven years old. Her mother was absent most of the day searching for work. There were socks to darn and dishes to wash. She had to bathe and dress her brothers. She had to amuse them, aid them with their lessons. The days were full of bleak effort in which great sacrifices were demanded of all of them. Though she experienced a tremendous relief in helping her mother, in serving her faithfully, she felt nevertheless that the color and the fragrance had gone out of their life. When she heard music, laughter and talk in the room where her mother gave singing lessons, she was saddened by the feeling of something lost.

And so, little by little, she shut herself up within the walls of her diary. She held long conversations with herself, through the diary. She talked to her diary, addressed it by name, as if it were a living person, her other self perhaps. Looking out the window which gave on their ugly back yard she imagined that she was looking at parks, castles, golden grilles, and exotic flowers. Within the covers of the diary she created another world wherein she told the truth, in contrast to the multiple lies which she spun when she was conversing with others, as, for instance, telling her playmates that she had traveled all around the world, describing to them the places which she had read about in her father's library.

The yearning for her father became a long, continuous plaint. Every page contained long pleas to him, invocations to God to reunite them. Hours and hours of suffocating moods, of dreams and reveries, of feverish restlessness, of morbid, somber memories and longings. She could not bear to listen to music, especially the arias her mother sang: "Ever since the day," "Some day he'll come," etc. Her mother seemed to choose only the songs which reminded her of him.

She felt crippled, lost, transplanted, rebellious. She was alone a great deal. Her mother was healthy, exuberant, full of plans for the future. When she was moody her mother chided her. If she confessed to her mother, she laughed at her. Her mother seemed to doubt the sincerity of her feelings. She attributed her moods to her overdeveloped imagination, or else to her blood. When her mother was angry she shouted: "*Mauvaise graine, va*!" She was often angry now, but not with them. She was obliged to fight for them every day of her life. It required all her courage, all her buoyancy and optimism, to face the world. New York was hostile, cold, indifferent. They were immigrants, and they were made to feel it. Even on Christmas Eve her mother had to sing at the church in order to earn a few pennies.

The great crime, her mother made them feel, was their resemblance to their father. Each flare of temper, each tragic outburst was severely condemned. Even her paleness served to remind her mother of him. He too always looked pale and ready to die, but it was all nonsense, she said. Every day she added a little touch to the image they had of him. Her younger brother's rages, his wildness, his destructiveness, all this came from their father. Her imagination, her exaggerations, her fantasies, her lies, these, too, sprang from their father.

It was true. Everything sprang from him, even the lies which originated from the books she had read in his library. When she told the children at school that she had once traveled through Russia in a covered wagon it was not a lie either, because in her mind she had made this journey through snow-covered Russia time and time again.

The cold of New York revived the memories of her father's books, of the journeys she had longed to take with him when he went away.

To face the cold of New York required superhuman efforts. Standing in the snow in Central Park, feeding the pigeons, she wanted to die. The dread of facing the snow and frost each morning paralyzed her. Their school was only around the corner, but she had not the courage to leave the house. Her mother had to ask the Negro janitor to drag her to school. "Po' thing," he would say, "you ought to live down South." He would lend her his woolen gloves and slap her back to get her warm.

Only in her diary could she reveal her true self, her true feelings. What she really desired was to be left alone with her diary and her dreams of her father. In solitude she was happy. Her head was seething with ideas. She described every phase of their life in detail, minute, childish details which seem ridiculous and absurd now, but which were intended to convey to her father the need that she felt for his presence. Though she detested New York, she painted a picture of it in glowing terms, hoping that it would entice him to come.

When, to amuse her brothers, she impersonated Marie Antoinette as she marched proudly to the guillotine, standing on a chariot of chairs with a lace cap, she wept real tears. She wept over the martyrdom of Marie Antoinette because she was aware of her own future sufferings. A million times her hair would turn white overnight and the crowd jeer at her. A million times she would lose her throne, her husband, her children, and her life. At eleven years of age she was searching in the lives of the great for analogies to the drama of her own life which she felt was destined to be shattered at every turn of the road. In acting the roles of other personages she felt that she was piecing together the fragments of her shattered life. Only in the fever of creation could she recreate her own lost life.

There was a passage in the diary wherein she wrote that she would like to relive her life in Spain. At that early age she was bemoaning the irreversibility of life.

Already she was aware of how the past dies. She re-examined what she had written about New York for her father because she felt that she had not done justice to it. She watched every minute of the day as she lived so that nothing would be lost. She regretted the minutes passing. She wept without knowing why, since she was young and had not yet known real suffering. But without being fully aware of it, she had already experienced her greatest sorrow, the irreparable loss of her father. She did not know it then, as indeed most of us never know when it is that we experience the full measure of joy or sorrow. But our feelings penetrate us like a poison of undetectable nature. We have sorrows of which we do not know the origin or name.

She remembered a night before Christmas when, in utter desperation, she began to believe that her father was coming, that he would arrive Christmas Day. Even though that very day she had received a postcard from him and she knew that he was too far away for her hopes to be realized, still a sense of the miraculous impelled her to expect what was humanly impossible. She got down on her knees and she prayed to God to perform a miracle. She looked for her father all Christmas Day, and again on her birthday, a month later. Today he will come. Or tomorrow. Or the next day. Each disappointment was baffling and terrifying to her.

Today he is coming. She is sure of it. But how can she be sure? She is standing on the edge of a crater.

Her true God was her father. At communion it was her father she received, and not God. She closed her eyes and swallowed the white bread with blissful tremors. She embraced her father in holy communion. Her exaltation fused into a semblance of holiness. She aspired to saintliness in order to conceal the secret love which she guarded so jealously in her diary. The voluptuous tears at night when she prayed to God, the joy without name when she stood in his presence, the inexplicable bliss at communion, because then she talked with her father and she kissed him.

She worshiped him passionately but as she grew older the form of his image grew blurred. But she had not lost him. His image was buried deep in the most mysterious region of her being. On the surface there remained the image created by her mother—his egoism, his neglectfulness, his irresponsibility, his love of luxury. When for a time her immense yearning appeared to have exhausted itself, when it seemed that she had almost forgotten this man whom her mother described so bitterly, it was only the announcement of the fact that his image had become fluid; it ran in subterranean channels, through her blood. Consciously she was no longer aware of him; but in another way his existence was even stronger than before. Submerged, yet magically ineffaceable, he floated in her blood.

At thirteen she recorded in her diary that she wanted to marry a man who looked like the Count of Monte Cristo. Apart from the mention of black eyes it was her father's portrait which she gave: "A man so strong . . . with very white teeth, a pale, mysterious face, . . . a grave walk, a distant smile. . . . I would like him to tell me all about his life, a very sad life, full of harrowing adventures . . . . I would like him to be proud and haughty . . . to play some instrument . . . ."

The image created by her mother, added to the blurred memories of a child, do not compose a being; yet in her haunting quest she fashioned an imagined individual she pursued relentlessly. The blue eyes of a boy in school, the talent of a young violinist, a pale face seen in the street—these fleeting aspects of the image that was buried deep in her blood moved her to tears . . . . To listen to music was unbearable. When her mother sang she exhausted herself in sobs.

In this record which she faithfully kept for twenty years she spoke of her diary as of her shadow, her double; "I say I will only marry my double." As far as she knew this double was the diary which was full of reflections like a mirror, which could change shape and color and serve all kinds of imaginative substitutions. This diary she had intended to send to her father, which was to be a revelation of her love for him, became by an accident of fate, a secretive thing, another wall between herself and that world which it seemed forbidden her ever to enter.

She would have liked great love and tenderness, confidence, openness. Her father, she felt certain, would have rejected her—his standards were too severe. She wrote him once that she thought he had abandoned her because she was not an intelligent or pretty enough daughter. She was a perpetually offended being who fancied that she was not wanted. This fear of not being wanted weighed down on her like a perpetual icy condemnation.

Today, when he arrives, will she be able to lift her head? Will she be able to keep her head lifted, will she be able to stand the cold look in his eyes when she raises her eyes to his? Will her body not tremble with fear when she hears his voice? After twenty years she is still obsessed by the fear of him. But now she felt that it was in his power to absolve her of all fear. Perhaps it is he who will fear her. Perhaps he is coming to receive the judgment which she alone can mete out to him. Today the circle of empty waiting will be broken. She is waiting for him to embrace her, to say that he loves her. She made a God of him and she was punished. Now when he comes she wants to make him a human father. She does not want to fear him any longer. She does not want to write another line in her diary. She wants him to smash this monument which she erected to him and accept her in her own right.

He is coming. She hears his steps.

* * *

She expected the man of the photographs, the young man of the photographs. She had not tried to imagine what the years had done to his face.

It was not any older, there were no wrinkles on it, but there was a mask over it. His face wore a mask. The skin did not match the skin of his wrists. It seemed made of earth and papier-mâché, not pure skin. There must have been a little space between it and the real face, a little partition through which the breeze could sing, and behind this mask another smile, another face, and skin like that of his wrists, white and vulnerable.

At the sight of her waiting on the doorstep he smiled, a feminine smile, and moved towards her with a neat, compact grace, ease, youthfulness. She felt unsettled. This man coming towards her did not seem at all like a father.

His first words were words of apology. After he had taken off his gloves, and verified by his watch that he was on time—it was very important to him to be on time—after he had kissed her and told her that she had become very beautiful, almost immediately it seemed to her that she was listening to an apology, an explanation of why he had left them. It was as if behind her there stood a judge, a tall judge he alone could see, and to this judge her father addressed a beautiful polished speech, a marvelous speech to which she listened with admiration, for the logic was so beautiful, the smooth change of phrases, the long and flawless story of her mother's imperfections, of all that he had suffered, the manner in which all the facts of their life were presented, all made a perfect and eloquent pleading, addressed to a judge she could not see and with whom she had nothing to do. He had not come out free of his past. Taking out a gold-tipped cigarette and with infinite care placing it in a holder which contained a filter for the nicotine, he related the story she had heard from her mother, all with an accent of apology and deference.

She had no time to tell him that she understood that they had not been made to live together, that it was not a question of faults and defects, but of alchemy, that this alchemy had created war, that there was no one to blame or to judge. Already her father was launched on an apology of why he had stayed all winter in the south; he did not say that he enjoyed it but that it had been absolutely essential to his health. It seemed to her as he talked that he was just as ashamed to have left them as he was of having spent the winter in the south when he should have been in Paris giving concerts.

She waited for him to lose sight of this judge standing behind her and then, plunging into the present, she said: "It's scandalous to have such a young father!"

"Do you know what I used to fear?" he said. "That you might come too late to see me laughing—too late for me to have the power to make you laugh. In June when I go south again you must come with me. They will take you for my mistress, that will be delightful."

She was standing against the mantelpiece. He was looking at her hands, admiring them. She leaned backwards, pushing the crystal bowl against the wall. It cracked and the water gushed forth as from a fountain, splashing all over the floor. The glass ship could no longer sail away—it was lying on its side, on the rock-crystal stones.

They stood looking at the broken bowl and at the water forming a pool on the floor.

"Perhaps I've arrived at my port at last," she said. "Perhaps I've come to the end of my wanderings. I have found you."

"We've both done a lot of wandering," he said. "I not only played the piano in every city of the world . . . sometimes when I look at the map, it seems to me that even the tiniest villages could be replaced by the names of women. Wouldn't it be funny if I had a map of women, of all the women I have known before you, of all the women I have had? Fortunately I am a musician, and my women remain incognito. When I think about them it comes out as a *do* or a *la*, and who could recognize them in a sonata? What husband would come and kill me for expressing my passion for his wife in terms of a quartet?"

When he was not smiling, his face was a Greek mask, his blue eyes enigmatic, the features sharp and willful.

He appeared cold and formal. She realized it was this mask which had terrorized her as a child. The softness came only in flashes swift as lightning, like breaks.

Unexpectedly, he broke when he smiled, the hardness broke and the softness which came was so feminine, so exposed, giving and seducing with the beauty of the teeth, exposing a dimple which he said was not a dimple at all, but a scar from the time he had slid down the banister.

As a child she had the obscure fear that this man could never be satisfied, by life, by human beings, by the world. Nothing but perfection would do. It was this sense of his exactingness which haunted her, an obscure awareness of his expectations which excited her to the great efforts she had made. But today she told herself that she had strained enough, that she wanted to rest, that she had waited a long time for it. She felt she did not want to appear before him until she was complete, and could satisfy him.

She wanted to enjoy. Her life had been a long strain, one long effort to surpass herself, to create, to perfect, a desperate and anxious flight upwards, always aiming higher, seeking greater difficulties, accumulating victories, loves, books, creations, always shedding yesterday's woman to pursue a new vision.

Today she wanted to enjoy....

They were walking into a new world together, into a new planet, a world of transparency where all that happened to them since that day she clung to him so desperately was reduced to its essence, to a skeleton, to a silhouette. His vision and his talk were abstract; his rigorous selection acted like an intense searchlight which annihilated everything around them: the color of the room, the smell of *Tabac Blond*, the warmth of the log fire, the spring sunlight showing its pale face on the studio window, the flash of his gold ring flashing his coat of arms, the immaculateness of his shirt cuffs. Everything vanished around them, the walls, the rug under their feet, the satin rays of her dress, the orange rim of her sleeve, the orange reflections of the walls, the books leaning against each other, the soft backs of the French books yielding under the stiff-backed English books, the lightness and swiftness of his Spanish voice, his Spanish words bowing and smiling between the French.

She could only see the point he watched, the intense focusing upon the meaning of their lives, the clear outline of their patterns, and his questions: What are you today? What do you believe? What do you think? What do you read? What do you love? What is your music? What is your language? What is your climate? What hour of the day do you love best? What are your whims? Your extravagances? Your antipathies? Who are your enemies? Who is your god? Who is your demon? What haunts you? What frightens you? What gives you courage? Whom do you love? What do you remember? What image do you have of me? What have you been? Are we strangers, with twenty years between us? Does your blood obey me? Have I made you? Are you my daughter? Are you my father? Have we dreamed? Are we real? Is our life real? Is anything real? Are we here? Do I understand you?

"You are my daughter. We think the same. We laugh the same things. You owe me nothing. You have created yourself alone, but I gave you the seed."

He was walking back and forth, the whole length of the studio, asking questions, and every answer she gave was the echo in his own soul. Echoes. Echoes. Echoes. Echoes. Blood echoes. Yes, yes to everything. Exactly. She knew it. That is what she hoped. The same: father and daughter. Unison. The same rhythm.

They were not talking. They were merely corroborating each other's theories. Their phrases interlocked.

She was a woman, she had to live in a world built by the man she loved, live by his system. In the world she made alone she was lonely. She, being a woman, had to live in a man-made world, could not impose her own, but here was her father's world, it fitted her. With him she could run through the world in seven-league boots. He thought and felt the same thing at the same time.

"Never knew anything but solitutude," said her father. "I never knew a woman I could take into my world."

They did not speak of the harm they had done each other. The disease they carried in them they did not reveal. He did not know that the tragedy which had marked the first years of her life still colored it today. He did not know that the feeling of being abandoned was still as strong in her despite the fact that she knew it was not she who had been abandoned but her mother, that he had not really abandoned her but simply tried to save his own life. He did not know that this feeling was still so strong in her that anything which resembled abandon created a violent inner storm in her: a door closed on her too brusquely, a letter unanswered, a friend going away on a trip, the maid leaving to get married, the least mark of absent-mindedness, two people talking and forgetting to include her, or someone sending greetings to someone and forgetting her.

The smallest incident could arouse an anguish as great as that caused by death, and could reawaken the pain of separation as keenly as she had experienced it the day her father had gone away.

In an effort to combat this anguish she had crowded her world richly with friends, loves and creations. But beyond the moment of conquest there was again a desert. The joys given to her by friendships, loves, or a book just written, were endangered by the fear of loss. Just as some people are perpetually aware of death, she was perpetually aware of the pain of separation and the inevitability of it.

And beyond this, she also treated the world as if it were an ailing, abandoned child. She never put an end to a friendship of her own accord. She never abandoned anyone; she spent her life healing others of this fear wherever she saw it shadowed, pitying the whole world and giving it the illusion of faithfulness, durability, solidity. She was incapable of scolding, of pushing away, of cutting ties, of breaking relationships, of interrupting a correspondence.

Her father was telling her the story of the homely little governess he had to love because otherwise she would never have known what love was. He took her out in his beautiful car and made her lie on the heather just as the sun was going down so he would not have to see too much of her face. He enjoyed her happiness at having an adventure, the only one she would ever have. When she came to his room in the hotel he covered the lamp with a handkerchief and again he enjoyed her happiness, and taught her how to do her hair, how to rouge her lips and powder her face. The adventure made her almost beautiful.

He was talking about his escapades, skirting the periphery of his life, dwelling on his adventures. He did not dare to venture into the realm of deep love, for fear of discovering she had given her life to another. They wanted to give each other the illusion of having been faithful to each other always, and of being free to devote their whole lives to each other, now that he had returned.

Love had not been mentioned yet. Yet it was love alone which obsessed them. Not music, not writing, not painting, not decorating, not costuming, but love, the orchestration of love, its metamorphosis. She was living in a furnace of love, a blaze all around. Obsessional love, passionate love, sensual love, love in mystery, in darkness, in resistance, in contrast, love in fraternity, gratitude, imagination.

"I do think," he said, "that we should give up all this for the sake of each other. These women mean nothing to me. But the idea of devoting my whole life to you, of sacrificing adventures to something far more marvelous and deep, appeals so much to me . . . ."

"But mine is no adventure . . . ."

"You should give him up. That isn't love at all. You know I've been your only great love . . . ."

She did not want to say: "Not my only great love," but he seemed to have guessed her thought because he turned his eyes completely away from her and added: "Remember, I am an old man, I haven't so many years left to enjoy you . . . ."

With this phrase, which was actually untrue because he was younger than most men of his age, he seemed to be asking her for her life, almost to be reaching out to take full possession of her life, just as he had taken her soul away with him when she was a child. It seemed to her that he wanted to take it away now again, when she was a full-blown woman. It seemed natural to him that she should have mourned his loss throughout her childhood. It was true that he was on the road to death, drawing nearer and nearer to it; it was also true that she loved him so much that perhaps a part of her might follow him and perish with him. Would she follow him from year to year, his withering, his vanishing? Was her love a separate thing, or a part of his life? Would she leave the earth with him today? He was asking her to leave the earth today, but this time she would not. This time she felt that she would fight against giving herself up wholly. She would not die a second time.

Having been so faithful to his image as she had been, having loved his image in other men, having been moved by the men who played the piano, the men who talked brilliantly, intellectuals, teachers, philosophers, doctors, every man with blue eyes, every man with an adventurous life, every Don Juan—was it not to give him her absolute love at the end? Why did she draw away, giving him the illusion he wanted but not the absolute?

* * *

In the south of France. Six silver-gray valises, the scent of *Tabac Blond,* the gleam of polished nails, the wave of immaculate hands. Her father leaped down from the train and already he was beginning a story.

"There was a woman on the train. She sent me a message. Would I have dinner with her? Knew all about me, had sung my songs in Norway. I was too tired, with this damnable lumbago coming on, and besides, I can't put my mind on women any longer. I can only think of my betrothed."

In the elevator he overtipped the boy, he asked for news of the Negro's wife who had been sick, he advised a medicine, he ordered an appointment with the hairdresser for the next day, he took stock of the weather predictions, he ordered special biscuits and a strict vegetarian diet. The fruit had to be washed with sterilized water. And was the flautist still in the neighborhood, the one who used to keep him awake?

In the room he would not let her help him unpack his bags. He was cursing his lumbago. He seemed to have a fear of intimacy, almost as if he had hidden a crime in his valises.

"This old carcass must be subjugated," he said.

He moved like a cat. Great softness. Yet when he wanted to he could show powerful muscles. He believed in concealing one's strength.

They walked out into the sun, he looking like a Spanish grandee. He could look straight into the sun, and the tenseness of his will when he said, for instance, "I want," made him rigid from head to foot, like silex.

As she watched him bending over so tenderly to pick up an insect from the road in order to lay it safely on a leaf, addressing it in a soft, whimsical tone, preaching to it about its recklessness in thus crossing a road on which so many automobiles passed, she asked herself why it was that as a child she could only remember him as a cruel person. Why could she remember no tenderness or care on his part? Nothing but fits of anger and severity, of annoyance when they were noisy, of beatings, of a cold reserved face at meals.

As she watched him playing with the concierge's dog she wondered why she could not remember him ever sitting down to play with them; she wondered whether this conception she had of her father's cruelty was not entirely imaginary. She could not piece together his gentleness with animals and his hardness towards his children. He lived in his world like a scientist occupied with the phenomena of nature. The ways of insects aroused his curiosity; he liked to experiment, but the phenomena which the lives of his children offered, their secrets, their perplexities, had no interest for him, or rather, they disturbed him.

It was really a myopia of the soul.

The day after he arrived he was unable to move from his bed. A special medicine had to be found. Samba, the elevator man, was sent out to hunt for it. The bus driver was dispatched to get a special brand of English crackers. Paris had to be phoned to make sure the musical magazines were being forwarded. Telegrams and letters, telephone calls, Samba perspiring, the bus man covered with dust, postpone the hairdresser, order a special menu for dinner, telephone the doctor, fetch a newspaper, Samba perspiring, the elevator running up and down....

There were no other guests in the hotel—the place seemed to be run for them. Their meals were brought to the room. Mosquito nettings were installed, the furniture was changed around, his linen sheets with large initials were placed on the bed, his silver hairbrushes on the dresser, the plumber ordered to subdue a noisy water pipe, the rusty shutters were oiled, the proprietor was informed that all hotel rooms should have double doors. Noise was his greatest enemy. His nerves, as vibrant as the strings of a violin, had endowed or cursed him with uncanny hearing. A fly in the room could prevent him from sleeping. He had to put cotton in his ears in order to dull his oversensitive hearing.

He began talking about his childhood, so vividly that she thought they were back in Spain. She could feel again the noonday heat, could hear the beaded curtains parting, footsteps on the tiled floors, the cool green shadows of shuttered rooms, women in white negligees, the smell of carnations, the holy water, the dried palms at the head of the bed, the pictures of the Virgin in lace and satin, wicker armchairs, the servants singing in the courtyard....

He used to read under his bed, by the light of a candle so that his father would not find him out. He was given only one penny a week to spend. He had to make cigarettes out of straw. He was always hungry.

They laughed together.

He didn't have enough money for the Merry-go-Round. His mother used to sew at night so that he could afford to rent a bicycle the next day.

He looked out of the window from his bed and saw the birds sitting on the telegraph wires, one on each wire.

"Look," he said, "I'll sing you the melody they make sitting up there." And he sang it. "It's all in the key of humor."

"When I was a child I used to write stories in which I was always left an orphan and forced to face the world alone."

"Did you want to get rid of me?" asked her father.

"I don't think so. I think I only wanted to struggle with life alone. I was proud, and that also prevented me from coming to you until I felt ready...."

"What happened in all those stories?"

"I met with gigantic difficulties and obstacles. I overcame them. I was handed a bigger portion of suffering than is usual. Without father or mother I fought the world, angry seas, hunger, monstrous stepparents, and there were mysteries, pursuits, tortures, all kinds of danger...."

"Don't you think you are still seeking that?"

"Perhaps. Then there was another story, a story of a boat in a garden. Suddenly I was sailing down a river and I went round and round for twenty years without landing anywhere."

"Was that because you didn't have me?"

"I don't know. Perhaps I was waiting to become a woman. In all the fairy tales where the child is taken way she either returns when she is twenty, or the father returns to the daughter when she is twenty."

"He waits till she gets beyond the stage of having to have her nose blown. He waits for the interesting age."

* * *

Her father's jealousy began with the reading of her diary. He observed that after two years of obsessional yearning for him she had finally exhausted her suffering and obtained serenity. After serenity she had fallen in love with an Irish boy and then with a violinist. He was offended that she had not died completely, that she had not spent the rest of her life yearning for him. He did not understand that she had continued to love him better by living than by dying for him. She had loved him in life, lived for him and created for him. She had written the diary for him. She had loved him by falling in love at the age of eleven with the ship's captain who might have taken her back to Spain. She had loved him by taking his place at her mother's side and becoming logical and intellectual in imitation of him, not through any natural gifts for either. She had loved him by playing the father to her brothers, the husband to her mother, by giving courage, strength, by denying her feminine, emotional self. She had loved him in life creatively by writing about him.

It is true that she did not die altogether—she lived in creations. Nor did she wear black nor turn her back on men and life.

But when she became aware of his jealousy she began immediately to give him what he desired. Understanding his jealousy she began to relate the incidents of her life in a deprecatory manner, in a mocking tone, in such a way that he might feel she had not loved deeply anything or anyone but him. Understanding his desire to be exclusively loved, to be at the core of every life he touched, she could not bring herself to talk with fervor or admiration of all she loved or enjoyed. To be so aware of his feelings forced her into a role. She gave a color to her past which could be interpreted as: nothing that happened before you came was of any importance....

The result was that nothing appeared in its true light and that she deformed her true self.

Today her father, looking at her, holding her book in his hand, studying her costumes, exploring her home, studying her ideas, says: "You are an Amazon. Until you came I felt that I was dying. Now I feel renewed and strengthened."

Her own picture of her life gave him the opportunity he loved of passing judgment, an ideal judgment upon the pattern of it.

But she was so happy to have found a father, a father with a strong will, a wisdom, an infallible judgment, that she forgot for the moment everything she knew, surrendered her own certainties. She forgot her own efforts, her own wisdom. It was so sweet to have a father, to believe that there could exist someone who was in life so many years ahead of her, and who looked back upon hers and her errors, who could guide and save her, give her strength. She relinquished her convictions just to hear him say: "In that case you were too believing," or: "That was a wasted piece of sacrifice. Why save junk? Let the failures die. It is something in them that make them failures."

To have a father, the seer, the god. She found it hard to look him in the eyes. She never looked at the food he put in his mouth. It seemed to her that vegetarianism was the right diet for a divine being. She had such a need to worship, to relinquish her power. It made her feel more the woman.

She thought again of his remark: "You are an Amazon. You are a force." She looked at herself in the mirror with surprise. Certainly not the *body* of an Amazon.

What was it her father saw? She was underweight, so light on her feet that a caricaturist had once pictured her as having floated up to the ceiling like a balloon and everybody trying to catch her with brooms and ladders. Not the woman in the mirror, then, but her words, her writing, her work. Strength in creation, in life, ideas. She had proved capable of building a world for herself. *Amazon!* Capable of every audacity in life, but vulnerable in love. . . .

She translated his remark to herself thus: Whenever anyone says *you are* they mean *I want you to be!* He wanted her to be an Amazon. One breast cut off as in the myth, so as to be able to use the bow and arrow. The other breast far too tender, too vulnerable.

Why? Because an Amazon did not need a father. Nor a lover, nor a husband. An Amazon was a law and a world all to herself.

He was abdicating his father role. A woman-ruled world was no hardship to him, the artist, for in it he had a privileged place. He had all the sweetness of her one breast, together with all her strength. He could lie down on that breast and dream, for at his side was a woman who carried a bow and arrow to defend him. He, the writer, the musician, the sculptor, the painter, he could lie down and dream by the side of the Amazon who could give him nourishment and fight the world for him as well. . . .

She looked at him. He was her own height. He was a little bowed by fatigue and the thought of his own frailness. His nerves, his sensitiveness, his dependence on women. He looked slenderer and paler. He said: "I used to be afraid that my present wife might die. What would I do without a wife? I used to plan to die with her. But now I have you. I know you are strong."

Many men had said this to her before. She had not minded. Protection was a rhythm. They could exchange roles. But this phrase from a father was different . . .A father.

All through the world . . . looking for a father . . . looking naively for a father . . . falling in love with gray hairs . . . the symbol . . . every symbol of the father . . . all through the world . . . an orphan . . . in need of man the leader . . to be made woman . . . and again to be asked . . . to be the mother . . . always the mother . . . always to draw the strength she had, but never to know where to rest, where to lay down her head and find new strength . . . always to draw it out of herself . . . from herself . . . strength . . . to pour out love . . . all through the world seeking a father . . . loving the father . . . awaiting the father . . . . and finding the child.

* * *

His lumabgo and the almost complete paralysis it brought about seemed to her like a stiffness in the joints of his soul, from acting and pretending. He had assumed so many roles, had disciplined himself to appear always gay, always immaculate, always shaved, always faultless; he played at love so often, that it was as if he suffered from a cramp due to the false positions too long sustained. He could never relax. The lumbago was like the stiffness and brittleness of emotions which he had constantly directed. It was something like pain for him to move about easily in the realm of impulses. He was now as incapable of an impulse as his body was incapable of moving, incapable of abandoning himself to the great uneven flow of life with its necessary disorder and ugliness. Every gesture of meticulous care taken to eat without vulgarity, to wash his teeth, to disinfect his hands, to behave ideally, to sustain the illusion of perfection, was like a rusted hinge, for when a pattern and a goal, when an aesthetic order penetrates so deeply into the motions of life, it eats into its spontaneity like rust, and this mental orientation, his forcing of nature to follow a pattern, this constant defeat of nature and control of it, had become rust, the rust which had finally paralyzed his body. . . .

She wondered how far back she would have to trace the current of his life to find the moment at which he had thus become congealed into an attitude. At what moment had his will petrified his emotions? What shock, what incident had produced this mineralization such as took place under the earth, due to pressure?

When he talked about his childhood she could see a luminous child always dancing, always running, always alert, always responsive. His whole nature was on tiptoes with expectancy, hope and ardor. His nose sniffed the wind with high expectations of storms, tragedies, adventures, beauty. The eyes did not retreat under the brow, but were opened wide like a clairvoyant's.

She could not trace the beginning of his disease, this cancer of jealousy. Perhaps far back in his childhood, in his jealousy of his delicate sister who was preferred by his father, in his jealousy of the man who took his fiancée away from him, in the betrayal of his fiancée, in the immense shock of pain which sent him out of Spain.

Today if he read a clipping which did not give him the first place in the realm of music, he suffered. If a friend turned his admiration away. . . . If in a room he was not the center of attention. . . . Wherever there was a rival, he felt the fever and the poison of self-doubt, the fear of defeat. In all his relations with man and woman there had to be a battle and a triumph.

He began by telling her first of all that she owed him nothing; then he began to look for all that there was in her of himself.

What he noted in her diary were only the passages which revealed their sameness. She began naturally enough to think that he loved in her only what there was of himself, that beyond the realm of self-discovery, self-love, there was no curiosity.

Her father said: "Although I was prevented from training you, your blood obeyed me." As he said this his face shone with the luminosity of early portraits, this luminosity the one trait which had never faded from her memory. He glowed with a joyous Greek wisdom.

"We must look for light and clarity," he said, "because we are too easily unbalanced."

She was sitting at the foot of his bed.

"You've got such strong wings," he said. "One feels there are no walls to your life."

The mistral was blowing hot and dry. It had been blowing for ten days.

"Now I see that all these women I pursued are all in you, and you are my daughter, and I can't marry you! You are the synthesis of all the women I loved."

"Just to have found each other will make us stronger for life."

Samba the Negro came in with mail. When her father saw the letters addressed her he said: "Am I to be jealous of your letters too?"

Between each two of these phrases there was a long silence. A great simplicity of tone. They looked at each other as if they were listening to music, not as if he were saying words. Inside both their heads, as they sat there, he leaning against a pillow and she against the foot of the bed, there was a concert going on. Two boxes filled with the resonances of an orchestra. A hundred instruments playing all at once. Two long spools of flutethreads interweaving between his past and hers, the strings of the violin constantly trembling like the strings inside their bodies, the nerves never still, the heavy poundings on the drum like the heavy pounding of sex, the throb of blood, the beat of desire which drowned all the vibrations, louder than any instrument, the harp singing god, god, and the angels, the purity in his brow, the clarity in his eyes, god god, god, and the drums pounding desire at the temples. The orchestra all in one voice now, for an instant, in love, in love with the harp singing god and the violins shaking their hair and she passing the violin bow gently between her legs, drawing music out of her body, her body foaming, the harp singing god, the drum beating, the cello singing a dirge under the level of tears, through subterranean roads with notes twinkling right and left, notes like stairways to the harp singing god, god, god, and the faun through the flute mocking the notes grown black and penitent, the black notes ascending the dust route of the cello's tears, an earth tremor splitting the music in two fallen walls, walls of their faith, the cello weeping, and the violins trembling, the beat of sex breaking through the middle and splitting the white notes and black notes apart, and the piano's stairway of sounds rolling into the inferno of silence because far away, behind and beyond the violins comes the second voice of the orchestra, the dark voice out of the bellies of the instruments, underneath the notes being pressed by hot fingers, in opposition to these notes comes the song from the bellies of the instruments, out of the pollen they contain, out of the wind of passing fingers, the carpet of notes mourn with voices of black lace and dice on telegraph wires. His sadnesses locked into the cello, their dreams wrapped in dust inside of the piano box, this box on their heads cracking with resonances, the past singing, an orchestra splitting with fullness, lost loves, faces vanishing, jealousy twisting like a cancer, eating the flesh, the letter that never came, the kiss that was not exchanged, the harp singing god, god, god, who laughs on one side of his face, god was the man with a wide mouth who could have eaten her whole, singing inside the boxes of their heads. Friends, treacheries, ecstasies. The voices that carried them into serenity, the voices which made the drum beat in them, the bow of the violins passing between the legs, the curves of women's backs yielding, the baton of the orchestra leader, the second voice of locked instruments, the strings snapping, the dissonances, the hardness, the flute weeping.

They danced because they were sad, they danced all through their life, and the golden top dancing inside them made the notes turn, the white and the black, the words they wanted to hear, the new faces of the world turning black and white, ascending and descending, up and down askew stairways from the bellies of the cello full of salted tears, the water rising slowly, a sea of forgetfulness.

Yesterday ringing through the bells and castanets, and today a single note all done, like their fear of solitude, quarreling, the orchestra taking their whole being together and lifting them clear out of the earth where pain is a long, smooth song that does not cut through the flesh, where love is one long smooth note like the wind at night, no blood-shedding knife to its touch of music from distance far beyond the orchestra which answered the harp, the flute the cello, the violins, the echoes on the roof, the taste on the roof of their palates, music in the tongue, in the fingers when the fingers seek the flesh, the red pistil of desire in the fingers on the violin cords, their cries rising and falling, borne on the wings of the orchestra, hurt and wounded by its knowledge of her, for thus they cried and thus they laughed, like the bells and the castanets, thus they rolled from black to white stairways, and dreaming spirals of desire.

Where is serenity? All their forces at work together, their fingers playing, their voices, their heads cracking with the fullness of sound, crescendo of exaltation and confusion, chaos, fullness, no time to gather all the notes together, sitting inside the spider web of their past, failures, defeats.

She writing a diary like a perpetual obsessional song, and he and she dancing with gold-tipped cigarettes, wrinkled clothes, vanity, and worship, faith and doubt, losing their blood slowly from too much love, love a wound in them, too many delicacies, too many thoughts around it, too many vibrations, fatigue, nervousness, the orchestra of their desire splitting with its many faces, sad songs, god songs, quest and hunger, idealization and cynicism, humor in the split-opened face of the trombone swelling with laughter. Walls falling under the pressure of wills, walls of the absolute falling with each part of them breathing music into instruments, their arms waving, their voices, their loves, hatreds, an orchestra of conflicts, a theme of disease, the song of pain, the song of things that are never still, for after the orchestra is silent in their heads the echoes last, the concert is eternal, the solo is a delusion, the others wait behind one to accompany, to stifle, to silence, to drown. Music spilling out from the eyes in place of tears, music spilling from the throat in place of words, music falling from his fingertips in place of caresses, music exchanged between them instead of love, yearning on five lines, the five lines of their thoughts, their reveries, their emotions, their unknown self, their giant self, their shadow.

The key sitting ironically, half a question mark, like their knowledge of destiny. But she sat on five lines cursing the world for the shocks, loving the world because it has jaws, weeping at the absolute unreachable, the fifth line and the voice, saying always: have faith, even curses make music. Five lines running together with simultaneous song.

The poverty, the broken hairbrush, the Alice blue gown, twilight of sensations, MUSIQUE ANCIENNE, *objects floating. One line saying all the time I believe in god, in a god, in a father who will lean over and understand all things. I need absolution! I believe in others' purity and I find myself never pure enough. I need absolution! Another line on which she was making colorful dresses, colorful houses, and dancing. Underneath ran the line of disease, doubt, life a danger, life a mockery with an evil mouth. Everything lived out simultaneously, the love, the impulse, the doubt of the love, the knowledge of the love's death, the love of life, the doubt, the ecstasy, the knowledge of its death germ, everything like an orchestra. Can we live in rhythm, my father? Can we feel in rhythm, my father? Can we think in rhythm, my father? Rhythm—rhythm—rhythm.*

* * *

At midnight she walked away from his room, down the very long corridor, under the arches, with the lamps watching, throwing her shadow on the carpets, passing mute doors in the empty hotel, the train of her silk dress caressing the floor, the mistral hooting.

As she opened the door of her room the window closed violently—there was the sound of broken glass. Doors, silent closed doors of empty rooms, arches like those of a convent, like opera settings, and the mistral blowing. . . .

Over her bed the white mosquito netting hung like an ancient bridal canopy. . . .

The mystical bride of her father. . . .

It was she who told the first lie, with deep sadness because she did not have the courage to say to her father: "Our love should be great enough to be above jealousy. Spare me those lies which we tell the weaker ones."

Something in his eyes, a quicker beat of the eyelid, a wavering of the blue surface, the small quiver by which she had learned to detect jealousy in a face, prevented her from saying this. Truth was impossible.

At the same time there were moments when she experienced dark, strange pleasure at the thought of deceiving him. She knew how deceptive he was. She felt deep down that he was incapable of truth, that sooner or later he would lie to her, fail her. And she wanted to deceive him first, in a deeper way. It gave her joy to be so far ahead of her father who was almost a professional deceiver.

When she saw her father at the station a great misery overcame her. She sat inert, remembering each word he had said, each sensation.

It seemed to her that she had not loved him enough, that he had come upon her like a great mystery, that again there was a confusion in her between god and father. His severity, luminousness, his music, seemed again to her not human elements. She had pretended to love him humanly.

Sitting in the train, shaken by the motion, the feeling of the ever-growing distance between them, suffocating with a cold mood, she recognized the signs of an inhuman love. By certain signs she recognized all her pretenses. Every time she had pretended to feel more than she felt, she experienced this sickness of heart, this cramp and tenseness of her body. By this sign she recognized her insincerities. At the core nothing ever was false. Her feeling never deceived her. It was only her imagination which deceived her. Her imagination could give a color, a smell, a beauty to things, even a warmth which her body knew very well to be unreal.

In her head there could be a great deal of acting and many strange things could happen in there, but her emotions were sincere and they revolted, they prevented her from getting lost down the deep corridors of her inventions. Through them she knew. They were her eyes, her divining rod, they were her truth.

Today she recognized an inhuman love.

Lying back on the chaise longue with cotton over her eyes, wrapped in coral blankets, her feet on a pillow. Lying back with a feeling like that of convalescence. All weight and anguish lifted from the body and life like cotton over the eyelids.

She recognized a state which recurred often, in spite of light and sound, in spite of the streets she walked, her activities. A mood between sleep and dream, where she caught the corner of two streets—

the street of dreams and the street of living—in the palm of her hand and looked at them simultaneously, as one looks at the lines of one's destiny.

There would come cotton over her eyes and long unbroken reveries, sharp, intense, and continuous. She began to see very clearly that what destroyed her in this silent drama with her father was that she was always trying to tell something that never happened, or rather, that everything that happened, the many incidents, the trip down south, all this produced a state like slumber and ether out of which she could only awake with great difficulty. It was a struggle with shadows, a story of not meeting the loved one but loving one's self in the other, of never seeing the loved one but of seeing reflections of his presence everywhere, in everyone; of never addressing the loved one except through a diary or a book written about him, because in reality there was no connection between them, there was no human being to connect with. No one had ever merged with her father, yet they had thought a fusion could be realized through the likeness between them but the likeness itself seemed to create greater separations and confusions. There was a likeness and no understanding, likeness and no nearness.

Now that the world was standing on its head and the figure of her father had become immense, like the figure of a myth, now that from thinking too much about him she had lost the sound of his voice, she wanted to open her eyes again and make sure that all this had not killed the light, the steadiness of the earth, the bloom of the flowers, and the warmth of her other loves. So she opened her eyes and she saw: the picture of her father's foot. One day down south, while they were driving, they stopped by the road and he took off his shoe which was causing him pain. As he pulled off his sock she saw the foot of a woman. It was delicate and perfectly made, sensitive and small. She felt as if he had stolen it from her: it was her foot she was looking at, her foot he was holding in his hand. She had the feeling that she knew this foot completely. It was her foot—the very same size and the very same color, the same blue veins showing and the same air of never having walked at all.

To this foot she could have said: "I know you." She recognized the lightness, the speed of it. "I know you, but if you are my foot I do not love you. I do not love my own foot."

A confusion of feet. She is not alone in the world. She has a double. He sits on the running board of the car and when he sits there she does not know where she is. She is standing there pitying his foot, and hating it, too, because of the confusion. If it were someone else's foot her love could flow out freely, all around, but here her love stands still inside of her, still with a kind of fright.

There is no distance for her to traverse; it chokes inside of her, like the coils of self-love, and she cannot feel any love for this sore foot because that love leaps back into her like a perpetually coiled snake, and she wants always to leap outside of herself. She wants to flow out, and here her love lies coiled inside and choking her, because her father is her double, her shadow, and she does not know which one is real. One of them must die so that the other may find the boundaries of himself. To leap out freely beyond the self, love must flow out and beyond this wall of confused identities. Now she is all confused in her boundaries. She doesn't know where her father begins, where she begins, where it is he ends, what is the difference between them.

The difference is this, she begins to see, that he wears gloves for gardening and so does she, but he is afraid of poverty, and she is not. Can she prove that? *Must* she prove that? Why? For herself. She must know wherein she is not like him. She must disentangle their two selves.

She walked out into the sun. She sat at a café. A man sent her a note by the garçon. She refused to read it. She would have liked to have seen the man. Perhaps she would have liked him. Some day she might like a very ordinary man, sitting at a café. It hadn't happened yet. Everything must be immense and deep. In this she was absolutely unlike her father who liked only the most superficial adventures.

Walking into the heart of a summer day, as into a ripe fruit. Looking down at her lacquered toenails, at the white dust on her sandals. Smelling the odor of bread in the bakery where she stopped for a roll. (This her father would not do.)

A cripple passed very close to her. Her face was burned, scarred, the color of iron. All traces of her features were lost, as on a leprous face. The whites of her eyes bloodshot, her pupils dilated and misty. In her flesh she saw the meat of an animal, the fat, the sinews, the blackening blood.

Her father had said once that she was ugly. He had said it because she was born full of bloom, dimpled, roseate, overflowing with health and joy. But at the age of two she had almost died of fever. She lost the bloom all at once. She reappeared before him very pale and thin, and the aesthete in him said coolly: "How ugly you are!" This phrase she had never been able to forget. It had taken her a lifetime to disprove it to herself. A lifetime to efface it. It took the love of others, the worship of the painters, to save her from its effects.

His paternal role could be summed up in the one word: criticism. Never an élan of joy, of contentment, of approval. Always sad, exacting, critical, blue eyes.

Out of this came her love of ugliness, her effort to see beyond ugliness, always treating the flesh as a mask, as something which never possessed the same shape, color and features as thought. Out of this came her love of men's creations. All that a man said or thought *was* the face, the body; all that a man invented was his walk, his flavor, his coloring; all that a man wrote, painted, sang was his skin, his hair, his eyes. People were made of crystal for her. She could see right through their flesh, through and beyond the structure of their bones. Her eyes stripped them of their defects, their awkwardness, their stuttering. She overlooked the big ears, the frame too small, the hunched back, the wet hands, the webbed-foot walk... she forgave ... she became clairvoyant. A new sense which had awakened in her uncovered the smell of their soul, the shadow cast by their sorrows, the glow of their desires. Beyond the words and the appearances she caught all that was left unsaid—the electric sparks of their courage, the expanse of their reveries, the lunar aspects of their moods, the animal breath of their yearning. She never saw the fragmented individual, never saw the grotesque quality or aspect, but always the complete self, the mask and the reality, the fulfillment and the intention, the core and the future, She saw always the actual and the potential man, the seed, the reverie, the intention as one....

Now with her love of her father this concern with the truth lying beneath the surface and the appearance became an obsession because in him the mask was more complete. The chasm between his appearance, his words, his gestures, and his true self was deeper.

Through this mask of coldness which had terrified her as a child she was better able as a woman to detect the malady of his soul. His soul was sick. He was very sick deep down. He was dying inside; his eyes could no longer see the warm, the near, the real. He seemed to have come from very far only to be leaving again immediately. He was always pretending to be there. His body alone was there, but his soul was absent: it always escaped through a hundred fissures, it was in flight always, towards the past, or towards tomorrow, anywhere but in the present.

They looked at each other across miles and miles of separation. Their eyes did not meet. His fear of emotion enwrapped him in glass. This glass shut out the warmth of life, its human odors. He had built a glass house around himself to shut out all suffering. He wanted life to filter through, to reach him distilled, sifted of crudities and shocks. The glass walls were a prism intended to eliminate the dangerous, and in this artifical elimination life itself was deformed. With the bad was lost the human warmth, the nearness.

There was no change in his love, but the mask was back again as soon as he returned to Paris. The whole pattern of his artificial life began again. He had stopped talking as he talked down south. He was conversing. It was the beginning of his salon life. There were always people around with whom he kept up a tone of lightness and humor. In the evenings she had to appear in his salon and talk with the tip of her tongue about everything that was far from her thoughts.

This was the winter of artifice.

In that salon, with its stained-glass windows, its highly polished floor, its dark couches rooted into the Arabian rugs, its soft lights and precious books, there was only a fashionable musician bowing.

Although in reality he had not abandoned her, she felt he had passed into a world she would not follow him into. She felt impelled to act out the scene of abandon from beginning to end. She wept at the isolation in which her father's superficiality left her. She told him she had surrendered all her friends and activities for him. She told him she could not live on the talks they had in his salon. Each phrase she uttered was almost automatic.

It was the scene she knew best, the one most familiar to her even though it became an utter lie. It was the same scene which had impressed her as a child, and out of which she had made a life pattern.

As she talked with tears in her eyes, she pitied herself for having loved and trusted her father again, for having given herself to him, for having expected everything from him. At the same time she knew that this was not true. Her mind ran in two directions as she talked, and so did her feelings. She continued the habitual scene of pain: "I gave myself to you once, and you hurt me. I am glad I did not give myself to you again. Deep down I have no faith at all in you, as a human being."

The scene which she acted best and felt the best was that of abandon. She felt impelled to act it over and over again. She knew all the phrases. She was familiar with the emotions it aroused. It came so easily to her, even though she knew all the time that, except for the moment when he left them years ago, she had never really experienced abandon except by way of her imagination, except through her fear of it, through her misinterpretation of reality.

There seemed to be a memory deeper than the usual one, a memory in the tissues and cells of the body on which we tattoo certain scenes which give a shape to one's soul and life habits. It was in this way she remembered most vividly that as a child a man had tortured her; still she could not help feeling tortured or interpreting the world today as it had appeared to her then in the light of her misunderstanding of people's motives. She could not help telling her father that he was destroying her absolute love; yet she knew this was not true because it was not he who was her absolute love. But this statement was untrue only in time; that is, it was her father who had endangered her faith in the absolute, it was his behavior which she did not understand as a child which destroyed her faith in life and in love.

She knew she had deceived her father as to the extent of her love, but the thought in her mind was: what would I be feeling now if I had entrusted all my happiness to my father, if I had truly depended on him for joy and sustenance? I would be thoroughly despairing. This thought increased her sadness, and her face betrayed such anguish that her father was overwhelmed.

After this scene he continued his marionette life: a chain of fashionable concerts, of soirées, hairdressers, shirtmakers, newspaper clippings, telephone calls. . . .

She began to hate him for evaporating into frivolity, for disguising his soul with such puerilities.

She was filled with doubts. She saw him in a perpetually haunting shadow of something he was not. This man that he was not interfered with her actual knowledge. These encounters where love never reached an understanding, where all ended in frustration, this love which created nothing, this love strangled her life. As soon as he was away she began again to imagine him as he might be. She imagined him talking to her deeply, she imagined tenderness and understanding.

Imagined! Like a contagious disease withering her actual life, this imaginary meeting, imaginary talk, on which she spent all her inventiveness. As soon as he came all these expectations were destroyed. His talk was empty, marginal. His whole ingenuity was spent circling away from everything vital, in remaining on the surface by adroit descriptions of nothing; by a swift chain of puerilities, by long speeches about trivialities, by lengthy expansions of empty facts.

This ghost of her potential father tormented her like a hunger for something which she knew had been invented or created solely by herself, but which she feared might never take human shape. Where was the man she really loved? The windows he had opened in the south had been windows on the past. The present or the future seemed to terrify him. Nothing was essential but to retain avenues of escape.

This constant yearning for the man beyond the mask, this disregard of the harm which the wearing of a mask inevitably produced. It was difficult for her to believe, as others did, that the mask tainted the blood, that the colors of the mask could run into the colors of nature and poison it. She could not believe that, like the women who had been painted in gold and died of the poison, the mask and the flesh could melt into each other and bring on infection.

Her love was based on faith in the purity of one's own nature. It made her oblivious of the deformities which could be produced in the soul by the wearing of a mask. It caused her to disregard the deterioration that might affect the real face, the habits which the mask could form if worn for a long time. She could not believe that if one pretended indifference long enough, the germ of indifference could finally grow, that the soul could be discolored by long pretense, that there could come a moment when the mask and the man melted into one another, that confusion between them corroded the vital core, destroyed the core. . . .

This deterioration in her father she could not yet believe. She expected a miracle to happen. So many times it had happened to her to see the hardness of a face fall, the curtain over the eyes draw away, the false voice change, and to be allowed to enter by her vision into the true self of others.

* * *

When she was sixteen she could feel his visitations. He would descend on her often when she was dancing and laughing. He came then like a blight, because when she felt his presence, she felt a curtain of criticism covering all things. She looked through his eyes then instead of her own. Her mother always said: laugh and dance, but her father in her was contemptuous. A strange intuition because she did not know then that her father could not dance.

Once she was dancing on the stage. She had just begun her first number. The Spanish music carried her away, whirled her into a state of delirium. She could feel the audience surrendering to her. She was dancing; carrying away their eyes, their senses, into her spinning and whirling.

Her eyes fell on the front row. She saw her father there. She saw his pale face half hidden in the audience. He was holding a program before his face in order not to be recognized. But she knew his hair, his brow, his eyes. It was her father. Her steps faltered, she lost her rhythm. Only for a moment. Then she swung around, stamping her feet, dancing wildly and never looking his way, until the end.

When she saw her father years later she asked him if he had been there. He answered that not only was he not there but that if he had had the power he would have prevented her from dancing because he did not want his daughter on the stage. Even from a distance she had felt his criticalness. Now she saw him as she had divined him, cold, formal, and conventional; and she was angry at the prison walls of his severity.

As soon as she left him everything began to sing again. Everybody she passed in the street seemed like a music box. She heard the street organ, the singing of the wheels rolling. Motion was music. Her father was the musican, but in life he arrested music. Music melts all the separate parts of our bodies together. Every rusty fragment, every scattered piece could be melted into one rhythm. A note was a whole, and it was in motion, ascending or descending, swelling in fullness or thrown away, thrown out in the air, but always moving.

As soon as she left her father she heard music again. It was falling from the trees, pouring from throats, twinkling from the street lamps, sliding down the gutter. It was her faith in the world which danced again. It was the expectation of miracles which made every misery sound like part of a symphony.

Not separateness but oneness was music.

* * *

Father, let me walk alone into the music of my faith. When I am with you the world is still and silent.

You give the command for stillness, and life stops like a clock that has fallen. You draw geometric lines around liquid forms, and what you extract from the chaos is already crystallized.

As soon as I leave you everything fixed falls into waves, tides, is transformed into water and flows. I hear my heart beating again with disorder. I hear the music of my gestures, and my feet begin to run as music runs and leaps. Music does not climb stairways. Music runs and I run with it. Faith makes music come out of the trees, out of wood, out of ivory.

I could never dance around you, my father, I could never dance around you!

You held the conductor's baton, but no music could come from the orchestra because of your severity. As soon as you left, my heart beat in great disorder. Everything melted into music, and I could dance through the streets singing, without an orchestra leader. I could dance and sing.

* * *

Walking down the Rue Saturne she heard the students of the Conservatoire playing the "*Sonate en Re Mineur*" of Bach. She also heard her mother's beautiful voice singing Schumann's "*J'ai pardonné.*" . . . Strange how her mother, who had never forgiven her father, could sing that song more movingly than anything else she sang.

Walking down the Rue Saturne she was singing "*J'ai pardonné*" under her breath and thinking at the same time how she hated this street because it was the one she always walked through on her way to her father's house. On winter evenings his luxurious home was heated like a hothouse, and she found him pale and tense, at work upon some trifling matter which he took very seriously. Or rehearsing, or else just coming down from his siesta.

This siesta he always took with religious care, as if the preservation of his life depended on it. At bottom he felt life to be a danger, a process not of growth but of deterioration. To love too deeply, he said, to talk too much, to laugh too much, was a wasting of one's energy. Life was an enemy to him, and every sign of its wear and tear gave him anxiety. He could not bear a crack in the ceiling, a bit of paint worn away, a stairway worn threadbare, a faded spot on the wallpaper. Since he never lived wholly in the moment a part of him was already preparing for the morrow.

When she saw her father coming out of his room after his siesta she always had the feeling that he was making artificial efforts to delay the process of growth, fruition, decay, disintegration, which is organic and inevitable.

He believed he was delaying death by preserving himself from life, when on the contrary, it was the fear of life and the efforts he made to avoid it which used up his strength. Living never wore one out as much as the effort not to live, she believed, and only if one lived fully and freely one also rested fully and deeply. Not trusting himself to life, not abandoning himself, he could not sink into deep sleep at night without fear of death.... She always left his house with a feeling of having come near to death because everything there was so clearly a fight against death.

She left the neatest, the most spotless street of Paris where the gardners were occupied in clipping and trimming a few rare potted bushes in small, still front gardens; where butlers were occupied in polishing door knobs; where slow cars rolled up silently and caught one by surprise; where stone lions watched fur-trimmed women kissing little dogs—everything that she had rejected—....

The light was very strong on the newly painted street sign. And then she saw that the name of the street was being changed. Already it said: "Anciennement Rue Saturne... now changed to..."

Now changed. As she was changed and beginning to move away from the past. She wanted to change with the city, that all the houses of the past may be finally torn down, that the whole city of the past may disappear. That all she had seen, heard, experienced would cease to walk with her down streets with changed names, through the labyrinth of loss and change where all is forgotten. . . .

Each step along the Rue Saturne corresponded to a million steps she had taken away from her father. In the same city in which he lived a thousand steps took her to a different milieu, different ideas, different people.

Walking in the rain to pass before his house, looking up at the stained-glass window, thinking: I have at least eluded you. Where it is I have my deeper life, you do not know. The deepest part of my being you never penetrated. The woman who stands here is not your daughter. It is the woman who has escaped the stigmata of parental love.

To escape him she had run away to the end of the world. To be free of him she had run away to places where he never went. She had lost him, by living in the opposite direction from him. She sought out the failures because he didn't like those who stuttered, those who stumbled; she sought out the ugly because he turned his face away; she sought out the weak because they irritated him. She sought out chaos because he insisted on logic. She traveled to the other end of life, to the drab, the loose, the weak, the wine-stained, wine-soggy, in whom she was sure not to find the least trace of him. No trace of him anywhere along the Boulevard Clichy where the market people passed with their vegetable carts; no trace of him at two in the morning in the little café opposite La Trinite; no trace of him in the sordid neighborhood of the Boulevard Jean-Jaures: no trace of him in the *cinema du quartier,* in the Bal Musette, in the burlesque theatre. Never anyone who had heard of him. Never anyone who smelled like him. Never a voice like his.

It was her father who thrust her out into the black, soiled corners of the world. Everything she loved she turned her back on because it was also what he loved. Luxury with its serpentine of light, its masquerade costume of gaiety, everything that shined, glittered, threw off perfume, would have reminded her of him. To efface such a love took her years of walking greasy streets, of sleeping between soiled sheets, of traversing the unknown. She was happy only when she finally succeeded in losing him.

Her father and she were walking through the Bois. On his lips she could still see the traces of a mordant kiss.

"We met at Notre Dame," he was saying. "She began with the most vulgar cross-examination, reproaching me for not loving her. So I proceeded with a slow analysis of her, telling her she had fallen in love with me in the way women usually fall in love with an artist who is handsome and who plays with vehemence and elegance; telling her that it had been a literary and imaginary affair kindled by the reading of my books, that our affair had no substantial basis, what with meetings interrupted by intervals of two years. I told her that no love could survive such thin nourishment and that besides she was too pretty a woman to have remained two years without a lover, especially in view of the fact that she cordially detested her husband. She said she felt that my heart was not in it. I answered that I didn't know whether or not my heart was in it when we had only twenty minutes together in a taxi without curtains in an overlit city."

"Did you talk to her in that ironic tone?" she asked.

"It was even more cutting than that. I was annoyed that she had been able to give me only twenty minutes."

(He had forgotten that he had come to tell her that he did not love her. What most struck him and annoyed him was that she had only been able to escape her husband's surveillance for twenty minutes.)

"She was so hurt," he added, "that I didn't even kiss her."

As they walked along she again looked carefully at his lip. It was slightly red, with a deeper, bluish tone in one corner, where no doubt the dainty tooth of the countess had bitten most fiercely. But she did not say anything. She was reconstructing the scene more accurately in her own head. Probably the little countess had arrived at the steps of Notre Dame, looking very earnest, very exalted. Probably her father had been touched. She did not believe that her father had been annoyed by the countess' jealousy and worship, but that it had touched his vanity. He was disguising his pleasure under an air of indifference, so that his listener might take him for a cynical Don Juan, the despair of women.

He repeated a story which he had told her before, of how the countess had slashed her face in order to justify her tardiness to her husband. This story had always seemed highly improbable to her, because a woman in love is not likely to endanger her beauty. Any explanation would have been simpler than this farfetched tale of an automobile accident.

But why did he have this need of falsifying all that happened to him? She had long before asked him to cease creating this illusion of an exclusive love, to be truthful with her. She had offered to be his confidante. He had promised . . . and now he was inventing again.

When she arrived the next day he had not slept at all, thinking: I am going to lose you. And if I lose you I cannot live any more. You are everything to me. My life was empty before you came. My life is a failure and a tragedy anyway.

He looked deeply sad. His fingers were wandering over the keys, hesitantly. His eyes looked as if he had been walking through a desert.

"You make me realize," he said, "how empty my activity is. In not being able to make you happy I miss the most vital reason for living."

He was again the man she had known in the south. His tone rang true. But he could not let her be. If she preferred Dostoevski to Anatole France he felt that his whole edifice of ideas was being attacked and endangered. He was offended if she did not smoke his cigarettes, if she did not go to all his concerts, if she did not admire all his friends.

And she—she wanted him to abandon his superficialities and vanities and deceptions. They could not accept each other.

Realizing more and more that she did not love him she felt a strange joy, as if she were witnessing a just punishment for his coldness as a father when she was a child. And this suffering, which in reality she made no effort to inflict since she kept her secret, gave her joy. It made her feel that she was balancing in herself all the injustice of life, that she was restoring in her own soul a kind of symmetry to the events of life.

It was the fulfillment of a spiritual symmetry. A sorrow here, a sorrow there. Abandon yesterday, abandon today. Betrayal today, betrayal tomorrow. Two equally poised columns. A deception here, a deception there, like twin colonades: a love for today, a love for tomorrow; a punishment to him, a punishment to the other... and one for herself.... Mystical geometry. The arithmetic of the unconscious which impelled this balancing of events.

She felt like laughing whenever her father repeated that he was lucid, simple, logical. She knew that this order and precision were only apparent. He had chosen to live on the surface, and she to descend deeper and deeper. His fundamental desire was to escape pain, hers to face all of life. Instead of coming out of his shell to face the disintegration of their relationship, he eluded the truth. He had not discovered as she had that by meeting the person she feared to meet, by reading the letter she feared to read, by giving life a chance to strike at her she had discovered that it struck less cruelly than her imagination. To imagine was far more terrible than reality, because it took place in a void, it was untestable. There were no hands with which to strike or defend oneself in that inner chamber of ghostly tortures. But in living the realization summoned energies, forces, courage, arms and legs to fight with so that war almost became a joy. To fight a real sorrow, a real loss, a real insult, a real disillusion, a real treachery was infinitely less difficult than to spend a night without sleep struggling with ghosts. The imagination is far better at inventing tortures than life because the imagination is a demon within us and it knows where to strike, where it hurts. It knows the vulnerable spot, and life does not, our friends and lovers do not, because seldom do they have the imagination equal to the task.

* * *

He told her that he had stayed awake all night wondering how he would bring himself to tell a singer that she had no voice at all.

"There was almost a drama here yesterday with Laura about that singer. I tried to dissuade her from falling in love with me by assuring her she was simply the victim of a mirage which surrounds every artist, that if she came close to me she would be disillusioned. So yesterday after the singing we talked for three quarters of an hour and when I told her I would not have an affair with her (at another period of my life I might have done it, for the game of it, but now I have other things to live for) she began to sob violently and the rimmel came off. When she had used up her handkerchief I was forced to lend her mine. Then she dropped her lipstick and I picked it up and wiped it with another of my handkerchiefs. After the first fits of tears she began to calmly make up her face, wiping off the rouge that had been messed up by the tears. When she left I threw the handkerchiefs into the laundry. The *femme de chambre* picked them up and left all the laundry just outside the door of my room while she was cleaning it. Laura passed by, saw them and immediately thought I had deceived her. I had to explain everything to her; I told her I had not told her about this woman because I did not want to seem to be boasting all the time about women pursuing me."

She did not mind his philandering, but she was eager for the truth. She knew that he was telling a lie, because when a woman weeps the rimmel comes off, but not the lipstick, and besides, all elegant women have acquired a technique of weeping which has no such fatal effect on the make-up. You wept just enough to fill the eyes with tears and no more. No overflow. The tears stay inside the cups of the eyes, the rimmel is preserved, and yet the sadness is sufficiently expressive. After a moment one can repeat the process with the same dexterity which enables the garçon to fill a liqueur glass exactly to the brim. One tear too much could bring about a catastrophe, but these only came uncontrolled in the case of a deep love.

She was smiling to herself at his naive lies. The truth probably was that he had wiped his own mouth after kissing the singer.

He was playing around now as before, but he hated to admit it to himself, and to her, because of the ideal image he carried in himself, the image of a man who could be so deeply disturbed and altered by the love of a long-lost daughter that his career as a Don Juan had come to an abrupt end.

This romantic gesture which he was unable to make attracted him so much that he had to pretend he was making it, just as she had often pretended to be taking a voyage by writing letters on the stationery of some famous ocean liner.

"I said to Laura: do you really think that if I wanted to deceive you I would do it in such an obvious and stupid way, right here in our own home where you might come in any moment?"

What her father was attempting was to create an ideal world for her in which Don Juan, for the sake of his daughter, renounced all women. But she could not be deceived by his inventions. She was too clairvoyant. That was the pity of it. She could not believe in that which she wanted others to believe in—in a world made as one wanted it, an ideal world. She no longer believed in an ideal world.

And her father, what did he want and need? The illusion, which she was fostering, of a daughter who had never loved any one but him? Or did he find it hard to believe her too? When she left him in the south, did he not doubt her reason for leaving him?

When she went about dreaming of satisfying the world's hunger for illusion did she know it was the most painful, the most insatiable hunger? Did she not know too that she suffered from doubt, and that although she was able to work miracles for others she had no faith that the fairy tale would ever work out for herself? Even the gifts she received were difficult for her to love, because she knew that they would soon be taken away from her, just as her father had been taken away from her when she loved him so passionately, just as every home she had as a child had been disrupted, sold, lost, just as every country she became attached to was soon changed for another country, just as all her childhood had been loss, change, instability.

When she entered his house which was all in brown, brown wood on the walls, brown rugs, brown furniture, she thought of Spengler writing about brown as the color of philosophy. His windows were not open on the street, he had no use for the street, and so he had made the windows of stained glass. He lived within the heart of his own home as Orientals live within their citadel. Out of reach of passers-by. The house might have been anywhere—in England, Holland, Germany, America. There was no stamp of nationality upon it, no air from the outside. It was the house of the self, the house of his thoughts. The wall of the self-created without connection with the crown, or country or race.

He was still taking his siesta. She sat near the long range of files, the long, beautiful, neat rows of files, with names which set her dreaming: China, Science, Photography, Ancient Instruments, Egypt, Morocco, Cançer, Radio, Inventions, The Guitar, Spain. It required hours of work every day: newspapers and magazines had to be read and clippings cut out, dated, glued. He wove a veritable spider web about himself. No man was ever more completely installed in the realm of possessions.

He spent hours inventing new ways of filling his cigarette holder with an anti-nicotine filter. He bought drugs in wholesale quantities. His closets were filled with photographs, with supplies of writing paper and medicines sufficient to last for years. It was as if he feared to find himself suddenly empty-handed. His house was a storehouse of supplies which revealed his way of living too far ahead of himself, a fight against the improvised, the unexpected. He had prepared a fortress against need, war and change.

In proportion to her father's capacity for becoming invisible, untouchable, unattainable, in proportion to his capacity for metamorphosis, he had made the most solid house, the strongest walls, the heaviest furniture, the most heavily loaded bookcases, the most completely filled and catalogued universe. Everything to testify to his presence, his duration, his signature to a contract to remain on earth, visible at moments through his possessions.

In her mind she saw him asleep upstairs, with his elbow under his chin, in the most uncomfortable position which he had trained himself to hold so as not to sleep with his mouth open because that was ugly. She saw him asleep without a pillow, because a pillow under the head caused wrinkles. She pictured the bottle of alcohol which her mother had laughingly said that he bottled himself in at night in order to keep young forever. . . .

He washed his hands continuously. He had a mania for washing and disinfecting himself. The fear of microbes played a very important part in his life. The fruit had to be washed with filtered water. His mouth must be disinfected. The silverware must be passed over an alcohol lamp like the doctor's instruments. He never ate the part of the bread which his fingers had touched.

Her father had never imagined that he may have been trying to cleanse and disinfect his soul of his lies, his callousness, his deceptions. For him the only danger came from the microbes which attacked the body. He had not studied the microbe of conscience which eats into the soul.

When she saw him washing his hands, while watching the soap foaming she could see him again arriving behind stage at a concert, with his fur-lined coat and white silk scarf, and being immediately surrounded by women. She was seven years old, dressed in a strarched dress and white gloves, and sitting in the front row with her mother and brothers. She was trembling because her father had said severely: "And above all, don't make a cheap family show of your enthusiasm. Clap discreetly. Don't have people notice that the pianist's children are clapping away like noisy peasants." This enthusiasm which must be held in check was a great burden for a child's soul. She had never been able to curb a joy or sorrow: to restrain meant to kill, to bury. This cemetery of strangled emotions—was it this her father was trying to wash away? And the day she told him she was pregnant and he said: "Now you're worth less on the market as a woman"... was this being washed away? No insight into the feelings of others. Passing from hardness to sentimentality. No intermediate human feeling, but extreme poles of indifference and weakness which never made the human equation. Too hot or too cold, blood cold and heart weak, blood hot and heart cold.

While he was washing his hand with that expression she had seen on the faces of people in India thrust into the Ganges, of Egyptians plunged into the Nile, of Negroes dipped into the Mississippi, she saw the fruit being washed and mineral water poured into his glass. Sterilized water to wash away the microbes, but his soul unwashed, unwashable, yearning to be free of the microbe of conscience.... All the water running from the modern tap, running from this modern bathroom, all the rivers of Egypt, of India, of America... and he unwashed... washing his modern body, washing... washing ... washing.... A drop of holy water with which to exorcise the guilt. Hands washed over and over again in the hope of a miracle, and no miracle comes from the taps of modern washstands, no holy water flows through leaden pipes, no holy water flows under the bridges of Paris because the man standing at the tap has no faith and no awareness of his soul: he believes he is merely washing the stain of microbes from his hands....

* * *

She told her father she must leave on a trip. He said: "You are deserting me!"

He talked rapidly, breathlessly, and left very hurriedly. She wanted to stop him and ask him to give her back her soul. She hated him for the way he descended the stairs as if he had been cast out, wounded by jealously.

She hated him because she could not remain detached, nor remain standing at the top of the stairs watching him depart. She felt herself going down with him, within him, because his pain and flight were so familiar to her. She descended with him, and lost herself, passed into him, became one with him like his shadow. She felt herself empty, and dissolving into his pain. She knew that when he reached the street he would hail a taxi, and feel relief at escaping from the person who had inflicted the wound. There was always the power of escape, and rebellion.

The organ grinder would play and the pain would gnaw deeper, bitterer. He would curse the lead-colored day which intensified the sorrow because they both were born inextricably woven into the moods of nature.

He would curse his pain which distorted faces and events into one long, continuous nightmare.

She wanted to beg her father to say that he had not felt all this, and assure her that she had stayed at the top of the stairs, with separate, distinct feelings. But she was not there. She was walking with him, and sharing his feeling. She was trying to reach out to him and reassure him. But everything about him was fluttering like a bird that had flown into a room by mistake, flying recklessly and blindly in utter terror. The pain he had eluded all his life had caught him between four walls. And he was bruising himself against walls and furniture while she stood there mute and compassionate. His terror so great that he did not sense her pity, and when she moved to open the window to allow him to escape he interpreted the gesture as a menace. To run away from his own terror he flew wildly against the window and crushed his feathers.

Don't flutter so blindly, my father!

* * *

She grew suddenly tired of seeing her father always in profile, of seeing him always walking on the edge of circles, always elusive. The fluidity, the evasiveness, the deviations made his life a shadow picture. He never met life full-face. His eyes never rested on anything, they were always in flight. His face was in flight. His hands were in flight. She never saw them lying still, but always curving like autumn leaves over a fire, curling and uncurling. Thinking of him she could picture him only in motion, either about to leave, or about to arrive; she could see better than anything else, as he was leaving, his back and the way his hair came to a point on his neck.

She wanted to bring her father out in the open. She was tired of his ballet dancing. She would struggle to build up a new relationship.

But he refused to admit he had been lying. He was pale with anger. No one ever doubted him before—so he said. To be doubted blinded him with anger. He was not concerned with the truth or falsity of the situation. He was concerned with the injury and insult she was guilty of, by doubting him.

"You're demolishing everything," he said.

"What I'm demolishing was not solid," she answered. "Let's make a new beginning. We created nothing together except a sand pile into which both of us sink now and then with doubts. I am not a child. I cannot believe your stories."

He grew still more pale and angry. What shone out of his angry eyes was pride in his stories, pride in his ideal self, pride in his delusions. And he was offended. He did not stop to ask himself if she were right. She could not be right. She could see that, for a moment at any rate, he believed implicitly in the stories he had told her. If he had not believed in them so firmly he would have been humiliated to see himself as a poor comedian, a man who could not deceive even his own daughter.

"You shouldn't be offended," she said. "Not to be able to deceive your own daughter is no disgrace. It's precisely because I have told you so many lies myself that I can't be lied to."

"Now," he said, "you are accusing me of being a Don Juan."

"I accuse you of nothing. I am only asking for the truth."

"What truth?"he said, "I am a moral being, far more moral than you."

"That's too bad. I thought we were above questions of good and evil. I am not saying you are bad. That does not concern me. I am saying only that you are *false* with me. I have too much intuition."

"You have no intuition at all concerning me."

"That might have affected me when I was a child. Today I don't mind what you think of me."

"Go on," he said. "Now tell me, tell me I have no talent, tell me I don't know how to love, tell me *all that your mother used to tell me.*"

"I have never thought any of these things."

But suddenly she stopped. She knew her father was not seeing her any more, but always that judge, that past which made him so uneasy. She felt as if she were not herself any more, but her mother, her mother with a body tired with giving and serving, rebelling at his selfishness and irresponsibility. She felt her mother's anger and despair. For the first time her own image fell to the floor. She saw her mother's image. She saw the child in him who demanded all love and did not know how to love. She saw the child incapable of an act of protection, strength, or self-denial. She saw the child hiding behind her courage, the same child hiding now under Laura's protection. She was her mother telling him again that as a human being he was a failure. And perhaps she had told him too that as a musician he had not given enough to justify his limitations as a human being. All his life he had been playing with people, with love, playing *at* love, playing *at* being a pianist, playing *at* composing. Playing because to no one or nothing could he give his whole soul.

There were two regions, two tracts of land, with a bridge in between, a slight, fragile bridge like the Japanese bridges in the miniature Japanese gardens. Whoever ventured to cross the bridge fell into the abyss. So it was with her mother. She had fallen through and been drowned. Her mother thought he had a soul. She had fallen there in that space where his emotions reached their limit, where the land opened in two, where circles fell open and rings were unsoldered.

Was it her mother talking now? She was saying: "I am only asking you to be honest with yourself. I admit when I lie, but you never admit it. I am not asking for anything except that you be real."

"Now say I am superficial."

"At this moment you are. I wanted you to face me and be truthful."

He paced up and down, pale with anger.

It seemed to her that her father was not quarreling with her but with his own past, that what was coming to light now was his underlying feeling of guilt towards her mother. If he saw in her now an avenger it was only because of his fear that his daughter might accuse him too. Against her judgment he had erected a huge defense: the approbation of the rest of the world. But in himself he had never quite resolved the right and the wrong. He, too, was driven now by a compulsion to say things he never intended to say, to make her the symbol of the one who had come to punish, to expose his deceptions, to prove his worthlessness.

And this was not the meaning of her struggle with him. She had not come to judge him but to dissolve the falsities. He feared so much that she had come to say: "the four persons you abandoned in order to live your own life, to save yourself, were crippled," that he did not hear her real words. The scene was taking place between two ghosts.

Her father's ghost was saying: "I cannot bear the slightest criticism. Immediately I feel judged, condemned."

Her own ghost was saying: "I cannot bear lies and deceptions. I need truth and sincerity."

They could not understand each other. They were gesticulating in space. Gestures of despair and anger. Her father pacing up and down, angry because of her doubts of him, forgetting that these doubts were well founded, forgetting to ask himself if she was right or not. And she in despair because her father would not understand, because the fragile little Japanese bridge between the two portions of his soul would not hold her even for a moment, she walking with such light feet, trying to bring messages from one side to another, trying to make connections between the real and the unreal.

She could not see her father any more. She could see only the hard profile cutting the air like a swift stone ship, a stone ship moving in a sea unknown to human beings, into regions made of granite rock. No more water, or warmth, or flow between them. All communication paralyzed by the falsity. Lost in the fog. Lost in a cold, white fog of falsity. Images distorted as if they were looking through a glass bowl. His mouth long and mocking, his eyes enormous but empty in their transparency. Not human. All human contours lost.

And she thinking: I stopped loving my father a long time ago. What remained was the slavery to a pattern. When I saw him I thought I would be happy and exalted. I pretended. I worked myself up into ecstasies. When one is pretending the entire body revolts. There come great eruptions and revolts, great dark ravages, and above all, a joylessness. A great, bleak joylessness. Everything that is natural brings joy. He was pretending too—he had to win me as a trophy, as a victory. He had to win me away from my mother, had to win my approbation. Had to win me because he feared me. He feared the judgment of his children. And when he could not win me he suffered in his vanity. He fought in me his own faults, just as I hated in him my own faults.

Certain gestures made in childhood seem to have eternal repercussions. Such was the gesture she had made to keep her father from leaving, grasping his coat and holding on to it so fiercely that she had to be torn away. This gesture of despair seemed to prolong itself all through her life. She repeated it blindly, fearing always that everything she loved would be lost.

It was so hard for her to believe that this father she was still trying to hold on to was no longer real or important, that the coat she was touching was not warm, that the body of him was not human, that her breathless, tragic desire had come to an end, and that her love had died.

Great forces had impelled her towards symmetry and balance, had impelled her to desert her father in order to close the fatal circle of desertion. She had forced the hourglass of pain to turn. They had pursued each other. They had tried to possess each other. They had been slaves of a pattern, and not of love. Their love had long ago been replaced by the other loves which gave them life. All those parts of the self which had been tied up in a tangle of misery and frustration had been loosened imperceptibly by life, by creation. But the feelings they had begun with twenty years back, he of guilt and she of love, had been like railroad tracks on which they had been launched at full speed by their obsessions.

Today she held the coat of a dead love.

This had been the nightmare—to pursue this search and poison all joys with the necessity of its fulfillment. To discover that such fulfillment was not necessary to life, but to the myth. It was the myth which had forbidden them to deny their first ideal love or to recognize its illusory substance. What they called their destiny—the railroad track of their obsessions.

At last she was entering the Chinese theater of her drama and could see the trappings of the play as well as the play itself, see that the settings were made of the cardboard of illusion. She was passing behind the stage and could stop weeping. The suffering was no longer real. She could see the strings which ruled the scenes, the false storms and the false lightning.

She was coming out of the ether of the past.

The world was a cripple. Her father was a cripple. In striking out for his own liberty, to save his life, he had struck at her, but he had poisoned himself with remorse.

No need to hate. No need to punish.

The last time she had come out of the ether it was to look at her dead child, a little girl with long eyelashes and slender hands. She was dead.

The little girl in her was dead too. The woman was saved. And with the little girl died the need of a father.

from Under a Glass Bell

HOUSEBOAT

The current of the crowd wanted to sweep me along with it. The green lights on the street corners ordered me to cross the street, the policeman smiled to invite me to walk between the silver-headed nails. Even the autumn leaves obeyed the current. But I broke away from it like a fallen piece. I swerved out and stood at the top of the stairs leading down to the Quays. Below me flowed the river. Not like the current I had just broken from, made of dissonant pieces colliding rustily, driven by hunger and desire.

Down the stairs I ran towards the water front, the noises of the city receding as I descended, the leaves retreating to the corner of the steps under the wind of my skirt. At the bottom of the stairs lay the wrecked mariners of the street current, the tramps who had fallen out of the crowd life, who refused to obey. Like me, at some point of the trajectory, they had all fallen out, and here they lay shipwrecked at the foot of the trees, sleeping, drinking. They had abandoned time, possessions, labor, slavery. They walked and slept in counter-rhythm to the world. They renounced houses and clothes. They sat alone, but not unique, for they all seemed to have been born brothers. Time and exposure made their clothes alike, wine and air gave them the same eroded skin. The crust of dirt, the swollen noses, the stale tears in the eyes, all gave them the same appearance. Having refused to follow the procession of the streets, they sought the river which lulled them. Wine and water. Every day,

From *Under A Glass Bell* (Swallow, 1948), pp. 11-25.

in front of the river, they reenacted the ritual of abandon. Against the knots of rebellion, wine and the river, against the cutting iron of loneliness, wine and water washing away everything in a rhythm of blurred silences.

They threw the newspapers into the river and this was their prayer: to be carried, lifted, borne down, without feeling the hard bone of pain in man, lodged in his skeleton, but only the pulse of flowing blood. No shocks, no violence, no awakening.

While the tramps slept, the fishermen in a trance pretended to be capturing fish, and stood there hypnotized for hours. The river communicated with them through the bamboo rods of their fishing tackle, transmitting its vibrations. Hunger and time were forgotten. The perpetual waltz of lights and shadows emptied one of all memories and terrors. Fishermen, tramps, filled by the brilliance of the river as by an anesthetic which permitted only the pulse to beat, emptied of memories as in dancing.

The houseboat was tied at the foot of the stairs. Broad and heavy on its keel, stained with patches of lights and shadows, bathing in reflections, it heaved now and then to the pressure of a deeper breathing of the river. The water washed its flanks lingeringly, the moss gathered around the base of it, just below the water line, and swayed like Naiad hair, then folded back again in silky adherence to the wood. The shutters opened and closed in obedience to the gusts of wind and the heavy poles which kept the barge from touching the shore cracked with the strain like bones. A shiver passed along the houseboat asleep on the river, like a shiver of fever in a dream. The lights and shadows stopped waltzing. The nose of the houseboat plunged deeper and shook its chains. A moment of anguish: everything was slipping into anger again, as on earth. But no, the water dream persisted. Nothing was displaced. The nightmare might appear here, but the river knew the mystery of continuity. A fit of anger and only the surface erupted, leaving the deep flowing body of the dream intact.

The noises of the city receded completely as I stepped on the gangplank. As I took out the key I felt nervous. If the key fell into the river, the key to the little door to my life in the infinite? Or if the houseboat broke its moorings and floated away? It had done this once already, breaking the chain at the prow, and the tramps had helped to swing it back in place.

As soon as I was inside of the houseboat, I no longer knew the name of the river or the city. Once inside the walls of old wood, under the heavy beams, I might be inside a Norwegian sailing ship traversing fjords, in a Dutch boyer sailing to Bali, a jute boat on the Brahmaputra. At night the lights on the shore were those of Constantinople or the Neva. The giant bells ringing the hours were those of the sunken Cathedral. Every time I inserted the key in the lock, I felt this snapping of cords, this lifting of anchor, this fever of departure. Once inside the houseboat, all the voyages began. Even at night with its shutters closed, no smoke coming out of its chimney, asleep and secret, it had an air of mysteriously sailing somewhere.

At night I closed the windows which overlooked the Quays. As I leaned over I could see dark shadows walking by, men with their collars turned up and their caps pushed over their eyes, women with wide long skirts, market women who made love with the tramps behind the trees. The street lamps high above threw no light on the trees and bushes along the big wall. It was only when the window rustled that the shadows which seemed to be one shadow split into two swiftly and then, in the silence, melted into one again.

At this moment a barge full of coal passed by, sent waves rolling behind it, upheaving all the other barges. The pictures on the walls swayed. The fishing net hung on the ceiling like a giant spider web swung, gently rocking a sea shell and a starfish caught in its meshes.

On the table lay a revolver. No harm could come to me on the water but someone had laid a revolver there believing I might need it. I looked at it as if it reminded me of a crime I had commited, with an irrepressible smile such as rises sometimes to people's lips in the face of great catastrophes which are beyond their grasp, the smile which comes at times on certain women's faces while they are saying they regret the harm they have done. It is the smile of nature quietly and proudly asserting its natural right to kill, the smile which the animal in the jungle never shows but by which man reveals when the animal re-enters his being and reasserts its presence. This smile came to me as I took up the revolver and pointed it out of the window, into the river. But I was so averse to killing that even shooting into the water I felt uneasy, as if I might kill the Unknown Woman of the Seine again—the woman who had drowned herself here years ago and who was so beautiful that at the Morgue they had taken a plaster cast of her face. The shot came faster than I had expected. The river swallowed it. No one noticed it, not from the bridge, not from the Quays. How easily a crime could be committed here.

Outside an old man was playing the violin feverishly, but no sound came out of it. He was deaf. No music poured from his instrument, no music, but tiny plaintive cries escaped from his trembling gestures.

At the top of the stairs two policemen were chatting with the prostitutes.

The windows overlooking the Quays now shut, the barge looked uninhabited. But the windows looking on the river were open. The dying summer breath entered into my bedroom, the room of shadows, the bower of the night. Heavy beams overhead, low ceilings, a heavy wooden sideboard along the walls. An Indian lamp threw charcoal patterns over walls and ceiling—a Persian design of cactus flowers, lace fans, palm leaves, a lamaist vajry-mandala flower, minarets, trellises.

(When I lie down to dream, it is not merely a dust flower born like a rose out of the desert sands and destroyed by a gust of wind. When I lie down to dream it is to plant the seed for the miracle and the fulfillment.)

The headboard opened like a fan over my head, a peacock feather opening in dark wood and copper threads, the wings of a great golden bird kept afloat on the river. The barge could sink, but not this wide heavy bed traveling throughout the nights spread over the deepest precipices of desire. Falling on it I felt the waves of emotion which sustained me, the constant waves of emotion under my feet. Burrowing myself into the bed only to spread fanwise and float into a moss-carpeted tunnel of caresses.

The incense was spiraling. The candles were burning with delicate oscillations of anguish. Watching them was like listening to a beloved heartbeat and fearing the golden hammer strokes might stop. The candles never conquered the darkness but maintained a disquieting duel with the night.

I heard a sound on the river, but when I leaned out of the window the river had become silent again. Now I heard the sound of oars. Softly, softly coming from the shore. A moat knocked against the barge. There was a sound of chains being tied.

I await the phantom lover—the one who haunts all women, the one I dream of, who stands behind every man, with a finger and head shaking—"Not him, he is not the one." Forbidding me each time to love.

* * *

The houseboat must have traveled during the night, the climate and the scenery were changed. Dawn was accelerated by a woman's shrieks. Shrieks interrupted by the sound of choking. I ran on deck. I arrived just as the woman who was drowning grasped the anchor's chain. Her shrieks grew worse as she felt nearer salvation, her appetite for life growing more violent. With the help of one of the drunken tramps, we pulled the chain up, with the woman clinging to it She was hiccuping, spitting, choking. The drunken tramp was shouting orders to imaginary sailors, telling them what to do for the drowned. Leaning over the woman he almost toppled over her, which reawakened her aggressiveness and helped her to rise and walk into the barge where we changed her clothes.

The barge was traversing a dissonant climate. The mud had come to the surface of the river, and a shoal of corks surrounded the barge. We pushed them away with brooms and poles; the corks seemed to catch the current and float away, only to encircle the barge magnetically.

The tramps were washing themselves at the fountain. Bare to the waist, they soaked their faces and shoulders, and then they washed their shirts, and combed themselves, dipping their combs in the river. These men at the fountain, they knew what was going to happen. When they saw me on deck, they gave me the news of the day, of the approach of war, of the hope of revolution. I listened to their description of tomorrow's world. An aurora borealis and all men out of prison.

The oldest tramp of all, who did not know about tomorrow, he was in the prison of his drunkenness. No escape. When he was filled like a barrel, then his legs gave way and he could only fall down.

When he was lifted by alcoholic wings and ready for flight, the wings collapsed into nausea. This gangplank of drunkenness led nowhere.

The same day at this post of anguish, three men quarreled on the Quays. One carried a ragpicker's bag over his shoulder. The second was brilliantly elegant. The third was a beggar with a wooden leg. They argued excitedly. The elegant one was counting out money. He dropped a ten-franc piece. The beggar placed his wooden leg on it and would not budge. No one could frighten him, and no one dared to push off the wooden leg. He kept it there all the time they argued. Only when the two others went off did he lean over to pick it up.

The street cleaner was sweeping the dead leaves into the river. The rain fell into the cracked letter box and when I opened my letters it looked as if my friends had been weeping when writing me.

A child sat on the edge of the river, his thin legs dangling. He sat there for two or three hours and then began to cry. The street cleaner asked him what was the matter. His mother had told him to wait there until she returned. She had left him a piece of dry bread. He was wearing his little black school apron. The street cleaner took his comb, dipped it in the river and combed the child's hair and washed his face. I offered to take him on the barge. The street cleaner said: "She'll never come back. That's how they do it. He's another for the Orphanage."

When the child heard the word orphanage he ran away so fast the street cleaner did not have time to drop his broom. He shrugged his shoulders: "They'll catch him sooner or later. I was one of them."

Voyage of despair.

The river was having a nightmare. Its vast whaleback was restless. It had been cheated of its daily suicide. More women fed the river than men—more wanted to die in winter than in summer.

Parasitic corks obeyed every undulation but did not separate from the barge, glued like waves of mercury. When it rained the water seeped through the top room and fell on my bed, on my books, on the black rug.

I awakened in the middle of the night with wet hair. I thought I must be at the bottom of the Seine; that the barge, the bed, had quietly sunk during the night.

It was not very different to look through water at all things. It was like weeping cool saltless tears without pain. I was not cut off altogether, but in so deep a region that every element was marrying in sparkling silence, so deep that I heard the music of the spinet inside the snail who carries his antennae like an organ and travels on the back of a harp fish.

In this silence and white communion took place the convolutions of plants turning into flesh, into planets. The towers were pierced by swordfishes, the moon of citron rotated on a sky of lava, the branches had thirsty eyes hanging like berries. Tiny birds sat on weeds asking for no food and singing no song but the soft chant of metamorphosis, and each time they opened their beaks the webbed stained-glass windows decomposed into snakes and ribbons of sulphur.

The light filtered through the slabs of mildewed tombs and no eyelashes could close against it, no tears could blur it, no eyelids could curtain it off, no sleep could dissolve it, no forgetfulness could deliver one from this place where there was neither night nor day. Fish, plant, woman, equally aware, with eyes forever open, confounded and confused in communion, in an ecstasy without repose.

I ceased breathing in the present, inhaling the air around me into the leather urns of the lungs. I breathed out into the infinite, exhaling the mist of a three-quarter-tone breath, a light pyramid of heart beats.

This breathing lighter than breathing, without pressure from the wind, like the windless delicacy of the air in Chinese paintings, supporting one winged black bird, one breathless cloud, bowing one branch, preceded the white hysteria of the poet and the red-foamed hysteria of woman.

When this inhaling of particles, of dust grains, of rust microbes, of all the ashes of past death ceased, I inhaled the air from the unborn and felt my body like a silk scarf resting outside the blue rim of the nerves.

The body recovered the calm of minerals, its plant juices, the eyes became gems again, made to glitter alone and not for the shedding of tears.

Sleep.

No need to watch the flame of my life in the palm of my hand, this flame as pale as the holy ghost speaking in many languages to which none have the secret.

The dream will watch over it. No need to remain with eyes wide open. Now the eyes are gems, the hair a fan of lace. Sleep is upon me.

The pulp of roots, the milk of cactus, the quicksilver drippings of the silver beeches is in my veins.

I sleep with my feet on moss carpets, my branches in the cotton of the clouds.

The sleep of a hundred years has transfixed all into the silver face of ecstasy.

* * *

During the night the houseboat traveled out of the landscape of despair. Sunlight struck the wooden beams, and the reflected light of the water danced on the wooden beams. Opening my eyes I saw the light playing around me and I felt as if I were looking through a pierced sky into some region far nearer to the sun. Where had the houseboat sailed to during the night?

The island of joy must be near. I leaned out of the window. The moss costume of the houseboat was greener, washed by cleaner waters. The corks were gone, and the smell of rancid wine. The little waves passed with great precipitation. The waves were so clear I could see the roots of the indolent algae plants that had grown near the edge of the river.

This day I landed at the island of joy.

I could now put around my neck the sea-shell necklace and walk through the city with the arrogance of my secret.

When I returned to the houseboat with my arms loaded with new candles, wine, ink, writing paper, nails for the broken shutters, the policeman stopped me at the top of the stairs: "Is there a holiday on the Quay?"

"A holiday? No."

As I ran down the stairs I understood. There was a holiday on the Quay! The policeman had seen it on my face. A celebration of lights and motion. Confetti of sun spots, serpentines of water currents, music from the deaf violinist. It was the island of joy I had touched in the morning. The river and I united in a long, winding, never-ending dream, with its deep undercurrents, its deeper undertows of dark activity, the river and I rejoicing at teeming obscure mysteries of river-bottom lives.

The big clock of the Sunken Cathedral rang twelve times for the feast. Barges passed slowly in the sun, like festive chariots throwing bouquets of lightning from their highly polished knobs. The laundry in blue, white and rose, hung out to dry and waving like flags, children playing with cats and dogs, women holding the rudder with serenity and gravity. Everything washed clean with water and light passing at a dream pace.

But when I reached the bottom of the stairs the festivity came to an abrupt end. Three men were cutting the algae plants with long scythes. I shouted but they worked on unconcerned, pushing them all away so that the current would sweep them off. The men laughed at my anger. One man said: "These are not your plants. Cleaning Department order. Go and complain to them." And with quicker gestures they cut all the algae and fed the limp green carpet to the current.

So passed the barge out of the island of joy.

* * *

One morning what I found in the letter box was an order from the river police to move on. The King of England was expected for a visit and he would not like the sight of the houseboats, the laundry exposed on the decks, the chimneys and water tanks in rusty colors, the gangplanks with teeth missing, and other human flowers born of poverty and laziness. We were all ordered to sail on, quite a way up the Seine, no one knew quite where because it was all in technical language.

One of my neighbors, a one-eyed cyclist, came to discuss the dispossessions and to invoke laws which had not been made to give houseboats the right to lie in the heart of Paris gathering moss. The fat painter who lived across the river, open-shirted and always perspiring, came to discuss the matter and to suggest we do not move at all as a form of protest. What could happen? At the worst, since there were no laws against our staying, the police would have to fetch a tugboat and move us all in a line, like a row of prisoners. That was the worst that could happen to us. But the one-eyed cyclist was overcome by this threat because he said his houseboat was not strong enough to bear the strain of being pulled between other heavier, larger barges. He had heard of a small houseboat being wrenched apart in such a voyage. He did not think mine would stand the strain either.

The next day the one-eyed man was towed along by a friend who ran one of the tourist steamers; he left at dawn like a thief, with his fear of collective moving. Then the fat painter moved, pulled heavily and slowly because his barge was the heaviest. He owned a piano and huge canvases, heavier than coal. His leaving left a vast hole in the alignment of barges, like a tooth missing. The fishermen crowded in this open space to fish and rejoiced. They had been wishing us away, and I believe it was their prayers which were heard rather than ours, for soon the letters from the police became more insistent.

I was the last one left, still believing I would be allowed to stay. Every morning I went to see the chief of police. I always believed an exception would be made for me, that laws and regulations broke down for me. I don't know why except that I had seen it happen very often. The chief of police was extremely hospitable; he permitted me to sit in his office for hours and gave me pamphlets to pass the time. I became versed in the history of the Seine. I knew the number of sunken barges, collided Sunday tourist steamboats, of people saved from suicide by the river police. But the law remained adamant, and the advice of the chief of police, on the sly, was for me to take my houseboat to a repair yard near Paris where I could have a few repairs made while waiting for permission to return. The yard being near Paris, I made arrangements for a tugboat to come for me in the middle of the day.

The tugboat's approach to the barge was very much like a courtship, made with great care and many cork protectors. The tugboat knew the fragility of these discarded barges converted into houseboats. The wife of the tugboat captain was cooking lunch while the maneuvers were carried out. The sailors were untying the ropes, one was stoking the fire. When the tugboat and the barge were tied together like twins, the captain lifted the gangplank, opened his bottle of red wine, drank a very full gulp and gave orders for departure.

Now we were gliding along. I was humming all over the houseboat, celebrating the strangest sensation I had ever known, this traveling along a river with all my possessions around me, my books, my diaries, my furniture, my pictures, my clothes in the closet. I leaned out of each little window to watch the landscape. I lay on the bed. It was a dream. I was a dream, this being a marine snail traveling with one's house all around one's neck.

A marine snail gliding through the familiar city. Only in a dream could I move so gently along with the small human heartbeat in rhythm with the tug tug heartbeat of the tugboat, and Paris unfolding, uncurling, in beautiful undulations.

The tugboat pulled its smokestacks down to pass under the first bridge. The captain's wife was serving lunch on deck. Then I discovered with anxiety that the barge was taking in water. It had already seeped through the floor. I began to work the pumps, but could not keep abreast of the leaks. Then I filled pails, pots and pans, and still I could not control the water, so I called out to the captain. He laughed. He said: "We'll have to slow down a bit." And he did.

The dream rolled on again. We passed under a second bridge with the tugboat bowing down like a salute, passed all the houses I had lived in. From so many of these windows I had looked with envy and sadness at the flowing river and passing barges. Today I was free, and traveling with my bed and my books. I was dreaming and flowing along with the river, pouring water out with pails, but this was a dream and I was free.

Now it was raining. I smelled the captain's lunch and I picked up a banana, The captain shouted: "Go on deck and say where it is you want to stop."

I sat on deck under an umbrella, eating the banana, and watching the course of the voyage. We were out of Paris, in that part of the Seine where the Parisians swim and canoe. We were traveling past the Bois de Boulogne, through the exclusive region where only the small yachts were allowed to anchor. We passed another bridge, and reached a factory section. Discarded barges were lying on the edge of the water. The boat yard was an old barge surrounded with rotting skeletons of barges, piles of wood, rusty anchors, and pierced water tanks. One barge was turned upside down, and the windows hung half wrenched on the side.

We were towed alongside and told to tie up against the guardian barge, that the old man and woman would watch mine until the boss came to see what repairing had to be done.

My Noah's Ark had arrived safely, but I felt as if I were bringing an old horse to the slaughterhouse.

The old man and woman who were the keepers of this cemetery had turned their cabin into a complete concierge's lodge to remind themselves of their ancient bourgeois splendor: an oil lamp, a tile stove, elaborate sideboards, lace on the back of the chairs, fringes and tassels on the curtains, a Swiss clock, many photographs, bric-a-brac, all the tokens of their former life on earth.

Every now and then the police came to see if the roof was done. The truth was that the more pieces of tin and wood the boss nailed to the roof, the more the rain came in. It fell on my dresses and trickled into my shoes and books. The policeman was invited to witness this because he suspected the length of my stay.

Meanwhile the King of England had returned home, but no law was made to permit our return. The one-eyed man made a daring entry back and was expelled the very next day. The fat painter returned to his spot before the Gare d'Orsay—his brother was a deputy.

So passed the barge into exile.

RAGTIME

The city was asleep on its right side and shaking with violent nightmares. Long puffs of snoring came out of the chimneys. Its feet were sticking out because the clouds did not cover it altogether. There was a hole in them and the white feathers were falling out. The city had untied all the bridges, like so many buttons, to feel at ease. Wherever there was a lamplight the city scratched itself until it went out.

Trees, houses, telegraph poles, lay on their side. The ragpicker walked among the roots, the cellars, the breathing sewers, the open pipeworks, looking for odds and ends, for remnants, for rags, broken bottles, paper, tin and old bread. The ragpicker walked in and out of the pockets of the sleeping city with his ragpicker's pick. In and out of the pockets over the watch chain on its belly, in and out of the sleeves, around its dusty collar, through the wands of its hair, picking the broken strands. The broken strands to repair mandolins. The fringe on the sleeve, the crumbs of bread, the broken watch face, the grains of tobacco, the subway ticket, the string, the stamp. The ragpicker worked in silence among the stains and smells.

His bag was swelling.

The city turned slowly on its left side, but the eyes of the houses remained closed, and the bridges unclasped. The ragpicker worked in silence and never looked at anything that was whole. His eyes sought the broken, the worn, the faded, the fragmented. A complete

From *Under A Glass Bell* (Swallow, 1948), pp. 58-62.

object made him sad. What could one do with a complete object? Put it in a museum. Not touch it. But a torn paper, a shoelace without its double, a cup without saucer, that was stirring. They could be transformed melted into something else. A twisted piece of pipe. Wonderful, this basket without a handle. Wonderful, this bottle without a stopper. Wonderful, the box without a key. Wonderful, half a dress, the ribbon off a hat, a fan with a feather missing. Wonderful, the camera plate without the camera, the lone bicycle wheel, half a phonograph disk. Fragments, incompleted worlds, rags, detritus, the end of objects, and the beginning of transmutations.

The ragpicker shook his head with pleasure. He had found an object without a name. It shone. It was round. It was inexplicable. The ragpicker was happy. He would stop searching. The city would be waking up with the smell of bread. His bag was full. There were even fleas in it, pirouetting. The tail of a dead cat for luck.

His shadow walked after him, bent, twice as long. The bag on the shadow was the hump of a camel. The beard the camel's muzzle. The camel's walk, up and down the sand dunes. The camel's walk, up and down. I sat on the camel's hump.

It took me to the edge of the city. No trees. No bridge. No pavement. Earth. Plain earth trodden dead. Shacks of smokestained wood from demolished buildings. Between the shacks, gypsy carts. Between the shacks and the carts a path so narrow that one must walk Indian file. Around the shacks, palisades. Inside the shack, rags. Rags for beds. Rags for chairs. Rags for tables. On the rags men, women, brats. Inside the women more brats. Fleas. Elbows resting on an old shoe. Head resting on a stuffed deer whose eyes hung loose on a string. The ragpicker gives the woman the object without a name. The woman picks it up and looks at the blank disk, then behind it. She hears tick, tick, tick, tick, tick. She says it is a clock. The ragpicker puts it to his ear and agrees it ticks like a clock but since its face is blank they will never know the time. Tick, tick, tick, the beat of time and no hour showing.

The tip of the shack is pointed like an Arab tent. The windows oblique like oriental eyes. On the sill a flower pot. Flowers made of beads and iron stems, which fell from a tomb. The woman waters them and the stems are rusty.

The brats sitting in the mud are trying to make an old shoe float like a boat. The woman cuts her thread with half a scissor. The ragpicker reads the newspaper with broken specs. The children go to the fountain with leaky pails. When they come back the pails are empty. The ragpickers crouch around the contents of their bags. Nails fall out. A roof tile. A signpost with letters missing.

Out of the gypsy cart behind them comes a torso. A torso on stilts, with his head twisted to one side. What had he done with his legs and arms? Were they under the pile of rags? Had he been thrown out of a window? A fragment of a man found at dawn.

Through the cracks in the shacks came the strum of a mandolin with one string.

The ragpicker looks at me with his one leaking eye. I pick a basket without bottom. The rim of a hat. The lining of a coat. Touch myself. Am I complete? Arms? Legs? Hair? Eyes? Where is the sole of my foot? I take off my shoe to see, to feel. Laugh. Glued to my sole is a blue rag. Ragged but blue like cobalt dust.

The rain falls. I pick up the skeleton of an umbrella. Sit on a hill of corks perfumed by the smell of wine. A ragpicker passes, the handle of a knife in his hand. With it he points to a path of dead oysters. At the end of the path is my blue dress. I had wept over its death. I had danced in it when I was seventeen, danced until it fell into pieces. I try to put it on and come out the other side. I cannot stay inside of it. Here I am, and there the dress, and I forever out of the blue dress I had loved, and I dance right through air, and fall on the floor because one of my heels came off, the heel I lost on a rainy night walking up a hill kissing my loved one deliriously.

Where are all the other things, I say, where are all the things I thought dead?

The ragpicker gave me a wisdom tooth, and my long hair which I had cut off. Then he sinks into a pile of rags and when I try to pick him up I find a scarecrow in my hands with sleeves full of straw and a high top hat with a bullet hole through it.

The ragpickers are sitting around a fire made of broken shutters, window frames, artificial beards, chestnuts, horse's tails, last year's holy palm leaves. The cripple sits on the stump of his torso, with his stilts beside him. Out of the shacks and the gypsy carts come the women and the brats.

Can't one throw anything away forever? I asked.

The ragpicker laughs out of the corner of his mouth, half a laugh, a fragment of a laugh, and they all begin to sing.

First came the breath of garlic which they hang like little red Chinese lanterns in their shacks, the breath of garlic followed by a serpentine song:

> Nothing is lost but it changes
> into the new string old string
> in the new bag old bag
> in the new pan old tin
> in the new shoe old leather
> in the new silk old hair
> in the new hat old straw
> in the new man the child
> and the new not new
> the new not new
> the new not new

All night the ragpicker sang the new not new the new not new until I fell asleep and they picked me up and put me in a bag.

BIRTH

"The child," said the doctor, "is dead."

I lay stretched on a table. I had no place on which to rest my legs. I had to keep them raised. Two nurses leaned over me. In front of me stood the doctor with the face of a woman and eyes protruding with anger and fear. For two hours I had been making violent efforts. The child inside of me was six months old and yet it was too big for me. I was exhausted, the veins in me were swelling with the strain. I had pushed with my entire being. I had pushed as if I wanted this child out of my body and hurled into another world.

"Push, push with all your strength!"

Was I pushing with all my strength? All my strength?

No. A part of me did not want to push out the child. The doctor knew it. That is why he was angry, mysteriously angry. He knew. A part of me lay passive, did not want to push out anyone, not even this dead fragment of myself, out in the cold, outside of me. All in me which chose to keep, to lull, to embrace, to love, all in me which carried, preserved and protected, all in me which imprisoned the whole world in its passionate tenderness, this part of me would not thrust out the child, even though it had died in me. Even though it threatened my life, I could not break, tear out, separate, surrender, open and dilate and yield up a fragment of a life like a fragment of the past, this part of me rebelled against

From *Under A Glass Bell* (Swallow, 1948) pp. 96-101.

pushing out the child, or anyone, out in the cold, to be picked up by strange hands, to be buried in strange places, to be lost, lost, lost. . . . He knew, the doctor. A few hours before he adored me, served me. Now he was angry. And I was angry with a black anger at this part of me which refused to push, to separate, to lose.

"Push! Push! Push with all your strength!"

I pushed with anger, with despair, with frenzy, with the feeling that I would die pushing, as one exhales the last breath, that I would push out everything inside of me, and my soul with all the blood around it, and the sinews with my heart inside of them, choked, and that my body itself would open and smoke would rise, and I would feel the ultimate incision of death.

The nurses leaned over me and they talked to each other while I rested. Then I pushed until I heard my bones cracking, until my veins swelled. I closed my eyes so hard I saw lightning and waves of red and purple. There was a stir in my ears, a beating as if the tympanum would burst. I closed my lips so tightly the blood was trickling. My legs felt enormously heavy, like marble columns, like immense marble columns crushing my body. I was pleading for someone to hold them. The nurse laid her knee on my stomach and shouted: "Push! Push! Push!" Her perspiration fell on me.

The doctor paced up and down angrily, impatiently. "We will be here all night. Three hours now. . . ."

The head was showing, but I had fainted. Everything was blue, then black. The instruments were gleaming before my eyes. Knives sharpened in my ears. Ice and silence. Then I heard voices, first talking too fast for me to understand. A curtain was parted, the voices still tripped over each other, falling fast like a waterfall, with sparks, and cutting into my ears. The table was rolling gently, rolling. The women were lying in the air. Heads. Heads hung where the enormous white bulbs of the lamps were hung. The doctor was still walking, the lamps moved, the heads came near, very near, and the words came more slowly.

They were laughing. One nurse was saying: "When I had my first child I was all ripped to pieces. I had to be sewn up again, and then I had another, and had to be sewn up, and then I had another. . . ."

The other nurse said: "Mine passed like an envelope through a letter box. But afterwards the bag would not come out. The bag would not come out. Out. Out. . . ." Why did they keep repeating themselves. And the lamps turning. And the steps of the doctor very fast, very fast.

"She can't labor any more, at six months nature does not help. She should have another injection."

I felt the needle thrust. The lamps were still. The ice and the blue that was all around came into my veins. My heart beat wildly. The nurses talked: "Now that baby of Mrs. L. last week, who would have thought she was too small, a big woman like that, a big woman like that, a big woman like that. . . ." The words kept turning, as on a disk. They talked, they talked, they talked. . . .

Please hold my legs! Please hold my legs! Please hold my legs! PLEASE HOLD MY LEGS! I am ready again. By throwing my head back I can see the clock. I have been struggling four hours. It would be better to die. Why am I alive and struggling so desperately? I could not remember why I should want to live. I could not remember anything. Everything was blood and pain. I have to push. I have to push. That is a black fixed point in eternity. At the end of a long dark tunnel. I have to push. A voice saying: "Push! Push! Push!" A knee on my stomach and the marble of my legs crushing me and the head so large and I have to push.

Am I pushing or dying? The light up there, the immense round blazing white light is drinking me. It drinks me slowly, inspires me into space. If I do not close my eyes it will drink all of me. I seep upward, in long icy threads, too light, and yet inside there is a fire too, the nerves are twisted, there is no rest from this long tunnel, or is the child being pushed out of me, or is the light drinking me. Am I dying? The ice in the veins, the cracking of the bones, this pushing in darkness, with a small shaft of light in the eyes like the edge of a knife, the feeling of a knife cutting the flesh, the flesh somewhere is tearing as if it were burned through by a flame, somewhere my flesh is tearing and the blood is spilling out. I am pushing in the darkness, in utter darkness. I am pushing until my eyes open and I see the doctor holding a long instrument which he swiftly thrusts into me and the pain makes me cry out. A long animal howl. That will make her push, he says to the nurse. But it does not. It paralyzes me with pain. He wants to do it again. I sit up with fury and I shout at him: "Don't you dare do that again, don't you dare!"

The heat of my anger warms me, all the ice and pain are melted in the fury. I have an instinct that what he has done is unnecessary, that he has done it because he is in a rage, because the hands on the clock keep turning, the dawn is coming and the child does not come out, and I am losing strength and the injection does not produce the spasm.

I look at the doctor pacing up and down, or bending to look at the head which is barely showing. He looks baffled, as before a savage mystery, baffled by this struggle. He wants to interfere with his instruments, while I struggle with nature, with myself, with my child and with the meaning I put into it all, with my desire to give and to hold, to keep and to lose, to live and to die. No instrument can help me. His eyes are furious. He would like to take a knife. He has to watch and wait.

I want to remember all the time why I should want to live. I am all pain and no memory. The lamp has ceased drinking me. I am too weary to move even towards the light, or to turn my head and look at the clock. Inside of my body there are fires, there are bruises, the flesh is in pain. The child is not a child, it is a demon strangling me. The demon lies inert at the door of the womb, blocking life, and I cannot rid myself of it.

The nurses begin to talk again. I say: let me alone. I put my two hands on my stomach and very softly, with the tips of my fingers I drum drum drum drum drum drum on my stomach in circles. Around, around, softly, with eyes open in great serenity. The doctor comes near with amazement on his face. The nurses are silent. Drum drum drum drum drum drum in soft circles, soft quiet circles. Like a savage. The mystery. Eyes open, nerves begin to shiver, . . . a mysterious agitation. I hear the ticking of the clock . . . inexorably, separately. The little nerves awake, stir. But my hands are so weary, so weary, they will fall off. The womb is stirring and dilating. Drum drum drum drum. I am ready! The nurse presses her knee on my stomach. There is blood in my eyes. A tunnel. I push into this tunnel, I bite my lips and push. There is a fire and flesh ripping and no air. Out of the tunnel! All my blood is spilling out. Push!

Push! Push! It is coming! It is coming! It is coming! I felt the slipperiness, the sudden deliverance, the weight is gone. Darkness. I hear voices. I open my eyes. I hear them saying: "It was a little girl. Better not show it to her." All my strength returns. I sit up. The doctor shouts: "Don't sit up"

"Show me the child!"

"Don't show it," says the nurse, "it will be bad for her." The nurses try to make me lie down. My heart is beating so loud I can hardly hear myself repeating: "Show it to me." The doctor holds it up. It looks dark and small, like a diminutive man. But it is a little girl. It has long eyelashes on its closed eyes, it is perfectly made, and all glistening with the waters of the womb.

HEJDA

The unveiling of women is a delicate matter. It will not happen overnight. We are all afraid of what we shall find.

Hejda was, of course, born in the Orient. Before the unveiling she was living in a immense garden, a little city in itself, filled with many servants, many sisters and brothers, many relatives. From the roof of the house one could see all the people passing, vendors, beggars, Arab going to the mosque.

Hejda was then a little primitive, whose greatest pleasure consisted in inserting her finger inside pregnant hens and breaking the eggs, or filling frogs with gasoline and setting a lighted match to them. She went about without underclothes in the house, without shoes, but once outside she was heavily veiled and there was no telling exactly the contours of her body, which were at an early age those of a full-blown woman, and there was no telling that her smile had that carnivorous air of smiles with large teeth.

In school she had a friend whose great sorrow was her dark color. The darkest skin in the many shaded nuances of the Arabian school. Hejda took her out into the farthest corner of the school garden one day and said to her: "I can make you white if you want me to. Do you trust me?"

"Of course I do."

Hejda brought out a piece of pumice stone. She very gently but very persistently began to pumic a piece of the girl's forehead. Only

From *Under A Glass Bell* (Swallow, 1948), pp. 86-95.

when the pain became unendurable did she stop. But for a week, every day, she continued enlarging the circle of scraped, scarred skin, and took secret pleasure in the strange scene of the girl's constant lamentations of pain and her own obstinate scraping. Until they were both found out and punished.

At seventeen she left the Orient and the veils, but she retained an air of being veiled. With the most chic and trim French clothes, which molded her figure, she still conveyed the impression of restraint and no one could feel sure of having seen her neck, arms or legs. Even her evening dresses seemed to sheathe her. This feeling of secrecy, which recalled constantly the women of Arabia as they walked in their many yards of white cotton, rolled like silk around a spool, was due in great part to her inarticulateness. Her speech revealed and opened no doors. It was labyrinthian. She merely threw off enough words to invite one into the passageway but no sooner had one started to walk towards the unfinished phrase than one met an impasse, a curve, a barrier. She retreated behind half admissions, half promises, insinuations.

This covering of the body, which was like the covering of the spirit, had created an unshatterable timidity. It had the effect of concentrating the light, the intensity in the eyes. So that one saw Hejda as a mixture of elegance, cosmetics, aesthetic plumage, with only the eyes sending signals and messages. They pierced the European clothes with the stabbing brilliancy of those eyes in the Orient which to reach the man had to pierce through the heavy aura of yards of white cotton.

The passageways that led one to Hejda were as tortuous and intricate as the passageways in the Oriental cities in which the pursued women lost themselves, but all through the vanishing, turning streets the eyes continued to signal to strangers like prisoners waving out of windows.

The desire to speak was there, after centuries of confinement and repression, the desire to be invaded and rescued from the secretiveness. The eyes were full of invitations, in great contradiction to the closed folds of the clothes, the many defenses of the silk around the neck, the sleeves around the arms.

Her language was veiled. She had no way to say: look at Hejda who is full of ideas. So she laid out cards and told fortunes like the women of the harem, or she ate sweets like a stunted woman who had been kept a child by close binding with yards of white cotton, as the feet of the Chinese women had been kept small by bandaging. All she could say was: I had a dream last night (because at breakfast time in the Orient, around the first cup of dark coffee, everyone told their dreams). Or she opened a book accidentally when in trouble and placed her finger on a phrase and decided on her next course of action by the words of this phrase. Or she cooked a dish as colorful as an Oriental market place.

Her desire to be noticed was always manifested, as in the Orient, by a bit of plumage, a startling jewel, a spangle pasted on her forehead between the eyes (the third eye of the Oriental was a jewel, as if the secret life so long preserved from openness had acquired the fire of precious stones).

No one understood the signals: look at Hejda, the woman of the Orient who wants to be a woman of tomorrow. The plumage and the aesthetic adornment diverted them like decoration on a wall. She was always being thrust back into the harem, on a pillow.

She had arrived in Paris, with all her invisible veils. When she laughed she concealed her mouth as much as possible, because in her small round face the teeth were extraordinarily large. She concealed her voraciousness and her appetites. Her voice was made small, again as the Chinese make their feet small, small and infantile. Her poses were reluctant and reserved. The veil was not in her timidities, her fears, in her manner of dressing, which covered her throat and compressed her overflowing breasts. The veil was in her liking for flowers (which was racial), especially small roses and innocent asexual flowers, in complicated rituals of politeness (also traditional), but above all in evasiveness of speech.

She wanted to be a painter. She joined the Academie Julien. She painted painstakingly on small canvases—the colors of the Orient, a puerile Orient of small flowers, serpentines, confetti and candy color, the colors of small shops with metallic lace-paper roses and butterflies.

In the same class there was a dark, silent, timid young Roumanian. He had decadent, aristocratic hands, he never smiled, he never talked. Those who approached him felt such a shriveling timidity in him, such a retraction, that they remained at a distance.

The two timidities observed each other. The two silences, the two withdrawals. Both were oriental interiors, without windows on the external world, and all the greenery in the inner patio, all their windows open on the inside of the house.

A certain Gallic playfulness presides in the painting class. The atmosphere is physical, warm, gay. But the two of them remain in their inner patio, listening to birds singing and fountains playing. He thinks: how mysterious she is. And she thinks: how mysterious he is.

Finally one day, as he is leaving, he watches her repainting the black line on the edge of her eyes out of a silver peacock. She nimbly lifts up the head of the peacock and it is a little brush that makes black lines around her Oriental eyes.

This image confounds him, ensorcells him. The painter is captivated, stirred, Some memory out of Persian legends now adorns his concept of her.

They marry and take a very small apartment where the only window gives on a garden.

At first they marry to hide together. In the dark caverns of their whisperings, confidences, timidities, what they now elaborate is a stalactitic world shut out from light and air. He initiates her into his aesthetic values. They make love in the dark and in the daytime make their place more beautiful and more refined.

In Molnar's hands she is being remolded, refashioned, stylized. He cannot remold her body. He is critical of her heaviness. He dislikes her breasts and will not let her ever show them. They overwhelm him. He confesses he would like her better without them. This shrinks her within herself and plants the seed of doubt of her feminine value. With these words he has properly subjugated her, given her a doubt which will keep her away from other men. He bound her femininity, and it is now oppressed, bound, even ashamed of its vulgarity, of its expansiveness. This is the reign of aesthetic value, stylization, refinement, art, artifice. He has established his domination in this. At every turn nature must be subjugated. Very soon, with his coldness, he represses her violence. Very soon he polishes her language, her manners, her impulses. He reduces and limits her hospitality, her friendliness, her desire for expansion.

It is her second veiling. It is the aesthetic veil of art and social graces. He designs her dresses. He molds her as far as he can into the stylized figures in his paintings. His women are transparent and lie in hammocks between heaven and earth. Hejda cannot reach this, but she can become an odalisque. She can acquire more silver peacocks, more poetic objects that will speak for her.

Her small canvases look childlike standing beside his. Slowly she becomes more absorbed in his painting than in her own. The flowers and gardens disappear.

He paints a world of stage settings, static ships, frozen trees, crystal fairs, the skeletons of pleasure and color, from which nature is entirely shut off. He proceeds to make Hejda one of the objects in this painting; her nature is more and more castrated by this abstraction of her, the obtrusive breasts more severely veiled. In his painting there is no motion, no nature, and certainly not the Hejda who liked to run about without underwear, to eat herbs and raw vegetables out of the garden.

Her breasts are the only intrusion in their exquisite life. Without them she could be the twin he wanted, and they could accomplish this strange marriage of his feminine qualities and her masculine ones. For it is already clear that he likes to be protected and she likes to protect, and that she has more power in facing the world of reality, more power to sell pictures, to interest the galleries in his work, more courage too. It is she who assumes the active role in contact with the world. Molnar can never earn a living, Hejda can. Molnar cannot give orders (except to her) and she can. Molnar cannot execute, realize, concretize as well as she can, for in execution and action she is not timid.

Finally it is Molnar who paints and draws and it is Hejda who goes out and sells his work.

Molnar grows more and more delicate, more vulnerable, and Hejda stronger. He is behind the scene, and she is in the foreground now.

He permits her love to flow all around him, sustain him, nourish him. In the dark he reconquers his leadership. And not by any sensual prodigality, but on the contrary, by a severe economy of pleasure. She is often left hungry. She never suspects for a moment that it is anything but economy and thinks a great abundance lies behind this aesthetic reserve. There is no delight or joy in their sensual contact. It is a creeping together into a womb.

Their life together is stilted, windowless, facing inward. But the plants and fountains of the patio are all artificial, ephemeral, immobile. A stage setting for a drama that never takes place. There are colonnades, friezes, backgrounds, plush drops but no drama takes place, no evolution, no sparks. His women's figures are always lying down, suspended in space.

But Hejda, Hejda feels compressed. She does not know why. She has never known anything but oppression. She has never been out of a small universe delimited by man. Yet something is expanding in her. A new Hejda is born out of the struggle with reality, to protect the weakness of Molnar. In the outer world she feels larger. When she returns home she must shrink back into submission to Molnar's proportions. The outgoing rhythm must cease. Molnar's whole being is one total negation; negation and rejection of the world, of social life, of other human beings, of success, of movement, of motion, of curiosity, of adventure, of the unknown.

What is he defending, protecting? No consuming passion for one person, but perhaps a secret consuming. He admits no caresses, no invitations to love-making. It is always "no" to her hunger, "no" to her tenderness, "no" to the flow of life. They were close in fear and concealment, but they are not close in flow and development. Molnar is now frozen, fixed. There is no emotion to propel him. And when she seeks to propel him, substitute her élan for his static stagnation, all he can do is break this propeller.

"Your ambitions are vulgar."

(She does not know how to answer: my ambitions are merely the balance to your inertia.)

A part of her wants to expand. A part of her being wants to stay with Molnar. This conflict tears her asunder. The pulling and tearing bring on illness.

Hejda falls.

Hejda is ill.

She cannot move forward because Molnar is tied, and she cannot break with him.

Because he will not move, his being is stagnant and filled with poison. He injects her every day with this poison.

She has taken his paintings into the real world, to sell, and in so doing she has connected with that world and found it larger, freer.

Now he does not let her handle the painting. He even stops painting. Poverty sets in.

Perhaps Molnar will turn about now and protect her. It is the dream of every maternal love: I have filled him with my strength. I have nourished his painting. My painting has passed his painting. I am broken and weak. Perhaps now he will be strong.

But not at all. Molnar watches her fall, lets her fall. He lets poverty install itself. He watches inertly the sale of their art possessions, the trips to the pawnbroker. He leaves Hejda without care. His passivity and inertia consume the whole house.

It is as if Hejda had been the glue that held the furniture together. Now it breaks. It is as if she had been the cleaning fluid and now the curtains turn gray. The logs in the fireplace now smoke and do not burn: was she the fire in the hearth too? Because she lies ill objects grow rusty. The food turns sour. Even the artificial flowers wilt. The paints dry on the palette. Was she the water, the soap too? Was she the fountain, the visibility of the windows, the gloss of the floors? The creditors buzz like locusts. Was she the fetish of the house who kept them away? Was she the oxygen in the house? Was she the salt now missing from the bread? Was she the delicate feather duster dispelling the webs of decay? Was she the silver polish?

Tired of waiting for her to get well—alone, he goes out.

* * *

Hejda and Molnar are now separated. She is free. Several people help her to unwind the binding wrapped around her personality first by the family life, then by the husband. Someone falls in love with her ample breasts, and removes the taboo that Molnar had placed upon them. Hejda buys herself a sheer blouse which will reveal her possessions.

When a button falls off she does not sew it on again.

Then she also began to talk.

She talked about her childhood. The same story of going about without underwear as a child which she had told before with a giggle of confusion and as if saying: "what a little primitive I was," was now told with the oblique glance of the strip-teaser, with a slight arrogance, the *agent provocateur* towards the men (for now exhibitionism placed the possibility in the present, not in the past).

She discards small canvases and buys very large ones. She paints larger roses, larger daisies, larger trellises, larger candied clouds, larger taffy seas. But just as the canvases grow larger without their content growing more important, Hejda is swelling up without growing. There is more of her. Her voice grows louder, her language, freed of Molnar's decadent refinement, grows coarser. Her dresses grow shorter. Her blouses looser. There is more flesh around her small body but Molnar is not there to corset it. There is more food on her table. She no longer conceals her teeth. She becomes proud of her appetite. Liberty has filled her to overflowing with a confidence that everything that was once secret and bound was of immense value. Every puerile detail of her childhood, every card dealer's intuition, every dream, becomes magnified.

And the stature of Hejda cannot bear the weight of her ambition. It is as if compression had swung her towards inflation. She is inflated physically and spiritually. And whoever dares to recall her to a sense of proportion, to a realization that there are perhaps other painters of value in the world, other women, becomes the traitor who must be banished instantly. On him she pours torrents of abuse like the abuse of the Oriental gypsies to whom one has refused charity—curses and maledictions.

It is not desire or love she brings to the lovers: I have discovered that I am very gifted for love making!

It is not creativity she brings to her painting: I will show Molnar that I was a better painter.

Her friendships with women are simply one long underground rivalry: to excel in startling dress or behavior. She enters a strained, intense competition. When everything fails she resorts to lifting her dress and arranging her garters.

Where are the veils and labyrinthian evasions?

She is back in the garden of her childhood, back to the native original Hejda, child of nature and succulence and sweets, of pillows and erotic literature.

The frogs leap away in fear of her again.

from *Children of the Albatross*

THE SEALED ROOM

Stepping off the bus at Montmartre Djuna arrived in the center of the ambulant Fair and precisely at the moment when she set her right foot down on the cobblestones the music of the merry-go-round was unleashed from its mechanical box and she felt the whole scene, her mood, her body, transformed by its gaiety exactly as in her childhood her life in the orphan asylum had been suddenly transformed from a heavy nightmare to freedom by her winning of a dance scholarship.

As if, because of so many obstacles, her childhood and adolescence had been painful, heavy walking on crutches and had suddenly changed overnight into a dance in which she discovered the air, space and the lightness of her own nature.

Her life was thus divided into two parts: the bare, the pedestrian one of her childhood, with poverty weighing her feet, and then the day when her interior monologue set to music led her feet into the dance.

Pointing her toe towards the floor she would always think: I danced my way out of the asylum, out of poverty, out of my past.

She remembered her feet on the bare floor of their first apartment. She remembered her feet on the linoleum of the orphan asylum. She remembered her feet going up and down the stairs of the home where she had been "adopted" and had suffered her jealousy of the affection bestowed on the legitimate children. She remembered her feet running away from that house.

From *Children of the Albatross* (Swallow, 1959), pp. 7-110.

She remembered her square-toed lusterless shoes, her mended stockings, and her hunger for new and shining shoes in shop windows.

She remembered the calluses of her feet from house work, from posing for painters, from working as a mannequin, from cold, from clumsy mendings and from ill-fitting shoes.

She remembered the day that her dreaming broke into singing, and became a monologue set to music, the day when the dreams became a miniature opera shutting out the harsh or dissonant sounds of the world.

She remembered the day when her feet became restless in their prison of lusterless leather and they began to vibrate in obedience to inner harmonizations, when she kicked off her shoes and, as she moved, her worn dress cracked under her arms and her skirt slit at the knees.

The flow of images set to music had descended from her head to her feet and she ceased to feel as one who had been split into two pieces by some great invisible sabre cut.

In the external world she was the woman who had submitted to mysterious outer fatalities beyond her power to alter, and in her interior world she was a woman who had built many tunnels deeper down where no one could reach her, in which she deposited her treasures safe from destruction and in which she built a world exactly the opposite of the one she knew.

But at the moment of dancing a fusion took place, a welding, a wholeness. The cut in the middle of her body healed, and she was all one woman moving.

Lifted and impelled by an inner rhythm, with a music box playing inside her head, her foot lifted from drabness and immobility, from the swamps and miasmas of poverty, carried her across continents and oceans, depositing her on the cobblestones of a Paris square on the day of the Fair, among shimmering colored tents, the flags of pleasure at full mast, the merry-go-rounds turning like dervish dancers.

She walked to a side street, knocked on a dark doorway opened by a disheveled concierge and ran down the stairway to a vast underground room.

As she came down the stairway she could already hear the piano, feet stamping, and the ballet master's voice. When the piano stopped there was always his voice scolding, and the whispering of smaller voices.

Sometimes as she entered the class was dissolving, and a flurry of little girls brushed by her in their moth ballet costumes, the little girls from the Opera, laughing and whispering, fluttering like moths on their dusty ballet slippers, flurries of snow in the darkness of the vast room, with drops of dew from exertion.

Djuna went down with them along the corridors to the dressing rooms which at first looked like a garden, with the puffed white giant daisies of ballet skirts, the nasturtiums and poppies of Spanish skirts, the roses of cotton, the sunflowers, the spider webs of hair nets.

The small dressing room overflowed with the smell of cold cream, face powder, and cheap cologne, with the wild confusion of laughter, confessions from the girls, with old dancing slippers, faded flowers and withering tulle.

As soon as Djuna cast off her city clothes it was the trepidating moment of metamorphosis.

The piano slightly out of tune, the floor's vibrations, the odor of perspiration swelled the mood of excitement born in this garden of costumes to the accompaniment of whisperings and laughter.

When she extended her leg at the bar, the ballet master placed his hand on it as if to guide the accuracy of her pointed toe.

He was a slender, erect, stylized man of forty, not handsome in face; only in attitudes and gestures. His face was undefined, his features blurred. It was as if the dance were a sculptor who had taken hold of him and had carved style, form elegance out of all his movements, but left the face unimportant.

She always felt his hand exceptionally warm whenever he placed it on her to guide, to correct, improve or change a gesture.

When he placed his hand on her ankle she became intensely aware of her ankle, as if he were the magician who caused the blood to flow through it; when he placed his hand on her waist she became intensely aware of her waist as if he were the sculptor who indented it.

When his hand gave the signal to dance then it was not only as if he had carved the form of her body and released the course of her blood but as if his hand had made the coordination between blood and gestures and form, and the *leçon de danse* became a lesson in living.

So she obeyed, she danced, she was flexible and yielding in his hands, plying her body, disciplining it, awakening it.

It became gradually apparent that she was the favorite. She was the only one at whom he did not shout while she was dressing. He was more elated at her progress, and less harsh about her faults.

She obeyed his hands, but he found it more imperative than with other pupils to guide her by touch or by tender inflections of his voice.

He gave of his own movements as if he knew her movements would be better if he made them with her.

The dance gained in perfection, a perfection born of an accord between their gestures; born of her submission and his domination.

When he was tired she danced less well. When his attention was fixed on her she danced magnificently.

The little girls of the ballet troupe, mature in this experience, whispered and giggled: you are the favorite!

Yet not for a moment did he become for her a man. He was the ballet master. If he ruled her body with this magnetic rulership, a physical prestige, it was as a master of her dancing for the purpose of the dance.

But one day after the lessons, when the little girls from the Opera had left and there still hung in the air only an echo of the silk, flurry, snow and patter of activities, he followed her into the dressing room.

She had not yet taken off the voluminous skirt of the dance, the full-blown petticoat, the tight-fitting panties, so that when he entered the dressing room it seemed like a continuation of the dance. A continuation of the dance when he approached her and bent one knee in gallant salutation, and put his arms around her skirt that swelled like a huge flower. She laid her hand on his head like a queen acknowledging his worship. He remained on one knee while the skirt like a full-blown flower opened to allow a kiss to be placed at the core.

A kiss enclosed in the corolla of the skirt and hidden away, then he returned to the studio to speak with the pianist, to tell her at what time to come the next day, and to pay her, while Djuna dressed, covering warmth, covering her tremor, covering her fears.

He was waiting for her at the door, neat and trim.

He said: "Why don't you come and sit at the café with me?"

She followed him. Not far from there was the Place Clichy, always animated but more so now as the site of the Fair.

The merry-go-rounds were turning swiftly. The gypsies were reading fortunes in little booths hung with Arabian rugs.

Workmen were shooting clay pigeons and winning cut-glass dishes for their wives.

The prostitutes were enjoying their watchful promenades, and the men their loitering.

The ballet master was talking to her: "Djuna (and suddenly as he said her name, she felt again where he had deposited his tribute), I am a simple man. My parents were shoemakers in a little village down south. I was put to work as a boy in an iron factory, where I handled heavy things and was on the way to becoming deformed by big muscles. But during my lunch hour I danced. I wanted to be a ballet dancer, and I practiced at one of the iron bars in front of a big furnace. And today—look!" He handed her a cigarette case all engraved with names of famous ballet dancers. "Today," he said proudly, "I have been the partner of all these women. If you would come with me, we could be happy. I am a simple man, but we could dance in all the cities of Europe. I am no longer young but I have a lot of dancing in me still. We could be happy. . . ."

The merry-go-round turned and her feelings with it, riding again the wooden horses of her childhood in the park, which was so much like flying, riding around from city to city reaching eagerly for the prizes, for bouquets, for clippings, for fame, flinging all of one's secret desires for pleasure on the outside like a red shawl, with this joyous music at the center always, the body recovered, the body dancing (hadn't she been the woman in quest of her body once lost by a shattering blow—submerged, and now floating again on the surface where uncrippled human beings lived in a world of pleasure like the Fair?).

How to explain to this simple man, how to explain. *There is something broken inside of me.* I cannot dance, live, love as easily as others. Surely enough, if we traveled around the world, I would break my leg somewhere. Because this inner break is invisible and unconvincing to others, I would not rest until I had broken something for everyone to see, to understand. How to explain to this simple man, I could not dance continuously with success, without breaking. *I am the dancer who falls,* always, into traps of depression, breaking my heart and my body almost at every turn, losing my tempo and my lightness, falling out of groups, out of grace, out of perfection. There is too often something wrong. Something you cannot help me with. . . . Supposing we found ourselves in a strange country, in a strange hotel. You are alone in a hotel room. Well, what of that? You can talk to the barman, or you can sit before your glass of beer and read the papers. Everything is simple. But when I am alone in a hotel room something happens to me at times which must be what happens to children when the lights are turned out. Animals and children. But the animals howl their solitude, and children can call for their parents and for lights. But I. . . .

"What a long time it takes you to answer me," said the ballet master.

"I'm not strong enough," said Djuna.

"That's what I thought when I first saw you. I thought you couldn't take the discipline of a dancer's life. But it isn't so. You look fragile and all that, but you're healthy. I can tell healthy women by their skin. Yours is shining and clear. No, I don't think you have the strength of a horse, you're what we call '*une petite nature.*' But you have energy and guts. And we'll take it easy on the road."

In the middle of a piece of music the merry-go-round suddenly stopped. Something had gone wrong with the motor! The horses slowed down their pace. The children lost their hilarity. The boss looked troubled, and the mechanic was called and like a doctor came with his bag.

The Fair lost its spinning frenzy.

When the music stopped, one could hear the dry shots of the amateur hunters and the clay pigeons falling behind the cardboard walls.

The dreams which Djuna had started to weave in the asylum as if they were the one net in which she could exist, leaping thus always out of reach of unbearable happenings and creating her own events parallel to the ones her feelings could not accept, the dreams which gave birth to worlds within worlds, which, begun at night when she was asleep, continued during the day as an accompaniment to acts which she now discovered were rendered ineffectual by this defensive activity, with time became more and more violent.

For at first the personages of the dream, the cities which sprang up, were distinct and bore no resemblance to reality. They were images which filled her head with the vapors of fever, a drug-like panorama of incidents which rendered her insensible to cold, hunger and fatigue.

The day her mother was taken to the hospital to die, the day her brother was injured while playing in the street and developed a gentle insanity, the day at the asylum when she fell under the tyranny of the only man in the place, were days when she noted an intensification of her other world.

She could still weep at these happenings, but as people might lament just before they go under an anesthetic. "It still hurts," says the voice as the anesthetic begins to take effect and the pain growing duller, the body complaining more out of a mere remembrance of pain, automatically, just before sinking into a void.

She even found a way to master the weeping.

No mirrors were allowed in the orphan asylum, but girls had made one by placing black paper behind one of the small windows. Once a week they set it up and took turns at looking at their faces.

Djuna's first glimpse of the adolescent face was in this black mirror, where the clear coloring of her skin was as if touched with mourning, as if reflected at the bottom of a well.

Even long afterwards it was difficult for her to overcome this first impression of her face painted upon black still waters.

But she discovered that if she was weeping, and she looked at the weeping in a mirror, the weeping stopped. It ceased to be her own. It belonged to another.

Henceforth she possessed this power: whatever emotion would ravish or torment her, she could bring it before a mirror, look at it, and separate herself from it. And she thought she had found a way to master sorrow.

There was a boy of her age who passed every day under her window and who had the power to move her. He had a lean, eager face, eyes which seemed liquid with tenderness, and his gestures were full of gentleness.

His passage had the power to make her happy or unhappy, warm or cold, rich or poor. Whether he walked abstractedly on the other side of the street or on her side, whether he looked up at her window or forgot to look up, determined the mood of her day.

Because of his manner, she felt she trusted him entirely, that if he should come to the door and ask her to follow him she would do so without hesitation.

In her dreams at night she dissolved in his presence, lost herself in him. Her feelings for him were the opposite of an almost continuous and painful tension whose origin she did not know.

In contrast to this total submission to the unknown boy's gentleness, her first encounter with man was marked with defiance, fear, hostility.

The man, called the Watchman by the girls, was about forty years old when Djuna was sixteen. He was possessed of unlimited power because he was the lover of the Directress. His main attribute was power. He was the only man in the asylum, and he could deal privileges, gifts, and give permissions to go out at night.

This unique role gave him a high prestige. He was polite, carried himself with confidence, and was handsome in a neutral way which adapted him easily to any kind of image the orphans wished to fashion of him.

He could pass for the tall man, the brown-haired man, the blond man; given a little leeway, he answered all the descriptions of gypsy card readers.

An added piquancy was attained by the common knowledge that he was the favorite of the Directress, who was very much hated. In winning his favor, one struck indirect blows at her authority, and achieved a subtle revenge for her severity.

The girls thought of him as possessing an even greater power than hers, for she who submitted to no one, had often been seen bowing her head before his reproaches.

The one he chose felt endowed immediately with greater beauty, greater charm and power than the other girls. He was appointed the arbiter, the connoisseur, the bestower of decorations.

To be chosen by the Watchman was to enter the realm of protection. No girl could resist this.

Djuna could distinguish his steps at a great distance. It seemed to her that he walked more evenly than anyone she knew, evenly and without stops or change of rhythm. He advanced through the hallways inexorably. Other people could be stopped, or eluded. But his steps were those of absolute authority.

He knew at what time Djuna would be passing through this particular hallway alone. He always came up to her, not a yard away, but exactly beside her.

His glance was always leveled at her breasts, and two things would happen simultaneously: he would offer her a present without looking at her face, as if he were offering it to her breasts, and then he would whisper: "Tonight I will let you out if you are good to me."

And Djuna would think of the boy who passed by under her window, and feel a wild beating of her heart at the possibility of meeting him outside, of talking to him, and her longing for the boy, for the warm, liquid tenderness of his eyes was so violent that no sacrifice seemed too great—her longing and her feeling that if he knew of this scene, he would rescue her, but that there was no other way to reach him, no other way to defeat authority to reach him than by this concession to authority.

In this barter there was no question of rebellion. The way the Watchman stood, demanded, gestured, was all part of a will she did not even question, a continuation of the will of the father. There was the man who demanded, and outside was the gentle boy who demanded nothing, and to whom she wanted to give everything, whose silence even, she trusted, whose way of walking she trusted with her entire heart, while this man she did not trust.

It was the *droit du seigneur.*

She slipped the Watchman's bracelet around the lusterless cotton of her dress, while he said: "The poorer the dress the more wonderful your skin looks, Djuna."

Years later when Djuna thought the figure of the Watchman was long since lost she would hear echoes of his heavy step and she would find herself in the same mood she had experienced so many times in his presence.

No longer a child, and yet many times she still had the feeling that she might be overpowered by a will stronger than her own, might be trapped, might be somehow unable to free herself, unable to escape the demands of man upon her.

Her first defeat at the hands of man the father had caused her such a conviction of helplessness before tyranny that although she realized that she was now in reality no longer helpless, the echo of this helplessness was so strong that she still dreaded the possessiveness and willfullness of older men. They benefited from this regression into her past, and could override her strength merely because of this conviction of unequal power.

It was as if maturity did not develop altogether and completely, but by little compartments like the airtight sections of a ship. A part of her being would mature, such as her insight, or interpretative faculties, but another could retain a childhood conviction that events, man and authority together were stronger than one's capacity for mastering them, and that one was doomed to become a victim of one's pattern.

It was only much later that Djuna discovered that this belief in the greater power of others became the fate itself and caused the defeats.

But for years, she felt harmed and defeated at the hands of men of power, and she expected the boy, the gentle one, the trusted one, to come and deliver her from tyranny.

Ever since the day of Lillian's concert when she had seen the garden out of the window, Djuna had wanted a garden like it.

And now she possessed a garden and a very old house on the very edge of Paris, between the city and the Park.

But it was not enough to possess it, to walk through it, sit in it. One still had to be able to live in it.

And she found she could not live in it.

The inner fever, the restlessness within her corroded her life in the garden.

When she was sitting in a long easy chair she was not at ease.

The grass seemed too much like a rug awaiting footsteps, to be trampled with hasty incidents. The rhythm of growth too slow, the falling of the leaves too tranquil.

Happiness was an absence of fever. The garden was feverless and without tension to match her tensions. She could not unite or commune with the plants, the languor, the peace. It was all contrary to her inward pulse. Not one pulsation of the garden corresponded to her inner pulsation which was more like a drum beating feverish time.

Within her the leaves did not wait for autumn, but were torn off prematurely by unexpected sorrows. Within her, leaves did not wait for spring to sprout but bloomed in sudden hothouse exaggerations. Within her there were storms contrary to the lazy moods of the garden, devastations for which nature had no equivalent.

Peace, said the garden, peace.

The day began always with the sound of crushed gravel by the automobiles.

The shutters were pushed open by the French servant, and the day admitted.

With the first crushing of the gravel under wheels came the barking of the police dog and the carillon of the church bells.

Cars entered through an enormous green iron gate, which had to be opened ceremoniously by the servant.

Everyone else walked through the small green gate that seemed like the child of the other, half covered with ivy. The ivy did not climb over the father gate.

When Djuna looked at the large gate through her window it took on the air of a prison gate. An unjust feeling, since she knew she could leave the place whenever she wanted, and since she knew more than anyone that human beings placed upon an object, or a person this responsibility of being the obstacle, when the obstacle lay within one's self.

In spite of this knowledge, she would often stand at the window staring at the large closed iron gate as if hoping to obtain from this contemplation a reflection of her inner obstacles to a full open life.

She mocked its importance; the big gate had a presumptuous

creak! Its rusty voice was full of dissonant affectations. No amount of oil could subdue its rheumatism, for it took a historical pride in its own rust: it was a hundred years old.

But the little gate, with its overhanging ivy like disordered hair over a running child's forehead, had a sleepy and sly air, an air of always being half open, never entirely locked.

Djuna had chosen the house for many reasons, because it seemed to have sprouted out of the earth like a tree, so deeply grooved it was within the old garden. It had no cellar and the rooms rested right on the ground. Below the rugs, she felt, was the earth. One could take root here, feel at one with the house and garden, take nourishment from them like the plants.

She had chosen it too because its symmetrical façade covered by a trellis overrun by ivy showed twelve window faces. But one shutter was closed and corresponded to no room. During some transformation of the house it had been walled up.

Djuna had taken the house because of this window which led to no room, because of this impenetrable room, thinking that someday she would discover an entrance to it.

In front of the house there was a basin which had been filled, and a well which had been sealed up. Djuna set about restoring the basin, excavated an old fountain and unsealed the well.

Then it seemed to her that the house came alive, the flow was re-established.

The fountain was gay and sprightly, the well deep.

The front half of the garden was trim and stylized like most French gardens, but the back of it some past owner had allowed to grow wild and become miniature jungle. The stream was almost hidden by overgrown plants, and the small bridge seemed like a Japanese bridge in a glass-bowl garden.

There was a huge tree of which she did not know the name, but which she named the Ink Tree for its black and poisonous berries.

One summer night she stood in the courtyard. All the windows of the house were lighted.

Then the image of the house with all its windows lighted—all but one—she saw as the image of the self, of the being divided into many cells. Action taking place in one room, now in another, was the replica of experience taking place in one part of the being, now in another.

The room of the heart in Chinese lacquer red, the room of the mind in pale green or the brown of philosophy, the room of the body in shell rose, the attic of memory with closets full of the musk of the past.

She saw the whole house on fire in the summer night and it was like those moments of great passion and deep experience when every cell of the self lighted simultaneously, a dream of fullness, and she hungered for this that would set aflame every room of the house and of herself at once!

In herself there was one shuttered window.

She did not sleep soundly in the old and beautiful house.

She was disturbed.

She could hear voices in the dark, for it is true that on days of clear audibility there are voices which come from within and speak in multiple tongues contradicting each other. They speak out of the past, out of the present, the voices of awareness—in dialogues with the self which mark each step of living.

There was the voice of the child in herself, unburied, who had long ago insisted: I want only the marvelous.

There was the low-toned and simple voice of the human being Djuna saying: I want love.

There was the voice of the artist in Djuna saying: I will create the marvelous.

Why should such wishes conflict with each other, or annihilate each other?

In the morning the human being Djuna sat on the carpet before the fireplace and mended and folded her stockings into little partitioned boxes, keeping the one perfect unmended pair for a day of high living, partitioning at the same time events into little separate boxes in her head, dividing (that was one of the great secrets against shattering sorrows) allotting and rearranging under the heading of one word a constantly fluid, mobile and protean universe whose multiple aspects were like quicksands.

This exaggerated sense, for instance, of a preparation for the love to come, like the extension of canopies, the unrolling of ceremonial carpets, the belief in the state of grace, of a perfection necessary to the advent of love.

As if she must first of all create a marvelous world in which to house it, thinking it befell her adequately to receive this guest of honor.

Wasn't it too oriental, said a voice protesting with mockery—such elaborate receptions, such costuming as if love were such an exigent guest?

She was like a perpetual bride preparing a trousseau. As other women sew and embroider, or curl their hair, she embellished her cities of the interior, painted, decorated, prepared a great *mise en scène* for a great love.

It was in this mood of preparation that she passed through her kingdom the house, painting here a wall through which the stains of dampness showed, hanging a lamp where it would throw Balinese theater shadows, draping a bed, placing logs in the fireplaces, wiping the dull-surfaced furniture that it might shine. Every room in a different tone like the varied pipes of an organ, to emit a wide range of moods—lacquer red for vehemence, gray for confidences, a whole house of moods with many doors, passageways, and changes of level.

She was not satisfied until it emitted a glow which was not only that of the Dutch interiors in Dutch paintings, a glow of immaculateness, but an effulgence which had caused Jay to dissert on the gold dust of Florentine paintings.

Djuna would stand very still and mute and feel: my house will speak for me. My house will tell them I am warm and rich. The house will tell them inside of me there are these rooms of flesh and Chinese lacquer, sea greens to walk through, inside of me there are lighted candles, live fires, shadows, spaces, open doors, shelters and air currents. Inside of me there is color and warmth.

The house will speak for me.

People came and submitted to her spell, but like all spells it was wonderful and remote. Not warm and near. No human being, they thought, made this house, no human being lived here. It was too fragile and too unfamiliar. There was no dust on her hands, no broken nails, no sign of wear and tear.

It was the house of the myth.

It was the ritual they sensed, tasted, smelled. Too different from the taste and smell of their own houses. It took them out of the present. They took on an air of temporary guests. No familiar landscape, no signpost to say: this is your home as well.

All of them felt they were passing, could not remain. They were tourists visiting foreign lands. It was a voyage and not a port.

Even in the bathroom there were no medicine bottles on the shelves proclaiming: soda, castor oil, cold cream. She had transferred all of them to alchemist bottles, and the homeliest drug assumed an air of philter.

This was a dream and she was merely a guide.

None came near enough.

There were houses, dresses, which created one's isolation as surely as those tunnels created by ferrets to elude pursuit of the male.

There were rooms and costumes which appeared to be made to lure but which were actually effective means to create distance.

Djuna had not yet decided what her true wishes were, or how near she wanted them to come. She was apparently calling to them but at the same time, by a great ambivalence and fear of their coming too near, of invading her, of dominating or possessing her, she was charming them in such a manner that the human being in her, the warm and simple human being, remained secure from invasion. She constructed a subtle obstacle to invasion at the same time as she constructed an appealing scene.

None came near enough. After they left she sat alone, and deserted, as lonely as if they had not come.

She was alone as everyone is every morning after a dream.

What was this that was weeping inside of her costume and house, something smaller and simpler than the edifice of spells?

She did not know why she was left hungry.

The dream took place. Everything had contributed to its perfection, even her silence, for she would not speak when she had nothing meaningful to say (like the silence in dreams between fateful events and fateful phrases, never a trivial word spoken in dreams!).

The next day, unknowing, she began anew.

She poured medicines from ugly bottles into alchemist bottles, creating minor mysteries, minor transmutations.

Insomnia. The nights were long.

Who would come and say: that is *my* dream, and take up the thread and make all the answers?

Or are all dreams made alone?

Lying in the fevered sheets of insomnia, there was a human being cheated by the dream.

Insomnia came when one must be on the watch, when one awaited an important visitor.

Everyone, Djuna felt, saw the dancer on light feet but no one seized the moment when she vacillated, fell. No one perceived or shared her difficulties, the mere technical difficulties of loving, dancing, believing.

When she fell, she fell alone, as she had in adolescence.

She remembered feeling this mood as a girl, that all her adolescence had proceeded by oscillations between weakness and strength. She remembered, too, that whenever she became entangled in too great a difficulty she had these swift regressions into her adolescent state. Almost as if in the large world of maturity, when the obstacle loomed too large, she shrank again into the body of the young girl for whom the world had first appeared as a violent and dangerous place, forcing her to retreat, and when she retreated she fell back into smallness.

She returned to the adolescent deserts of mistrust of love.

Walking through snow, carrying her muff like an obsolete wand no longer possessed of the power to create the personage she needed, she felt herself walking through a desert of snow.

Her body muffled in furs, her heart muffled like her steps, and the pain of living muffled as by the deepest rich carpets, while the thread of Ariadne which led everywhere, right and left, like scattered footsteps in the snow, tugged and pulled within her memory and she began to pull upon this thread (silk for the days of marvel and cotton for the bread of everyday living which was always a little stale) as one pulls upon a spool, and she heard the empty wooden spool knock against the floor of different houses.

Holding the silk or cotton began to cut her fingers which bled from so much unwinding, or was it that the thread of Ariadne had led into a wound?

The thread slipped through her fingers now, with blood on it, and the snow was no longer white.

Too much snow on the spool she was unwinding from the tightly wound memories. Unwinding snow as it lay thick and hard around the edges of her adolescence because the desire of men did not find a magical way to open her being.

The only words which opened her being were the muffled words of poets so rarely uttered by human beings. They alone penetrated her without awakening the bristling guards on watch at the gateways, costumed like silver porcupines armed with mistrust, barring the way to the secret recesses of her thoughts and feelings.

Before most people, most places, most situations, most words, Djuna's being, at sixteen, closed hermetically into muteness. The sentinels bristled: someone is approaching! And all the passages to her inner self would close.

Today as a mature woman she could see how these sentinels had not been content with defending her, but they had constructed a veritable fort under this mask of gentle shyness, forts with masked holes concealing weapons built by fear.

The snow accumulated every night all around the rim of her young body.

Blue and crackling snowbound adolescence.

The young men who sought to approach her then, drawn by her warm eyes, were startled to meet with such harsh resistance.

This was no mere flight of coquetry inviting pursuit. It was a fort of snow (for the snowbound, dream-swallower of the frozen fairs). An unmeltable fort of timidity.

Yet each time she walked, muffled, protected, she was aware of two women walking: one intent on creating trap doors of evasion, the other wishing someone might find the entrance that she might not be so alone.

With Michael it was as if she had not heard him coming, so gentle were his steps, his words. Not the walk or words of the hunter, of the man of war, the determined entrance of older men, not the dominant walk of the father, the familiar walk of the brother, not like any other man she knew.

Only a year older than herself, he walked into her blue and white climate with so light a tread that the guards did not hear him!

He came into the room with a walk of vulnerability, treading softly as upon a carpet of delicacies. He would not crush the moss, no gravel would complain under his feet, no plant would bow its head or break.

It was a walk like a dance in which the gentleness of the steps carried him through air, space and silence in a sentient minuet in accord with his partner's mood, his leaf-green eyes obeying every rhythm, attentive to harmony, fearful of discord, with an excessive care for the other's intent.

The path his steps took, his velvet words, miraculously slipped between the bristles of her mistrust, and before she had been fully aware of his coming, by his softness he had entered fully into the blue and white climate.

The mists of adolescence were not torn open, not even disturbed by his entrance.

He came with poems, with worship, with flowers not ordered from the florist but picked in the forest near his school.

He came not to plunder, to possess, to overpower. With great gentleness he moved towards the hospitable regions of her being, towards the peaceful fields of her interior landscape, where white flowers placed themselves against green backgrounds as in Botticelli paintings of spring.

At his entrance her head remained slightly inclined towards the right, as it was when she was alone, slightly weighed down by pensiveness, whereas on other occasions, at the least approach of a stranger, her head would raise itself tautly in preparation for danger.

And so he entered into the flowered regions behind the forts, having easily crossed all the moats of politeness.

His blond hair gave him the befitting golden tones attributed to most legendary figures.

Djuna never knew whether this light of sun he emitted came out of his own being or was thrown upon him by her dream of him, as later she had observed the withdrawal of this light from those she had ceased to love. She never knew whether two people woven together by feelings answering each other as echoes threw off a phosphorescence, the chemical sparks of marriage, or whether each one threw upon the other the spotlight of his inner dream.

Transient or everlasting, inner or outer, personal or magical, there was now this lighting falling upon both of them and they could only see each other in its spanning circle which dazzled them and separated them from the rest of the world.

Through the cocoon of her shyness her voice had been hardly audible, but he heard every shading of it, could follow its nuances even when it retreated into the furthest impasse of the ear's labyrinth.

Secretive and silent in relation to the world, she became exalted and intense once placed inside of this inner circle of light.

This light which enclosed two was familiar and natural to her.

Because of their youth, and their moving still outside of the center of their own desires blindly, what they danced together was not a dance in which either took possession of the other, but a kind of minuet, where the aim consisted in *not* appropriating, *not* grasping, *not* touching, but allowing the maximum space and distance to flow between the two figures. To move in accord without collisions, without merging. To encircle, to bow in worship, to laugh at the same absurdities, to mock their own movements, to throw upon the walls twin shadows which will never become one. To dance around this danger: the danger of becoming one! To dance keeping each to his own path. To allow parallelism, but no loss of the self into the other. To play at marriage, step by step, to read the same book together, to dance a dance of elusiveness on the rim of desire, to remain within circles of heightened lighting without touching the core that would set the circle on fire.

A deft dance of unpossession.

They met once at a party, imprinted on each other forever the first physical image: she saw him tall, with an easy bearing, an easily flowing laughter. She saw all: the ivory color of the skin, the gold metal sheen of the hair, the lean body carved with meticulous economy as for racing, running, leaping; tender fingers touching objects as if all the world were fragile; tender inflections of the voice without malice or mockery; eyelashes always ready to fall over the eyes when people spoke harshly around him.

He absorbed her dark, long, swinging hair, the blue eyes never at rest, a little slanted, quick to close their curtains too, quick to laugh, but more often thirsty, absorbing like a mirror. She allowed the pupil to receive these images of others but one felt they did not vanish altogether as they would on a mirror: one felt a thristy being absorbing reflections and drinking words and faces into herself for a deep communion with them.

She never took up the art of words, the art of talk. She remained always as Michael had first seen her: a woman who talked with her Naiad hair, her winged eyelashes, her tilted head, her fluent waist and rhetorical feet.

She never said: I have a pain. But laid her two arms over the painful area as if to quiet a rebellious child, rocking and cradling this angry nerve. She never said: I am afraid. But entered the room on tiptoes, her eyes watching for ambushes.

She was already the dancer she was to become, eloquent with her body.

They met once and then Michael began to write her letters as soon as he returned to college.

In these letters he appointed her Isis and Arethusa, Iseult and the Seven Muses.

Djuna became the woman with the face of all women.

With strange omissions: he was neither Osiris nor Tristram, nor any of the mates or pursuers.

He became uneasy when she tried to clothe *him* in the costume of myth figures.

When he came to see her during vacations they never touched humanly, not even by a handclasp. It was as if they had found the most intricate way of communicating with each other by way of historical personages, literary passions, and that any direct touch even of finger tips would explode this world.

With each substitution they increased the distance between their human selves.

Djuna was not alarmed. She regarded this with feminine eyes: in creating this world Michael was merely constructing a huge, superior, magnificent nest in some mythological tree, and one day he would ask her to step into it with him, carrying her over the threshold all costumed in the trappings of his fantasy, and he would say: this is our home!

All this to Djuna was an infinitely superior way of wooing her, and she never doubted its ultimate purpose, or climax, for in this the most subtle women are basically simple and do not consider mythology or symbolism as a subtitute for the climaxes of nature, merely as adornments!

This mist of adolescence, prolonging and expanding the wooing, was merely an elaboration of the courtship. His imagination continued to create endless detours as if they had to live first of all through all the loves of history and fiction before they could focus on their own.

But the peace in his moss-green eyes disturbed her, for in her eyes there now glowed a fever. Her breasts hurt her at night, as if from overfullness.

His eyes continued to focus on the most distant points of all, but hers began to focus on the near, the present. She would dwell on a detail of his face. On his ears for instance. On the movements of his lips when he talked. She failed to hear some of his words because she was following with her eyes and her feelings the contours of his lips moving as if they were moving on the surface of her skin.

She began to understand for the first time the carnation in Carmen's mouth. Carmen was eating the mock orange of love: the white blossoms which she bit were like skin. Her lips had pressed around the mock-orange petals of desire.

In Djuna all the moats were annihilated: she stood perilously near to Michael glowing with her own natural warmth. Days of clear visibility which Michael did not share. His compass still pointed to the remote, the unknown.

Djuna was a woman being dreamed.

But Djuna had ceased to dream: she had tasted the mock orange of desire.

More baffling still to Djuna grown warm and near, with her aching breasts, was that the moss-green serenity of Michael's eyes was going to dissolve into jealousy without pausing at desire.

He took her to a dance. His friends eagerly appropriated her. From across the room full of dancers, for the first time he saw not her eyes but her mouth, as vividly as she had seen his. Very clear and very near, and he felt the taste of it upon his lips.

For the first time, as she danced away from him, encircled by young men's arms, he measured the great space they had been swimming through, measured it exactly as others measure the distance between planets.

The mileage of space he had put between himself and Djuna. The lighthouse of the eyes alone could traverse such immensity!

And now, after such elaborations in space, so many figures interposed between them, the white face of Iseult, the burning face of Catherine, all of which he had interpreted as mere elaborations of his enjoyment of her, now suddenly appeared not as ornaments but as obstructions to his possession of her.

She was lost to him now. She was carried away by other young men, turning with them. They had taken her waist as he never had, they bent her, plied her to the movements of the dance, and she answered and responded: they were mated by the dance.

As she passed him he called out her name severely, reproachfully, and Djuna saw the green of his eyes turned to violet with jealousy.

"Djuna! I'm taking you home."

For the first time he was willful, and she liked it.

"Djuna!" He called again, angrily, his eyes darkening with anger.

She had to stop dancing. She came gently towards him, thinking: "He wants me all to himself," and she was happy to yield to him.

He was only a little taller than she was, but he held himself very erect and commanding.

On the way home he was silent.

The design of her mouth had vanished again, his journey towards her mouth had ceased the moment it came so near in reality to his own. It was as if he dared to experience a possibility of communion only while the obstacle to it was insurmountable, but as the obstacle was removed and she walked clinging to his arm, then he could only commune with her eyes, and the distance was again reinstated.

He left her at her door without a sign of tenderness, with only the last violet shadows of jealousy lurking reproachfully in his eyes. That was all.

Djuna sobbed all night before the mystery of his jealousy, his anger, his remoteness.

She would not question him. He confided nothing. They barred all means of communication with each other. He would not tell her that at this very dance he had discovered an intermediate world from which all the figures of women were absent. A world of boys like himself in flight away from woman, mother, sister, wife or mistress.

In her ignorance and innocence then, she could not have pierced with the greatest divination where Michael, in his flight from her, gave his desire.

In their youthful blindness they wounded each other. He excused his coldness towards her: "You're too slender. I like plump women." Or again: "You're too intelligent. I feel better with stupid women." Or another time he said: "You're too impulsive, and that frightens me."

Being innocent, she readily accepted the blame.

Strange scenes took place between them. She subdued her intelligence and became passive to please him. But it was a game, and they both knew it. Her ebullience broke through all her pretenses at quietism.

She swallowed countless fattening pills, but could only gain a pound or two. When she proudly asked him to note the improvements, his eyes turned away.

One day he said: "I feel your clever head watching me, and you would look down on me if I failed."

Failed?

She could not understand.

With time, her marriage to another, her dancing which took her to many countries, the image of Michael was effaced.

But she continued to relate to other Michaels in the world. Some part of her being continued to recognize the same gentleness, the same elusiveness, the same mystery.

Michael reappeared under different bodies, guises, and each time she responded to him, discovering each time a little more until she pierced the entire mystery open.

But the same little dance took place each time, a little dance of insolence, a dance which said to the woman: "I dance alone, I will not be possessed by a woman."

The kind of dance tradition had taught woman as a ritual to provoke aggression! But this dance made by young men before the women left them at a loss for it was not intended to be answered.

* * *

Years later she sat at a café table in Paris between Michael and Donald.

Why should she be sitting between Michael and Donald?

Why were not all cords cut between herself and Michael when she married and when he gave himself to a succession of Donalds?

When they met in Paris again, he had this need to invent a trinity: to establish a connecting link between Djuna and all the changing, fluctuating Donalds.

As if some element were lacking in his relation to Donald.

Donald had a slender body, like an Egyptian boy. Dark hair, wild like that of a child who had been running. At moments the extreme softness of his gestures made him appear small, at others when he stood stylized and pure in line, erect, he seemed tall and firm.

His eyes were large and entranced, and he talked flowingly like a medium. His eyelids fell heavily over his eyes like a woman's, with a sweep of the eyelashes. He had a small straight nose, small ears, and strong boyish hands.

When Michael left for cigarettes they looked at each other, and immediately Donald ceased to be a woman. He straightened his body and looked at Djuna unflinchingly.

With her he asserted his strength. Was it her being a woman which challenged his strength? He was now like a grave child in the stage of becoming a man.

With the smile of a conspirator he said: "Michael treats me as if I were a woman or a child. He wants me not to work and to depend on him. He wants to go and live down south in a kind of paradise."

"And what do you want?"

"I am not sure I love Michael. . . ."

That was exactly what she expected to hear. Always this admission of incompleteness. Always one in flight or the three sitting together, always one complaining or one loving less than the other.

All this accompanied by the most complicated harmonization of expressions Djuna had ever seen. The eyes and mouth of Donald suggesting an excitement familiar to drug addicts, only in Donald it did not derive from any artificial drugs but from the strange flavor he extracted from difficulties, from the maze and detours and unfulfillments of his loves.

In Donald's eyes shone the fever of futile watches in the night, intrigue, pursuits of the forbidden, all the rhythms and moods unknown to ordinary living. There was a quest for the forbidden and it was this flavor he sought, as well as the strange lighting which fell on all the unknown, the unfamiliar, the tabooed, all that could remind him of those secret moments of childhood when he sought the very experiences most forbidden by the parents.

But when it came to the selection of one, to giving one's self to one, to an open simplicity and an effort at completeness, some mysterious impulse always intervened and destroyed the relationship. A hatred of permanency, of anything resembling marriage.

Donald was talking against Michael's paradise as it would destroy the bitter-sweet, intense flavor he sought.

He bent closer to Djuna, whispering now like a conspirator. It was his conspiracy against simplicity, against Michael's desire for a peaceful life together.

"If you only knew, Djuna, the first time it happened! I expected the whole world to change its face, be utterly transformed, turned upside down. I expected the room to become inclined, as after an earthquake, to find that the door no longer led to a stairway but into space, and the windows overlooked the sea. Such excitement, such anxiety, and such a fear of not achieving fulfillment. At other times I have the feeling that I am escaping a prison, I have a fear of being caught again and punished. When I signal to another like myself in a café I have the feeling that we are two prisoners who have found a laborious way to communicate by a secret code. All our messages are colored with the violent colors of danger. What I find in this devious way has a taste like no other object overtly obtained. Like the taste of those dim and secret afternoons of our childhood when we performed forbidden acts with great anxiety and terror of punishment. The exaltation of danger, I'm used to it now, the fever of remorse. This society which condemns me... do you know how I am revenging myself? I am seducing each one of its members slowly, one by one...."

He talked softly and exultantly, choosing the silkiest words, not disguising his dream of triumphing over all those who had dared to forbid certain acts, and certain forms of love.

At the same time when he talked about Michael there came to his face the same expression women have when they have seduced a man, an expression of vain glee, a triumphant, uncontrollable celebration of her power. And so Donald was celebrating the feminine wiles and ruses and charms by which he had made Michael fall so deeply in love with him.

It his flight from woman, it seemed to Djuna, Michael had merely fled to one containing all the minor flaws of women.

Donald stopped talking and there remained in the air the feminine intonations of his voice, chanting and never falling into deeper tones.

Michael was back and sat between them offering cigarettes.

As soon as Michael returned Djuna saw Donald change, become woman again, tantalizing and provocative. She saw Donald's body dilating into feminine undulations, his face open in all nakedness. His face expressed a dissolution like that of a woman being taken. Everything revealed, glee, the malice, the vanity, the childishness. His gestures like those of a second-rate actress receiving flowers with a batting of the eyelashes, with an oblique glance like the upturned cover of a bedspread, the edge of a petticoat.

He had the stage bird's turns of the head, the little dance of alertness, the petulance of the mouth pursed for small kisses that do not shatter the being, the flutter and perk of prize birds, all adornment and change, a mockery of the evanescent darts of invitation, the small gestures of alarm and promise made by minor women.

Michael said: "You two resemble each other. I am sure Donald's suits would fit you, Djuna."

"But Donald is more truthful," said Djuna, thinking how openly Donald betrayed that he did not love Michael, whereas she might have sought a hundred oblique routes to soften this truth.

"Donald is more truthful because he loves less," said Michael.

Warmth in the air. The spring foliage shivering out of pure coquetry, not out of discomfort. Love flowing now between the three, shared, transmitted, contagious, as if Michael were at last free to love Djuna in the form of a boy, through the body of Donald to reach Djuna whom he could never touch directly, and Djuna through the body of Donald reached Michael—and the missing dimension of their love accomplished in space like an algebra of imperfection, as abstract drama of incompleteness at last resolved for one moment by this trinity of woman sitting between two incomplete men.

She could look with Michael's eyes at Donald's finely designed body, the narrow waist, the square shoulders, the stylized gestures and dilated expression.

She could see that Donald did not give his true self to Michael. He acted for him a caricature of woman's minor petulances and caprices. He ordered a drink and then changed his mind, and when the drink came he did not want it at all.

Djuna thought: "He is like a woman without the womb in which such great mysteries take place. He is a travesty of a marriage that will never take place."

Donald rose, performed a little dance of salutation and flight before them, eluding Michael's pleading eyes, bowed, made some whimsical gesture of apology and flight, and left them.

This little dance reminded her of Michael's farewells on her doorsteps when she was sixteen.

And suddenly she saw all their movements, hers with Michael, and Michael's with Donald, as a ballet of unreality and unpossession.

"Their greatest form of activity is flight!" she said to Michael.

To the tune of Debussy's *Ile Joyeuse,* they gracefully made all the steps which lead to no possession.

(When will I stop loving these airy young men who move in a realm like the realm of the birds, always a little quicker than most human beings, always a little above, or beyond humanity, always in flight, out of some great fear of human beings, always seeking the open space, wary of enclosures, anxious for their freedom, vibrating with a multitude of alarms, always sensing danger all around them....)

"Birds," said a research scientist, "live their lives with an intensity as extreme as their brilliant colors and their vivid songs. Their body temperatures are regularly as high as 105 to 110 degrees, and anyone who has watched a bird at close range must have seen how its whole body vibrates with the furious pounding of its pulse. Such engines must operate at forced draft: and that is exactly what a bird does. The bird's indrawn breath not only fills its lungs, but also passes on through myriads of tiny tubules into air sacs that fill every space in the bird's body not occupied by vital organs. Furthermore the air sacs connect with many of the bird's bones, which are not filled with marrow as animal's bones are, but are hollow. These reserve air tanks provide fuel for the bird's intensive life, and at the same time add to its buoyancy in flight."

Paul arrived as the dawn arrives, mist-laden, uncertain of his gestures. The sun was hidden until he smiled. Then the blue of his eyes, the sleepy eyelids, were all illuminated by the wide, brilliant smile. Mist, dew, the uncertain hoverings of his gestures were dispelled by the full, firm mouth, the strong even teeth.

Then the smile vanished again, as quickly as it had come. When he entered her room he brought with him this climate of adolescence which is neither sun nor full moon but the intermediate regions.

Again she noticed the shadows under his eyes, which made a soft violet-tinted halo around the intense blue of the pupils.

He was mantled in shyness, and his eyelids were heavy as if from too much dreaming. His dreaming lay like the edges of a deep slumber on the rim of his eyelids. One expected them to close in a hypnosis of interior fantasy as mysterious as a drugged state.

This constant passing from cloudedness to brilliance took place within a few instants. His body would sit absolutely still, and then would suddenly leap into gaiety and lightness. Then once again his face would close hermetically.

He passed in the same quick way between phrases uttered with profound maturity to sudden innocent inaccuracies.

It was difficult to remember he was seventeen.

He seemed more preoccupied with uncertainty as to how to carry himself through this unfamiliar experience than with absorbing or enjoying it.

Uncertainty spoiled his plesure in the present, but Djuna felt he was one to carry away his treasures into secret chambers of remembrance and there he would lay them all out like the contents of an opium pipe being prepared, these treasures no longer endangered by uneasiness in living, the treasures becoming the past, and there he would touch and caress every word, every image, and make them his own.

In solitude and remembrance his real life would begin. Everything that was happening now was merely the preparation of the opium pipe that would later send volutes into space to enchant his solitude, when he would be lying down away from danger and unfamiliarity, lying down to taste of an experience washed of the dross of anxiety.

He would lie down and nothing more would be demanded of the dreamer, no longer expected to participate, to speak, to act, to decide. He would lie down and the images would rise in chimerical visitations and form a tale more marvelous in every detail than the one taking place at this moment marred by apprehension.

Having created a dream beforehand which he sought to preserve from destruction by reality, every movement in life became more difficult for the dreamer, for Paul, his fear of errors being like the opium dreamer's fear of noise or daylight.

And not only his dream of Djuna was he seeking to preserve like some fragile essence easily dispelled but even more dangerous, his own image of what was expected of him by Djuna, what he imagined Djuna expected of him—a heavy demand upon a youthful Paul, his own ideal exigencies, which he did not know to be invented by himself, creating a difficulty in every act or word in which he was merely re-enacting scenes rehearsed in childhood in which the child's naturalness was always defeated by the severity of the parents, giving him the perpetual feeling that no word and no act came up to this impossible standard set for him. A more terrible compression than when the Chinese bound the feet of their infants, bound them with yards of cloth to stunt the natural growth. Such tyrannical cloth worn too long, unbroken, uncut, would in the end turn one into a mummy. . . .

Djuna could see the image of the mother binding Paul in the story he told her: He had a pet guinea pig, once, which he loved. And his mother had forced him to kill it.

She could see all the bindings when he added: "I destroyed a diary I kept in school."

"Why?"

"Now that I was home for a month, my parents might have read it."

Were the punishments so great that he was willing rather to annihilate living parts of himself, a loved pet, a diary reflecting his inner self?

"There are many sides of yourself you cannot show your parents."

"Yes." An expression of anxiety came to his face. The effect of their severity was apparent in the way he sat, stood—even in the tone of resignation in which he said: "I have to leave soon."

Djuna looked at him and saw him as the prisoner he was—a prisoner of school, of parents.

"But you have a whole month of freedom now."

"Yes," said Paul, but the word freedom had no echo in his being.

"What will you do with it?"

He smiled then. "I can't do much with it. My parents don't want me to visit dancers."

"Did you tell them you were coming to visit me?"

"Yes."

"Do they know you want to be a dancer yourself?"

"Oh, no." He smiled again, a distressed smile, and then his eyes lost their direct, open frankness. They wavered, as if he had suddenly lost his way.

This was his most familiar expression: a nebulous glance, sliding off people and objects.

He had the fears of a child in the external world, yet he gave at the same time the impression of living in a larger world. This boy, thought Djuna tenderly, is lost. But he is lost in a large world. His dreams are vague, infinite, formless. He loses himself in them. No one knows what he is imagining and thinking. He does not know, he cannot say, but it is not a simple world. It expands beyond his grasp, he senses more than he knows, a bigger world which frightens him.

He cannot confide or give himself. He must have been too often harshly condemned.

Waves of tenderness flowed out to him from her eyes as they sat without talking. The cloud vanished from his face. It was as if he sensed what she was thinking.

Just as he was leaving Lawrence arrived breathlessly, embraced Djuna effusively, pranced into the studio and turned on the radio.

He was Paul's age, but unlike Paul he did not appear to carry a little snail house around his personality, a place into which to retreat and vanish. He came out openly, eyes aware, smiling, expectant, in readiness for anything that might happen. He moved propelled by sheer impulse, and was never still.

He was carrying a cage which he laid in the middle of the room. He lifted its covering shaped like a miniature striped awning.

Djuna knelt on the rug to examine the contents of the cage and laughed to see a blue mouse nibbling at a cracker.

"Where did you find a turquoise mouse?" asked Djuna.

"I bathed her in dye," said Lawrence. "Only she licks it all away in a few days and turns white again, so I had to bring her this time right after her bath."

The blue mouse was nibbling eagerly. The music was playing. They were sitting on the rug. The room began to glitter and sparkle.

Paul looked on with amazement.

(This pet, his eyes said, need not be killed. Nothing is forbidden here.)

Lawrence was painting the cage with phosphorescent paint so that it would shine in the dark.

"That way she won't be afraid when I leave her alone at night!"

While the paint dried Lawrence began to dance.

Djuna was laughing behind her veil of long hair.

Paul looked at them yearningly and then said in a toneless voice: "I have to leave now." And he left precipitately.

"Who is the beautiful boy?" asked Lawrence.

"The son of tyrannical parents who are very worried he should visit a dancer."

"Will he come again?"

"He made no promise. Only if he can get away."

GO TO P156

READ 156 first

rocks. He would always come back smiling: "Oh, Djuna, you remember Hilda? I was so crazy about her. Do you know what she did? She tried to palm off some false money on me. Yes, with all her lovely eyes, manners, sensitiveness, she came to me and said so tenderly: let me have change for this ten-dollar bill. And it was a bad one. And then she tried to hide some drugs in my room, and to say I was the culprit. I nearly went to jail. She pawned my typewriter, my box of paints. She finally took over my room and I had to sleep for the night on a park bench."

But the next morning he was again full of faith, love, trust, impulses.

Dancing and believing.

In his presence she was again ready to believe.

To believe in Paul's eyes, the mystery and the depth in them, the sense of some vast dream lying coiled there, undeciphered.

Lawrence had finished the phosphorescent painting. He closed the curtains and the cage shone in the dark. Now he decided to paint with phosphorescence everything paintable in the room.

The next day Lawrence appeared with a large pot of paint and he was stirring it with a stick when Paul telephoned: "I can get away for a while. My I come?"

"Oh, come, come," said Djuna.

"I can't stay very late. . . ." His voice was muffled, like that of a sick person. There was a plaintiveness in it so plainly audible to Djuna's heart.

"The prisoner is allowed an hour's freedom," she said.

When Paul came Lawrence handed him a paintbrush and in silence the two of them worked at touching up everything paintable in the room. They turned off the lights. A new room appeared.

Luminous faces appeared on the walls, new flowers, new jewels, new castles, new jungles, new animals, all in filaments of light.

Mysterious translucence like their unmeasured words, their impulsive acts, wishes, enthusiasms. Darkness was excluded from their world, the darkness of loss of faith. It was now the room with a perpetual sparkle, even in darkness.

(They are making a new world for me, felt Djuna, a world of greater lightness. It is perhaps a dream and I may not be allowed

GO TO P157

"We'll go and visit him."

Djuna smiled. She could imagine Lawrence arriving at Paul's formal home with a cage with a blue mouse in it and Paul's mother saying: "You get rid of that pet!"

Or Lawrence taking a ballet leap to touch the tip of a chandelier, or singing some delicate obscenity.

"C'est une jeune fille en fleur," he said now, clairvoyantly divining Djuna's fear of never escaping from the echoes and descendants of Michael.

Lawrence shrugged his shoulders. Then he looked at her with his red-gold eyes, under his red-gold hair. Whenever he looked at her it was contagious: that eager, ardent glance falling amorously on everyone and everything, dissolving the darkest moods.

No sadness could resist this frenzied carnival of affection he dispensed every day, beginning with his enthusiasm for his first cup of coffee, joy at the day's beginning, an immediate fancy for the first person he saw, a passion at the least provocation for man, woman, child or animal. A warmth even in his collisions with misfortunes, troubles and difficulties.

He received them smiling. Without money in his pocket he rushed to help. With generous excess he rushed to love, to desire, to possess, to lose, to suffer, to die the multiple little deaths everyone dies each day. He would even die and weep and suffer and lose with enthusiasm, with ardor. He was prodigal in poverty, rich and abundant in some invisible chemical equivalent to gold and sun.

Any event would send him leaping and prancing with gusto: a concert, a play, a ballet, a person. Yes, yes, yes, cried his young firm body every morning. No retractions, no hesitations, no fears, no caution, no economy. He accepted every invitation.

His joy was in movement, in assenting, in consenting, in expansion.

Whenever he came he lured Djuna into a swirl. Even in sadness they smiled at each other, expanding in sadness with dilated eyes and dilated hearts.

"Drop every sorrow and dance!"

Thus they healed each other by dancing, perfectly mated in enthusiasm and fire.

The waves which carried him forward never dropped him on the

BACK TO P155

to stay. They treat me as one of their own, because I believe what they believe, I feel as they do. I hate the father, authority, men of power, men of wealth, all tyranny, all authority, all crystallizations. I feel as Lawrence and Paul: outside there lies a bigger world full of cruelties, dangers and corruptions, where one sells out one's charms, one's playfulness, and enters a rigid world of discipline, duty, contracts, accountings. A thick opaque world without phosphorescence. I want to stay in this room forever, not with man the father but with man the son, carving, painting, dancing, dreaming, and always beginning, born anew every day, never aging, full of faith and impulse, turning and changing to every wind like the mobiles. I do not love those who have ceased to flow, to believe, to feel. Those who can no longer melt, exult, who cannot let themselves be cheated, laugh at loss, those who are bound and frozen.)

She laid her head on Lawrence's shoulder with a kind of gratitude. (Nowhere else as here with Lawrence and with Paul was there such an iridescence in the air; nowhere else so far from the threat of hardening and crystallizing. Everything flowing. . . .)

Djuna was brushing her hair with her fingers, in long pensive strokes, and Lawrence was talking about the recurrent big problem of a job. He had tried so many. How to work without losing one's color, one's ardor, personal possessions and freedom. He was very much like a delicate Egyptian scarab who dreaded to lose his iridescence in routine, in duty, in monotony. The job could kill one, or maim one, make one a robot, an opaque personage, a future undertaker, a man of power with gouty limbs and a hardening of the arteries of faith!

Lawrence was now working in a place which made decorations for shop windows. He liked to work at night, to go on strange expeditions in the company of mannequins, papier-mâché horses, to live on miniature stages building jungles, sea landscapes, fabulous animals. To flirt with naked mannequins whose arms came off as easily as other women's gloves, who deposited their heads on the floor and took off their wigs when they took off their hats. He became an expert at dismantling women!

Lawrence lived and breathed color and there was no danger of his dying of drabness, for even accidents took on a most vivid shade and a spoiled pot of *gouache* was still a delight to the eyes.

He brought Djuna gifts of chokers, headdresses, earrings made of painted clay which crumbled quickly like the trappings for a costume play.

She had always liked objects without solidity. The solid ones bound her to permanency. She had never wanted a solid house, enduring furniture. All these were traps. Then you belonged to them forever. She preferred stage trappings which she could move into and out of easily, without regret. Soon after they fell apart and nothing was lost. The vividness alone survived.

She remembered once hearing a woman complain that armchairs no longer lasted twenty years, and Djuna answered: "But I couldn't love an armchair for twenty years!"

And so change, mutations like the rainbow, and she preferred Lawrence's gifts from which the colored powder and crystals fell like the colors on the wings of butterflies after yielding their maximum of charm.

Paul was carving a piece of copper, making such fine incisions with the scissors that the bird which finally appeared between his slender fingers bristled with filament feathers.

He stood on the table and hung it by a thread to the ceiling. The slightest breath caused it to turn slowly.

Paul had the skin of a child that had never been touched by anything of this earth: no soap, no washrag, no brush, no human kiss could have touched his skin! Never scrubbed, rubbed, scratched, or wrinkled by a pillow. The transparency of the child skin, of the adolescent later to turn opaque. What do children nourish themselves with that their skin has this transparency, and what do they eat of later which brings on opaqueness?

The mothers who kiss them are eating light.

There is a phosphorescence which comes from the magic world of childhood.

Where does this illumination go later? Is it the substance of faith which shines from their bodies like phosphorescence from the albatross, and what kills it?

Now Lawrence had discovered a coiled measuring tape of steel in Djuna's closet while delving for objects useful for charades.

When entirely pulled out of its snail covering it stretched like a long snake of steel which under certain manipulations could stand rigid like a sword or undulate like silver-tipped waves, or flash like lightning.

Lawrence and Paul stood like expert swordsmen facing each other for a duel of light and steel.

The steel band flexed, then hardened between them like a bridge, and at each forward movement by one it seemed as if the sword had pierced the body of the other.

At other moments it wilted, wavered like a frightened snake, and then it looked bedraggled and absurd and they both laughed.

But soon they learned never to let it break or waver and it became like a thunderbolt in their hands. Paul attacked with audacity and Lawrence parried with swiftness.

At midnight Paul began to look anxious. His luminosity clouded, he resumed his hesitant manner. He ceased to occupy the center of the room and moved out of the focus of light and laughter. Like a sleepwalker, he moved away from gaiety.

Djuna walked with him towards the door. They were alone and then he said: "My parents have forbidden me to come here."

"But you were happy here, weren't you?"

"Yes, I was happy."

"This is where you belong."

"Why do you think I belong here?"

"You're gifted for dancing, for painting, for writing. And this is your month of freedom."

"Yes, I know. I wish . . . I wish I were free. . . ."

"If you wish it deeply enough you will find a way."

"I would like to run away, but I have no money."

"If you run away we'll all take care of you."

"Why?"

"Because we believe in you, because you're worth helping."

"I have nowhere to go."

"We'll find you a room somewhere, and we will adopt you. And you will have your month of life."

"Of life" he repeated with docility.

"But I don't want you to do it unless you feel ready, unless you want it so much that you're willing to sacrifice everything else. I only want you to know you can count on us, but it must be your decision, or it will not mean anything."

"Thank you." This time he did not clasp her hand, he laid his hand within hers as if nestling it there, folded, ivory smooth and gentle, at rest, in an act of trustingness.

Then before leaving the place he looked once more at the room as if to retain its enfolding warmth. At one moment he had laughed so much that he had slid from his chair. Djuna had made him laugh. At that moment many of his chains must have broken, for nothing breaks chains like laughter, and Djuna could not remember in all her life a greater joy than this spectacle of Paul laughing like a released prisoner.

Two days later Paul appeared at her door with his valise.

Djuna received him gaily as if this were the beginning of a holiday, asked him to tie the velvet bows at her wrist, drove him to where Lawrence lived with his parents and where there was an extra room.

She would have liked to shelter him in her own house, but she knew his parents would come there and find him.

He wrote a letter to his parents. He reminded them that he had only a month of freedom for himself before leaving for India on the official post his father had arranged for him, that during this month he felt he had a right to be with whatever friends he felt a kinship with. He had found people with whom he had a great deal to share and since his parents had been so extreme in their demands, forbidding him to see his friends at all, he was being equally extreme in his assertion of his freedom. Not to be concerned about him, that at the end of the month he would comply with his father's plans for him.

He did not stay in his room. It had been arranged that he would have his meals at Djuna's house. An hour after he had laid down his valise in Lawrence's room he was at her house.

In his presence she did not feel herself a mature woman, but again a girl of seventeen at the beginning of her own life. As if the girl of seventeen had remained undestroyed by experience—like some deeper layer in a geological structure which had been pressed but not obliterated by the new layers.

(He seems hungry and thirsty for warmth, and yet so fearful. We are arrested by each other's elusiveness. Who will take flight first? If we move too hastily, fear will spring up and separate us. I am fearful of his innocence, and he of what he believes to be my knowingness. But neither one of us knows what the other wants, we are both arrested and ready to vanish, with such a fear of being hurt. His oscillations are like mine, his muteness like mine at his age, his fears like my fears.)

She felt that as he came nearer there was a vibration through his body. Through all the mists as her body approached to greet him there was an echo of her movements within him.

With his hand within hers, at rest, he said: "Everyone is doing so much for me. Do you think that when I grow up I will be able to do the same for someone else?"

"Of course you will." And because he had said so gently "when I grow up" she saw him suddenly as a boy, and her hand went out swiftly towards the strand of boyish hair which fell over his eyes and pulled it.

That she had done this with a half-frightened laugh as if she expected retaliation made him feel at ease with her.

He did retaliate by trying jiujitsu on her arm until she said: "You hurt me." Then he stopped, but the discovery that her bones were not as strong as the boys' on whom he had tested his knowledge made him feel powerful. He had more strength than he needed to handle her. He could hurt her so easily, and now he was no longer afraid when her face came near his and her eyes grew larger and more brilliant, or when she danced and her hair accidentally swung across her face like a silk whip, or when she sat like an Arab holding conversation over the telephone in answer to invitations which might deprive him of her presence. No matter who called, she always refused, and stayed at home to talk with him.

The light in the room became intensely bright and they were bathed in it, bright with the disappearance of his fear.

He felt at ease to sit and draw, to read, to paint, and to be silent. The light around them grew warm and dim and intimate.

By shedding in his presence the ten years of life which created distance between them, she felt herself re-entering a smaller house of innocence and faith, and that what she shed was merely a role: she had played a role of woman, and this had been the torment, she had been pretending to be a woman, and now she knew she had not been at ease in this role, and now with Paul she felt she was being transformed into a stature and substance nearer to her true state.

With Paul she was passing from an insincere pretense at maturity into a more vulnerable world, escaping from the more difficult role of tormented woman to a smaller room of warmth.

For one moment, sitting there with Paul, listening to the Symphony in D minor of César Franck, through his eyes she was allowed behind the mirror into a smaller silk-lined house of faith.

In art, in history, man fights his fears, he wants to live forever, he is afraid of death, he wants to work with other men, he wants to live forever. He is like a child afraid of death. The child is afraid of death, of darkness, of solitude. Such simple fears behind all the elaborate constructions. Such simple fears as hunger for light, warmth, love. Such simple fears behind the elaborate constructions of art. Examine them all gently and quietly through the eyes of a boy. There is always a human being lonely, a human being afraid, a human being lost, a human being confused. Concealing and disguising his dependence, his needs, ashamed to say: I am a simple human being in too vast and too complex a world. Because of all we have discovered about a leaf. . . it is still a leaf. Can we relate to a leaf, on a tree, in a park, a simple leaf: green, glistening, sun-bathed or wet, or turning white because the storm is coming. Like the savage, let us look at the leaf wet or shining with sun, or white with fear of the storm, or silvery in the fog, or listless in too great heat, or falling in the autumn, drying, reborn each year anew. Learn from the leaf: simplicity. In spite of all we know about the leaf: its nerve structure phyllome cellular papilla parenchyma stomata venation. Keep a human relation—leaf, man, woman, child. In tenderness. No matter how immense the world, how elaborate, how contradictory, there is always man, woman, child, and the leaf. Humanity makes everything warm and simple. Humanity. Let the waters of humanity flow through the abstract city, through abstract art, weeping like rivulets cracking rocky mountains, melting icebergs. The frozen worlds in empty cages of mobiles where hearts lie exposed like wires in an electric bulb. Let them burst at the tender touch of a leaf.

The next morning Djuna was having breakfast in bed when Lawrence appeared.

"I'm broke and I'd like to have breakfast with you."

He had begun to eat his toast when the maid came and said: "There's a gentleman at the door who won't give his name."

"Find out what he wants. I don't want to dress yet."

But the visitor had followed the servant to the door and stood now in the bedroom.

Before anyone could utter a protest he said in the most classically villainous tone: "Ha, ha, having breakfast, eh?"

"Who are you? What right have you to come in here," said Djuna.

"I have every right: I'm a detective."

"A detective!"

Lawrence's eyes began to sparkle with amusement.

The detective said to him: "And what are you doing here, young man?"

"I'm having breakfast." He said this in the most cheerful and natural manner, continuing to drink his coffee and buttering a piece of toast which he offered Djuna.

"Wonderful!" said the detective. "So I've caught you. Having breakfast, eh? While your parents are breaking their hearts over your disappearance. Having breakfast, eh? When you're not eighteen yet and they can force you to return home and never let you out again." And turning to Djuna he added: "And what may your interest in this young man be?"

Then Djuna and Lawrence broke into irrepressible laughter.

"I'm not the only one," said Lawrence.

At this the detective looked like a man who had not expected his task to be so easy, almost grateful for the collaboration.

"So you're not the only one!"

Djuna stopped laughing. "He means anyone who is broke can have breakfast here."

"Will you have a cup of coffee?" said Lawrence with an impudent smile.

"That's enough talk from you," said the detective. "You'd better come along with me, Paul."

"But I'm not Paul."

"Who are you?"

"My name is Lawrence."

"Do you know Paul—? Have you seen him recently?"

"He was here last night for a party."

"A party? And where did he go after that?"

"I don't know," said Lawrence. "I thought he was staying with his parents."

"What kind of a party was this?" asked the detective.

But now Djuna had stopped laughing and was becoming angry. "Leave this place immediately," she said.

The detective took a photograph out of his pocket, compared it with Lawrence's face, saw there was no resemblance, looked once more at Djuna's face, read the anger in it, and left.

As soon as he left her anger vanished and they laughed again. Suddenly Djuna's playfulness turned into anxiety. "But this may become serious, Lawrence. Paul won't be able to come to my house any more. And suppose it had been Paul who had come for breakfast!"

And then another aspect of the situation struck her and her face became sorrowful. "What kind of parents has Paul that they can consider using force to bring him home."

She took up the telephone and called Paul. Paul said in a shocked voice: "They can't take me home by force!"

"I don't know about the law, Paul. You'd better stay away from my house. I will meet you somewhere—say at the ballet theater—until we find out."

For a few days they met at concerts, galleries, ballets. But no one seemed to follow them.

Djuna lived in constant fear that he would be whisked away and that she might never see him again. Their meetings took on the anxiety of repeated farewells. They always looked at each other as if it were for the last time.

Through this fear of loss she took longer glances at his face, and every facet of it, every gesture, every inflection of his voice thus sank deeper into her, to be stored away against future loss—deeper and deeper it penetrated, impregnated her more as she fought against its vanishing.

She felt that she not only saw Paul vividly in the present but Paul in the future. Every expression she could read as an indication of future power, future discernment, future completion. Her vision of the future Paul illumined the present. Others could see a young man experiencing his first drunkenness, taking his first steps in the world, oscillating or contradicting himself. But she felt herself living with a Paul no one had seen yet, the man of the future, willful, and with a power in him which appeared intermittently.

Then the clouds and mists of adolescence would vanish, what a complete and rich man he would become, with this mixture of sensibility and intelligence motivating his choices, discarding shallowness, never taking a step into mediocrity, with an unerring instinct for the extraordinary.

To send a detective to bring him home by force, how little his parents must know this Paul of the future, possessed of that deep-seated mine of tenderness hidden below access but visible to her.

She was living with a Paul no one knew as yet, in a secret relationship far from the reach of the subtlest detectives, beyond the reach of the entire world.

Under the veiled voice she felt the hidden warmth, under the hesitancies a hidden strength, under the fears a vaster dream more difficult to seize and to fulfill.

Alone, after an afternoon with him, she lay on her bed and while the bird he had carved gyrated lightly in the center of the room, tears came to her eyes so slowly she did not feel them at first until they slid down her cheeks.

Tears from this unbearable melting of her heart and body—a complete melting before the face of Paul, and the muted way his body spoke, the gentle way he was hungering, reaching, groping, like a prisoner escaping slowly and gradually, door by door, room by room, hallway by hallway, towards the light. The prison that had been built around him had been of darkness: darkness about himself, about his needs, about his true nature.

The solitary cell created by the parents.

He knew nothing, nothing about his true self. And such blindness was as good as binding him with chains. His parents and his teachers had merely imposed upon him a false self that seemed right to them.

This boy they did not know.

But this melting, it must not be. She turned her face away, to the right now, as if to turn away from the vision of his face, and murmured: "I must not love him, I must not love him."

The bell rang. Before she could sit up Paul had come in.

"Oh, Paul, this is dangerous for you!"

"I had to come."

As he stopped in his walking towards her his body sought to convey a message. What was his body saying? What were his eyes saying?

He was too near, she felt his eyes possessing her and she rushed away to make tea, to place a tray and food between them, like some very fragile wall made of sand, in games of childhood, which the sea could so easily wash away!

She talked, but he was not listening, nor was she listening to her own words, for his smile penetrated her, and she wanted to run away from him.

"I would like to know..." he said, and the words remained suspended.

He sat too near. She felt the unbearable melting, the loss of herself, and she struggled to close some door against him. "I must not love him, I must not love him!"

She moved slightly away, but his hair was so near her hand that her fingers were drawn magnetically to touch it lightly, playfully.

"What do you want to know?"

Had he noticed her own trembling? He did not answer her. He leaned over swiftly and took her whole mouth in his, the whole man in him coming out in a direct thrust, firm, willful, hungry. With one kiss he appropriated her, asserted his possessiveness.

When he had taken her mouth and kissed her until they were both breathless they lay side by side and she felt his body strong and warm against hers, his passion inflexible.

He laid his hand over her with hesitations. Everything was new to him, a woman's neck, a shoulder, a woman's hooks and buttons.

Between the journeys of discovery he had flickering instant of uncertainties until the sparks of pleasure guided his hand.

Where he passed his hand no one else had ever passed his hand. New cells awakened under his delicate fingers never wakened before to say: this is yours.

A breast touched for the first time is a breast never touched before.

He looked at her with his long blue eyes which had never wept and her eyes were washed luminous and clear, her eyes forgot they had wept.

He touched her eyelashes with his eyelashes of which not one had fallen out and those of hers which had been washed away by tears were replaced.

His hair which had never been crushed between feverish pillows, knotted by nightmares, mingled with hers and untangled it.

Where sadness had carved rich caverns he sank his youthful grasping endless sources of warmth.

Only before the last mystery of the body did he pause. He had thrust and entered and now he paused.

Did one lie still and at peace in the secret place of woman?

In utter silence they lay.

Fever mounting in him, the sap rising, the bodies taut with a need of violence.

She made one undulatory movement, and this unlocked in him a whirlpool of desire, a dervish dance of all the silver knives of pleasure.

When they awakened from their trance, they smiled at each other, but he did not move. They lay merged, slimness to slimness, legs like twin legs, hip to hip.

The cotton of silence lay all around them, covering their bodies in quilted softness.

The big wave of fire which rolled them washed them ashore tenderly into small circles of foam.

On the table there was a huge vase filled with tulips. She moved towards them, seeking something to touch, to pour her joy into, out of the exaltation she felt.

Every part of her body that had been opened by his hands yearned to open the whole world in harmony with her mood.

She looked at the tulips so hermetically closed, like secret poems, like the secrets of the flesh. Her hands took each tulip, the ordinary tulip of everyday living, and she slowly opened them, petal by petal, opened them tenderly.

They were changed from plain to exotic flowers, from closed secrets to open flowering.

Then she heard Paul say: "Don't do that!"

There was a great anxiety in his voice. He repeated: "Don't do that!"

She felt a great stab of anxiety. Why was he so disturbed?

She looked at the flowers. She looked at Paul's face lying on the pillow, clouded with anxiety, and she was struck with fear. Too soon. She had opened him to love too soon. He was not ready.

Even with tenderness, even with delicate fingers, even with the greatest love, it had been too soon! She had forced time, as she had forced the flowers to change from the ordinary to the extraordinary. He was not ready!

Now she understood her own hesitations, her impulse to run away from him. Even though he had made the first gesture, she, knowing, should have saved him from anxiety.

(Paul was looking at the opened tulips and seeing in them something else, not himself but Djuna, the opening body of Djuna. Don't let her open the flowers as he had opened her. In the enormous wave of silence, the hypnosis of hands, skin, delight, he had heard a small moan, yet in her face he had seen joy. Could the thrust into her have hurt her? It was like stabbing someone, this desire.)

"I'm going to dress, now," she said lightly. She could not close the tulips again, but she could dress. She could close herself again and allow him to close again.

Watching her he felt a violent surge of strength again, stronger than his fears. "Don't dress yet."

Again he saw on her face a smile he had never seen there in her gayest moments, and then he accepted the mystery and abandoned himself to his own joy.

His heart beat wildly at her side, wildly in panic and joy together at the moment before taking her. This wildly beating heart at her side, beating against hers, and then the cadenced, undulating blinding merging together, and no break between their bodies afterwards.

After the storm he lay absolutely still over her body, dreaming, quiet, as if this were the place of haven. He lay given, lost, entranced. She bore his weight with joy, though after a while it numbed and hurt her. She made a slight movement, and then he asked her: "Am I crushing you?"

"You're flattening me into a thin wafer," she said, smiling, and he smiled back, then laughed.

"The better to eat you, my dear."

He kissed her again as if he would eat her with delight.

Then he got up and made a somersault on the carpet, with light exultant gestures.

She lay back watching the copper bird gyrating in the center of the room.

His gaiety suddenly overflowed, and taking a joyous leap in the air, he came back to her and said:

"I will call up my father!"

She could not understand. He leaned over her body and keeping his hand over her breast he dialed his father's telephone number.

Then she could see on his face what he wanted to tell his father: call his father, tell him what could not be told, but which his entire new body wanted to tell him: I have taken a woman! I have a woman of my own. I am your equal, Father! I am a man!

When his father answered Paul could only say the ordinary words a son can say to his father, but he uttered these ordinary words with exultant arrogance, as if his father could see him with his hand on Djuna's body: "Father, I am here."

"Where are you?" answered the father severely. "We're expecting you home. You can continue to see your friends but you must come home to please your mother. Your mother has dinner all ready for you!"

Paul laughed, laughed as he had never laughed as a boy, with his hand over the mouth of the telephone.

On such a day they are expecting him for dinner!

They were blind to the miracle. Over the telephone his father should hear and see that he had a woman of his own: she was lying there smiling.

How dare the father command now, doesn't he hear the new voice of the new man in his son?

He hung up.

His hair was falling over his eager eyes. Djuna pulled at it. He stopped her. "You can't do that any more, oh, no." And he sank his teeth into the softest part of her neck.

"You're sharpening your teeth to become a great lover," she said.

When desire overtook him he always had a moment of wildly beating heart, almost of distress, before the invading tide. Before closing his eyes to kiss her, before abandoning himself, he always carefully closed the shutters, windows and doors.

This was the secret act, and he feared the eyes of the world upon him. The world was full of eyes upon his acts, eyes watching with disapproval.

That was the secret fear left from his childhood: dreams, wishes, acts, pleasures which aroused condemnation in the parents' eyes. He could not remember one glance of approval, of love, of admiration, of consent. From far back he remembered being driven into secrecy because whatever he revealed seemed to arouse disapproval or punishment.

He had read the *Arabian Nights* in secret, he had smoked in secret, he had dreamed in secret.

His parents had questioned him only to accuse him later.

And so he closed the shutters, curtains, windows, and then went to her and both of them closed their eyes upon their caresses.

There was a knitted blanket over the couch which he particularly liked. He would sit under it as if it were a tent. Through the interstices of the knitting he could see her and the room as through an oriental trellis. With one hand out of the blanket he would seek her little finger with his little finger and hold it.

As in an opium dream, this touching and interlacing of two little fingers became an immense gesture, the very fragile bridge of their relationship. By this little finger so gently and so lightly pulling hers he took her whole self as no one else had.

He drew her under the blanket, thus, in a dreamlike way, by a small gesture containing the greatest power, a greater power than violence.

Once there they both felt secure from all the world, and from all threats, from the father and the detective, and all the taboos erected to separate lovers all over the world.

Lawrence rushed over to warn them that Paul's father had been seen driving through the neighborhood.

Paul and Djuna were having dinner together and were going to the ballet.

Paul had painted a feather bird for Djuna's hair and she was pinning it on when Lawrence came with the warning.

Paul became a little pale, then smiled and said: "Wafer, in case my father comes, could you make yourself less pretty?"

Djuna went and washed her face of all make-up, and then she unpinned the airy feather bird from her hair, and they sat down together to wait for the father.

Djuna said: "I'm going to tell you the story of Caspar Hauser, which is said to have happened many years ago in Austria. Caspar Hauser was about seventeen years old when he appeared in the city, a wanderer, lost and bewildered. He had been imprisoned in a dark room since childhood. His real origin was unknown, and the cause for the imprisonment. It was believed to be a court intrigue, that he might have been put away to substitute another ruler, or that he might have been an illegitimate son of the Queen. His jailer died and the boy found himself free. In solitude he had grown into manhood with the spirit of a child. He had only one dream in his possession, which he looked upon as a memory. He had once lived in a castle. He had been led to a room to see his mother. His mother stood behind a door. But he had never reached her. Was it a dream or a memory? He wanted to find this castle again, and his mother. The people of the city adopted him as a curiosity. His honesty, his immediate, childlike instinct about people, both infuriated and interested them. They tampered with him. They wanted to impose their beliefs on him, reach him, possess him. But the boy could sense their falsities, their treacheries, their self-interest. He belonged to his dream. He gave his whole faith only to the man who promised to take him back to his home and to his mother. And this man betrayed him, delivered him to his enemies. Just before his death he had met a woman, who had not dared to love him because he was so young, who had stifled her feeling. If she had dared he might have escaped his fate."

"Why didn't she dare?" asked Paul.

"She saw only the obstacle," said Djuna. "Most people see only the obstacle, and are stopped by it."

(No harm can befall you now, Paul, no harm can befall you. You have been set free. You made a good beginning. You were loved by the first object of your desire. Your first desire was answered. I made such a bad beginning! I began with a closed door. This harmed me, but you at least began with fulfillment. You were not hurt. You were not denied. I am the only one in danger. For that is all I am allowed to give you, a good beginning, and then I must surrender you.)

They sat and waited for the father.

Lawrence left them. The suspense made him uneasy.

Paul was teaching Djuna how to eat rice with chopsticks. Then he carefully cleaned them and was holding them now as they talked as if they were puppets representing a Balinese shadow theater of the thoughts neither one dared to formulate.

They sat and waited for the father.

Paul was holding the chopsticks like impudent puppets, gesticulating, then he playfully unfastened the first button of her blouse with them, deftly, and they laughed together.

"It's time for the ballet," said Djuna. "Your father is evidently not coming, or he would be here already."

She saw the illumination of desire light his face.

"Wait, Djuna." He unfastened the second button, and the third.

Then he laid his head on her breast and said: "Let's not go anywhere tonight, let's stay here."

Paul despised small and shallow waves. He was drawn to a vastness which corresponded to his boundless dreams. He must possess the world in some big way, rule a large kingdom, expand in some absolute leadership.

He felt himself a king as a child feels king, over kingdoms uncharted by ordinary men. He would not have the ordinary, the known. Only the vast, the unknown could satisfy him.

Djuna was a woman with echoes plunging into an endless past he could never explore completely. When he tasted her, he tasted a suffering which had borne a fragrance, a fragrance which made deeper grooves. It was enough that he sensed the dark forests of experience, the unnamed rivers, the enigmatic mountains, the rich mines under the ground, the overflowing caves of secret knowledges. A vast ground for an intrepid adventurer.

Above all she was his "ocean" as he wrote her. "When a man takes a woman to himself he possesses the sea."

The waves, the enormous waves of a woman's love!

She was a sea whose passions could rise sometimes into larger waves than he felt capable of facing!

Much as he loved danger, the unknown, the vast, he felt too the need of taking flight, to put distance and space between himself and the ocean for fear of being submerged!

Flight: into silence, into a kind of invisibility by which he could be sitting there on the floor while yet creating an impression of absence, able to disappear into a book, a drawing, into the music he listened to.

She was gazing at his little finger and the extreme fragility and sensitiveness of it astonished her.

(He is the transparent child.)

Before this transparent finger so artfully carved, sensitively wrought, boned, which alighted on objects with a touch of air and magic, at the marvel of it, the ephemeral quality of it, a wave of passion would mount within her and exactly like the wave of the ocean intending merely to roll over, cover the swimmer with an explosion of foam, in a rhythm of encompassing, and withdrawing, without intent to drag him to the bottom.

But Paul, with the instinct of the new swimmer, felt that there were times when he could securely hurl himself into the concave heart of the wave and be lifted into ecstasy and be delivered back again on the shore safe and whole; but that there were other times when this great inward curve disguised an undertow, times when he measured his strength and found it insufficient to return to shore. Then he took up again the lighter games of his recently surrendered childhood.

Djuna found him gravely bending over a drawing and it was not what he did which conveyed his remoteness, but his way of sitting hermetically closed like some secret Chinese box whose surface showed no possibility of opening.

He sat then as children do, immured in his particular lonely world then, having built a magnetic wall of detachment.

It was then that he practiced as deftly as older men the great objectivity, the long-range view by which men eluded all personal difficulties: he removed himself from the present and the personal by entering into the most abstruse intricacies of a chess game, by explaining to her what Darwin had written when comparing the eye to a microscope, by dissertating on the pleuronectidae or flat fish, so remarkable for their asymmetrical bodies.

And Djuna followed this safari into the worlds of science, chemistry, geology with an awkwardness which was not due to any laziness of mind, but to the fact that the large wave of passion which had been roused in her at the prolonged sight of Paul's little finger was so difficult to dam, because the feeling of wonder before this spectacle was to her as great as that of the explorers before a new mountain peak, of the scientists before a new discovery.

She knew what excitement enfevered men at such moments of their lives, but she did not see any difference between the beauty of a high flight above the clouds and the subtly colored and changing landscape of adolescence she traversed through the contemplation of Paul's little finger.

A study of anthropological excavations made in Peru was no more wonderful to her than the half-formed dreams unearthed with patience from Paul's vague words, dreams of which they were only catching the prologue; and no forest of precious woods could be more varied than the oscillations of his extreme vulnerability which forced him to take cover, to disguise his feelings, to swing so movingly between great courage and a secret fear of pain.

The birth of his awareness was to her no lesser miracle than the discoveries of chemistry, the variations in his temperature, the mysterious angers, the sudden serenities, no less valuable than the studies of remote climates.

But when in the face of too large a wave, whose dome seemed more than a mere ecstasy of foam raining over the marvelous shape of his hands, a wave whose concaveness seemed more than a temporary womb in which he could lie for the fraction of an instant, the duration of an orgasm, he sat like a Chinese secret box with a surface revealing no possible opening to the infiltrations of tenderness or the flood of passion, then her larger impulse fractured with a strange pain into a multitude of little waves capped with frivolous sun-spangles, secretly ashamed of its wild disproportion to the young man who sat there offering whatever he possessed—his intermittent manliness, his vastest dreams and his fear of his own expansions, his maturity as well as his fear of this maturity which was leading him out of the gardens of childhood.

And when the larger wave had dispersed into smaller ones, and when Paul felt free of any danger of being dragged to the bottom, free of that fear of possession which is the secret of all adolescence, when he had gained strength within his retreat, then he returned to tease and stir her warmth into activity again, when he felt equal to plunging into it, to lose himself in it, feeling the intoxication of the man who had conquered the sea....

Then he would write to her exultantly: you are the sea....

But she could see the little waves in himself gathering power for the future, preparing for the moment when he would be the engulfing one.

Then he seemed no longer the slender adolescent with dreamy gestures but a passionate young man rehearsing his future scenes of domination.

He wore a white scarf through the gray streets of the city, a white scarf of immunity. His head resting on the folds was the head of the dreamer walking through the city selecting by a white magic to see and hear and gather only according to his inner needs, slowly and gradually building as each one does ultimately, his own world out of the material at hand from which he was allowed at least a freedom of selection.

The white scarf asserted the innumerable things which did not touch him: choked trees, broken windows, cripples, obscenities penciled on the walls, the lascivious speeches of the drunks, the miasmas and corrosions of the city.

He did not see or hear them.

After traversing desert streets, immured in his inner dream, he would suddenly open his eyes upon an organ grinder and his monkey.

What he brought home again was always some object by which men sought to overcome mediocrity: a book, a painting, a piece of music to transform his vision of the world, to expand and deepen it.

The white scarf did not lie.

It was the appropriate flag of his voyages.

His head resting fittingly on its white folds was immune to stains. He could traverse sewers, hospitals, prisons, and none left their odor upon him. His coat, his breath, his hair, when he returned, still exhaled the odor of his dream.

This was the only virgin forest known to man: this purity of selection.

When Paul returned with his white scarf gleaming it was all that he rejected which shone in its folds.

He was always a little surprised at older people's interest in him.

He did not know himself to be the possessor of anything they might want, not knowing that in his presence they were violently carried back to their first dream.

Because he stood at the beginning of the labyrinth and not in the heart of it, he made everyone aware of the turn where they had lost themselves. With Paul standing at the entrance of the maze, they recaptured the beginning of their voyage, they remembered their first intent, their first image, their first desires.

They would don his white scarf and begin anew.

And yet today she felt there was another purity, a greater purity which lay in the giving of one's self. She felt pure when she gave herself, and Paul felt pure when he withdrew himself.

The tears of his mother, the more restrained severity of his father, brought him home again.

His eighteenth birthday came and this was the one they could not spend together, this being his birthday in reality, the one visible to his parents. Whereas with Djuna he had spent so many birthdays which his parents could not have observed, with their limited knowledge of him.

They had not attended the birthday of his manhood, the birthday of his roguish humorous self, of his first drunkenness, his first success at a party; or the birthday of his eloquent self on the theme of poetry, painting or music. Or the birthday of his imagination, his fantasy, of his new knowledge of people, of his new assertions and his discoveries of unknown powers in himself.

This succession of birthdays that had taken place since he left home was the highest fiesta ever attended by Djuna, the spectacle of unpredictable blooms, of the shells breaking around his personality, the emergence of the man.

But his real birthday they could not spend together.

His mother made dinner for him, and he played chess with his father—they who loved him less and who had bound and stifled him with prohibitions, who had delayed his manhood.

His mother made a birthday cake iced and sprinkled with warnings against expansion, cautions against new friends, designed a border like those of formal gardens as if to outline all the proprieties with which to defeat adventure.

His father played chess with him silently, indicating in the carefully measured moves a judgment upon all the wayward dances of the heart, the caprices of the body, above all a judgment upon such impulses as had contributed to Paul's very presence there, the act of conjunction from which had been formed the luminous boy eating at their table.

The cake they fed him was the cake of caution: to fear all human beings and doubt the motivations of all men and women not listed in the Social Directory.

The candles were not lit to celebrate his future freedom, but to say: only within the radius lighted by these birthday candles, only within the radius of father and mother are you truly safe.

A small circle. And outside of this circle, evil.

And so he ate of this birthday cake baked by his mother, containing all the philters against love, expansion and freedom known to white voodoo.

A cake to prevent and preserve the child from becoming man!

No more nights together, when to meet the dawn together was the only marriage ceremony accorded to lovers.

But he returned to her one day carrying the valise with his laundry. On his return home he had packed his laundry to have it washed at home. And his mother had said: "Take it back. I won't take care of laundry you soiled while living with strangers."

So quietly he brought it back to Djuna, to the greater love that would gladly take care of his belongings as long as they were the clothes he soiled in his experience with freedom.

The smallness of his shirts hurt her, like a sign of dangers for him which she could not avert. He was still slender enough, young enough to be subjected to tyranny.

They were both listening to César Franck's Symphony in D Minor.

And then the conflicting selves in Djuna fused into one mood as they do at such musical crossroads.

The theme of the symphony was gentleness.

She had first heard it at the age of sixteen one rainy afternoon and associated it with her first experience of love, of a love without climax which she had known with Michael. She had interwoven this music with her first concept of the nature of love as one of ultimate, infinite gentleness.

In César Franck's symphony there was immediate exaltation, dissolution in feeling and the evasion of violence. Over and over again in this musical ascension of emotion, the stairway of fever was climbed and deserted before one reached explosion.

An obsessional return to minor themes, creating an endless tranquillity, and at sixteen she had believed that the experience of love was utterly contained in this gently flowing narcotic, in the delicate spirals, cadences and undulations of this music.

César Franck came bringing messages of softness and trust, accompanying Paul's gestures and attitudes, and for this she trusted him, a passion without the storms of destruction.

She had wanted such nebulous landscapes, such vertiginous spirals without explosions: the drug.

Listening to the symphony flowing and yet not flowing (for there was a static groove in which it remained imprisoned, so similar to the walled-in room of her house, containing a mystery of stillness), Djuna saw the Obelisk in the Place de la Concorde, the arrow of stone placed at the center of a gracefully turbulent square, summating gardens, fountains and rivers of automobiles. One pointed dart of stone to pierce the night, the fog, the rain, the sun, aiming faultlessly into the clouds.

And there was the small, crazy woman Matilda, whom everyone knew, who came every morning and sat on one of the benches near the river, and stayed there all day, watching the passers-by, eating sparingly and lightly of some mysterious food in crumbs out of a paper bag, like the pigeons. So familiar to the policeman, to the tourists, and the permanent inhabitants of the Place de la Concorde, that not to see her there would have been as noticeable, as disturbing, as to find the Obelisk gone, and the square left without its searchlight into the sky.

Matilda was known for her obstinacy in sitting there through winter and summer, her indifference to climate, her vague answers to those who sought her reasons for being there, her tireless watchfulness, as if she were keeping a rendezvous with eternity.

Only at sundown did she leave, sometimes gently incited by the policeman.

Since there was no total deterioration in her clothes, or in her health, everyone surmised she must have a home and no one was ever concerned about her.

Djuna had once sat beside her and Matilda at first would not speak, but addressed herself to the pigeons and to the falling autumn leaves, murmuring, whispering, muttering by turn. Then suddenly she said to Djuna, very simply and clearly: "My lover left me sitting here and said he would come back."

(The policeman had said: I have seen her sitting there for twenty years.)

"How long have you been sitting here and waiting?" Djuna asked.

"I don't know."

She ate of the same bread she was feeding the pigeons. Her face was wrinkled but not aged, through the wrinkles shone an expression which was not of age, which was the expression of alert waiting, watchfulness, expectation of the young.

"He will come back," she said, for the first time a look of defiance washing her face of its spectator's pallor, the pallor of the recluse who lives without intimate relationship to stir the rhythms of the blood, this glazed expression of those who watch the crowd passing by and never recognize a face.

"Of course he will," said Djuna, unable to bear even the shadow of anxiety on the woman's face.

Matilda's face recovered its placidity, its patience.

"He told me to sit here and wait."

A mortal blow had stopped the current of her life, but had not shattered her. It had merely paralyzed her sense of time, she would sit and wait for the lost lover and the years were obliterated by the anesthesia of the deadened cell of time: five minutes stretched to infinity and kept her alive, alive and ghostly, with the cell of time, the little clock of reality inside the brain forever damaged. A faceless clock pointing to anguish. And with time was linked pain, lodged in the same cell (neighbors and twins), time and pain in more or less intimate relationship.

And what was left was this shell of a woman immune to cold and heat, anesthetized by a great loss into immobility and timelessness.

Sitting there beside Matilda Djuna heard the echoes of the broken cell within the little psychic stage of her own heart, so well enacted, so neat, so clear, and wondered whether when her father left the house for good in one of his moods of violence as much damage had been done to her, and whether some part of her being had not been atrophied, preventing complete openness and complete development in living.

By his act of desertion he had destroyed a cell in Djuna's being, an act of treachery from a cruel world setting her against all fathers, while retaining the perilous hope of a father returning under the guise of the men who resembled him, to re-enact again the act of violence.

It was enough for a man to possess certain attributes of the father —any man possessed of power—and then her being came alive with fear as if the entire situation would be re-enacted inevitably: possession, love and desertion, replacing her on a bench like Matilda, awaiting a denouement.

Looking back there had been a momentous break in the flow, a change of activity.

Every authoritarian step announced the return of the father and danger. For the father's last words had been: "I will come back."

Matilda had been more seriously injured: the life flow had stopped. She had retained the first image, the consciousness that she must wait, and the last words spoken by the lover had been a command for eternity: wait until I come back.

As if these words had been uttered by a proficient hypnotist who had then cut off all her communications with the living, so that she was not permitted even this consolation allowed to other deserted human beings: the capacity to transfer this love to another, to cheat the order given, to resume life with others, to forget the first one.

Matilda had been mercifully arrested and suspended in time, and rendered unconscious of pain.

But not Djuna.

In Djuna the wound had remained alive, and whenever life touched upon this wound she mistook the pain warning her and guiding her to deflect from man the father to man the son.

She could see clearly all the cells of her being, like the rooms of her house which had blossomed, enriched, developed and stretched far beyond all experiences, but she could see also the cell of her being like the walled-in room of her house in which was lodged violence as having been shut and condemned within her out of fear of disaster.

There was a little cell of her being in which she still existed as a child, which only activated with a subtle anger in the presence of the father, for in relation to him she lost her acquired power, her assurance, she was rendered small again and returned to her former state of helplessness and dependence.

And knowing the tragic outcome of this dependence she felt hostility and her route towards the man of power bristled with this hostility—an immediate need to shut out violence.

Paul and Djuna sat listening to César Franck's Symphony in D Minor, in this little room of gentleness and trust, barring violence from the world of love, seeking an opiate against destruction and treachery.

So she had allied herself with the son against the father. He had been there to forbid and thus to strengthen the desire. He had been there, large and severe, to threaten the delicate, precarious bond, and thus to render it desperate and make each encounter a reprieve from death and loss.

The movements of the symphony and her movements had been always like Paul's, a ballet of oscillations, peripheral entrances and exits, figures designed to become invisible in moments of danger, pirouetting with all the winged knowledge of birds to avoid collision with violence and severity.

Together they had taken leaps into the air to avoid obstacles.

from Seduction of the Minotaur

Some voyages have their inception in the blueprint of a dream, some in the urgency of contradicting a dream. Lillian's recurrent dream of a ship that could not reach the water, that sailed laboriously, pushed by her with great effort, through city streets, had determined her course toward the sea, as if she would give this ship, once and for all, its proper sea bed.

She had landed in the city of Golconda, where the sun painted everything with gold, the lining of her thoughts, the worn valises, the plain beetles, Golconda of the golden age, the golden aster, the golden eagle, the golden goose, the golden fleece, the golden robin, the goldenrod, the goldenseal, the golden warbler, the golden wattles, the golden wedding, and the gold fish, and the gold of pleasure, the goldstone, the gold thread, the fool's gold.

With her first swallow of air she inhaled a drug of forgetfulness well known to adventurers.

Tropic, from the Greek, signified change and turning. So she changed and turned, and was metamorphosed by the light and caressing heat into a spool of silk. Every movement she made from that moment on, even the carrying of her valise, was softened and pleasurable. Her nerves, of which she had always been sharply aware, had become instead strands from a spool of silk, spiraling through the muscles.

"How long do you intend to stay?" asked the official. "How much

From *Seduction of the Minotaur* (Swallow, 1961), pp. 5-36.

money do you carry with you? In what currency? Do you have a return ticket?"

You had to account for every move, arrival or exit. In the world there was a conspiracy against improvisation. It was only permitted in jazz.

The guitars and the singing opened fire. Her skin blossomed and breathed. A heavy wave of perfume came down the jungle on the right, and a fine spray of waves came from the left. On the beach the natives swung in hammocks of reeds. The tender Mexican voices sang love songs which cradled and rocked the body as did the hammocks.

Where she came from only jewels were placed in satinlined cushioned boxes, but here it was thought and memories which the air, the scents, and the music conspired to hypnotize by softness.

But the airport official who asked cactus-pointed questions wore no shirt, nor did the porters, so that Lillian decided to be polite to the smoothest torso and show respect only to the strongest muscle.

The absence of uniforms restored the dignity and importance of the body. They all looked untamed and free, in their bare feet, as if they had assumed the duties of receiving the travelers only temporarily and would soon return to their hammocks, to swimming and singing. Work was one of the absurdities of existence. Don't you think so, Senorita? said their laughing eyes while they appraised her from head to toes. They looked at her openly, intently, as children and animals do, with a physical vision, measuring only physical attributes, charm, aliveness, and not titles, possessions, or occupations. Their full, complete smile was not always answered by the foreigners, who blinked at such sudden warmth of smile as they did at the dazzling sun. Against the sun they wore dark glasses, but against these smiles and open naked glances they could only defend their privacy with a half-smile. Not Lillian. Her very full, rounded lips had always given such a smile. She could respond to this naked curiosity, naked interest, proximity. Thus animals and children stare, with their whole, concentrated attentiveness. The natives had not yet learned from the white man his inventions for traveling away from the present, his scientific capacity for analyzing warmth into a chemical substance, for abstracting human beings into symbols. The white man had invented glasses which made objects too near or too far, cameras, telescopes, spyglasses, objects which put glass between living and vision. It was the image he sought to possess, not the texture, the living warmth, the human closeness.

The natives saw only the present. This communion of eyes and smiles was elating. Where Lillian came from people seemed intent on not seeing each other. Only children looked at her with this unashamed curiosity. Poor white man, wandering and lost in his proud possession of a dimension in which bodies became invisible to the naked eye, as if staring were an immodest act. Already she felt incarnated, in full possession of her own body because the porter was in full possession of his, and this concentration upon the present allowed no interruption or short circuits of the physical contact. When she turned away from the porter it was to find a smiling taxi driver who seemed to be saying: "I am not keen on going anywhere. It is just as good right here, right now. . . ."

He was scratching his luxuriant black hair, and he carried his wet bathing suit around his neck.

The guitars kept up their musical fire. The beggars squatted around the airport. Blind or crippled, they smiled. The festivities of nature bathed them in gold and anesthetized their suffering.

Clothes seemed ponderous and superfluous in the city of Golconda.

Golconda was Lillian's private name for this city which she wanted to rescue from the tourist-office posters and propaganda. Each one of us possesses in himself a separate and distinct city, a unique city, as we possess different aspects of the same person. She could not bear to love a city which thousands believed they knew intimately. Golconda was hers. True, it had been at first a pearl-fishing village. True, a Japanese ship had been wrecked here, slave ships had brought Africans, other ships delivered spices, and Spanish ships had brought the art of filigree, of lace making. A shipwrecked Spanish galley had scattered on the beach baptism dresses which the women of southern Mexico had adopted as headgear.

The legend was that when the Japanese pearl divers had been driven away they had destroyed the pearl caches, and Golconda became a simply fishing village. Then the artists had come on donkeys, and discovered the beauty of the place. They had been followed by the real-estate men and hotelkeepers. But none could destroy Golconda. Golconda remained a city where the wind was like velvet, where the sun was made of radium, and the sea as warm as a mother's womb.

The porters were deserting before all the baggage was distributed. They had earned enough, just enough for the day for food, beer, a swim, and enough to take a girl dancing, and they did not want any more. So the little boys of ten and twelve, who had been waiting for this opening, were seeking to carry bags bigger than themselves.

The taxi driver, who was in no hurry to go anywhere in his dilapidated car, saw his car filling up, and decided it was time to put on his clean laundry-blue shirt.

The three men who were to share the taxi with Lillian were already installed. Perhaps because they were in city clothes or perhaps because they were not smiling, they seemed to be the only subjects the sun could not illumine. The sea's aluminum reflectors had even penetrated the old taxi and found among the cracked leather some stuffing which had come out of the seat and which the sun transformed into angel hair such as grows on Christmas trees.

One of the men helped her into the car and introduced himself with Spanish colonial courtesy: "I am Doctor Hernandez."

He had the broad face she had seen in Mayan sculpture, the round high cheekbones, the aquiline nose, the full mouth slanting downward while the eyes slanted upward. His skin was a light olive which came from the mixture of Indian and Spanish blood. His smile was like the natives', open and total, but it came less often and faded quickly, leaving a shadow over his face.

She looked out the window to explore her new territory of pleasure. Everything was novel. The green of the foliage was not like any other greens: it was deeper, lacquered, and moist. The leaves were heavier, fuller, the flowers bigger. They seemed surcharged with sap, and more alive, as if they never had to close against the frost, or even a colder night. As if they had no need of sleep.

The huts made of palm leaves recalled Africa. Some were pointed on top and on stilts. Others had slanting roofs, and the palm leaves extended far enough to create shadows all around the house.

The lagoon on the left of the road showed a silver surface which sometimes turned to sepia. It was half filled with floating lagoon flowers. Trees and bushes seemed like new vegetation, also on stilts, dipping twisted roots into the water as the reeds dipped their straight and flexible roots. Herons stood on one leg. Iguanas slithered away, and parrots became hysterically gay.

Lillian's eyes returned to the Doctor. His thoughts were elsewhere, so she looked at the American who had introduced himself as Hatcher. He was an engineer who had come to Mexico years before to build roads and bridges, and had remained and married a Mexican woman. He spoke perfect Spanish, and was a leathery-skinned man who had been baked by the sun as dark as the natives. The tropics had not relaxed his forward-jutting jaw and shoulders. He looked rigid, lean, hard-fleshed. His bare feet were in Mexican sandals, the soles made of discarded rubber tires. His shirt was open at the neck. But on him the negligent attire still seemed a uniform to conquer, rather than a way of submitting to, the tropics.

"Golconda may seem beautiful to you, but it's spoiled by tourism. I found a more beautiful place farther on. I had to hack my way to it. I have a beach where the sand is so white it hurts the eyes like a snow slope. I'm building a house. I come to Golconda once a week to shop. I have a jeep. If you like you can drive out with me for a visit. Unless, like most Americans, you have come here to drink and dance...."

"I'm not free to drink and dance. I have to play every night with the jazz orchestra."

"Then you must be Lillian Beye," said the passenger who had not yet spoken. He was a tall blond Austrian who spoke a harsh Spanish but with authority. "I'm the owner of the Black Pearl. I engaged you."

"Mr. Hansen?"

He shook her hand without smiling. He was fairskinned. The tropics had not been able to warm him, or to melt the icicle blue eyes.

Lillian felt that these three men were somehow interfering with her own tasting of Golconda. They seemed intent on giving her an image of Golconda she did not want. The Doctor wanted her to notice only that the children were in need of care, the American wanted her to recoil from tourism, and the owner of the Black Pearl made the place seem like a night club.

The taxi stopped for gasoline. An enormously fat American, unshaved for many days, rose from hammock to wait on them.

"Hello, Sam," said Doctor Hernandez. "How is Maria? You didn't bring her to me for her injection."

Sam shouted to a woman dimly visible inside the palmleaf shack. She came to the door. Her long black shawl was fastened to her shoulders and her baby was cradled in the folds of it as if inside a hammock.

Sam repeated the Doctor's question. She shrugged her shoulders: "No time," she said and called: "Maria!"

Maria came forward from a group of children, carrying a boat made out of a coconut shell. She was small for her age, delicately molded, like a miniature child, as Mexican children often are. In the eyes of most Mexican painters, these finely chiseled beings with small hands and feet and slender necks and waists become larger than nature, with the sinews and muscles of giants. Lillian saw them tender and fragile and neat. The Doctor saw them ill.

The engineer said to Lillian: "Sam was sent here twenty years ago to build bridges and roads. He married a native. He does nothing but sleep and drink."

"It's the tropics," said Hansen.

"You've never been to the Bowery," said Lillian.

"But in the tropics all white men fall apart. ."

"I've heard that but I never believed it. Any more than I believe all adventurers are doomed. I think such beliefs are merely an expression of fear, fear of expatriation, fear of adventure."

"I agree with you," said the Doctor. "The white man who falls apart in the tropics is the same one who would fall apart anywhere. But in foreign lands they stand out more because they are few, and we notice them more."

"And then at home, if you want to fall apart, there are so many people to stop you. Relatives and friends foil your attempts! You get sermons, lectures, threats, and you are even rescued."

The Austrian laughed: "I can't help thinking how much encouragement you would get here."

"You, Mr. Hatcher, didn't disintegrate in the tropics!"

Hatcher answered solemnly: "But I am a happy man. I have succeeded in living and feeling like a native."

"Is that the secret, then? It's those who don't succeed in going native, in belonging, who get desperately lonely and self-destructive?"

"Perhaps," said the Doctor pensively. "It may also be that you Americans are work-cultists, and work is the structure that holds you up, not the joy of pure living."

His words were accompanied by a guitar. As soon as one guitar moved away, the sound of another took its place, to continue this net of music that would catch and maintain you in flight from sadness, suspended in a realm of festivities.

Just as every tree carried giant brilliant flowers playing chromatic scales, runs and trills of reds and blues, so the people vied with them in wearing more intense indigoes, more flaming oranges, more platinous whites, or else colors which resembled the purple insides of mangoes, the flesh tones of pomegranates.

The houses were covered with vines bearing bell-shaped flowers playing coloraturas. The guitars inside of the houses or on the doorsteps took up the color chromatics and emitted sounds which evoked the flavor of guava, papaya, cactus figs, anise, saffron, and red pepper.

Big terra-cotta jars, heavily loaded donkeys, lean and hungry dogs, all recalled images from the Bible. The houses were all open; Lillian could see babies asleep in hammocks, holy pictures on the white stucco walls, old people on rocking chairs, and photographs of relatives pinned on the walls together with old palm leaves from the Palm Sunday feast.

The sun was setting ostentatiously, with all the pomp of embroidered silks and orange tapestries of Oriental spectacles. The palms had a naked elegance, and wore their giant plumes like languid feather dusters sweeping the tropical sky of all clouds, keeping it as transparent as a sea shell.

Restaurants served dinner out in the open. On one long communal table was a bowl of fish soup and fried fish. Inside the houses people had begun to light the oil lamps which had a more vivacious flicker than candles.

The Doctor had been talking about illness. "Fifteen years ago this place was actually dangerous. We had malaria, dysentery, elephantiasis, and other illnesses you would not even know about. They had no hospital and no doctor until I came. I had to fight dysentery alone, and teach them not to sleep in the same bed with their farm animals."

"How did you happen to come here?"

"We have a system in Mexico. Before obtaining their degrees, young medical students have to have a year of practice in whatever small town needs them. When I first came here I was only eighteen. I was irresponsible, and a bit sullen at having to take care of fishermen who could neither read nor write nor follow instructions of any kind. When I was not needed, I read French novels and dreamed of the life in large cities which I was missing. But gradually I came to love my fishermen, and when the year was over I chose to stay."

The eyes of the people were full of burning life. They squatted like Orientals next to their wide flat baskets filled with fruits and vegetables. The fruit was not piled negligently but arranged in a careful Persian design of decorative harmonies. Strings of chili hung from the rafters, chili to wake them from their dreams, dreams born of scents and rhythms, and the warmth that fell from the sky like the fleeciest blanket. Even the twilight came without a change of temperature or alteration in the softness of the air.

It was not only the music from the guitars but the music of the body that Lillian heard—a continuous rhythm of life. There was a rhythm in the way the women lifted the water jugs onto their heads, and walked balancing them. There was a rhythm in the way the shepherds walked after their lambs and their cows. It was not just the climate, but the people themselves who exuded a more ardent life.

Hansen was looking out the taxi window with a detached and bored expression. He did not see the people. He did not notice the children who, because of their black hair cut in square bangs and their slanted eyes, sometimes looked like Japanese. He questioned Lillian on entertainers. What entertainers from New York or Paris or London should he bring to the Black Pearl?

The hotel was at the top of the hill, one main building and a cluster of small cottages hidden by olive trees and cactus. It faced the sea at a place where huge boiling waves were trapped by crevices in the rocks and struck at their prison with cannon reverberations. Two narrow gorges were each time assaulted, the waves sending foam high in the air and leaping up as if in a fury at being restrained.

The receptionist at the desk was dressed in rose silk, as if registering guests and handing out keys were part of the festivities. The manager came out, holding out his hand paternally, as though his immense bulk conferred on him a patriarchy, and said: "You are free to enjoy yourself tonight. You won't have to start playing until tomorrow night. Did you see the posters?"

He led her to the entrance where her photograph, enlarged, faced her like the image of a total stranger. She never recognized herself in publicity photographs. I look pickled, she thought.

A dance was going on, on the leveled portion of the rock beside the hotel. The music was intermittent, for the wind carried some of the notes away, and the sound of the sea absorbed others, so that these fragments of mambos had an abstract distinction like the music of Erik Satie. It also made the couples seem to be dancing sometimes in obedience to it, and sometimes in obedience to the gravitations of their secret attractions.

A barefoot boy carried Lillian's bags along winding paths. Flowers brushed her face as she passed. Both music and sea sounds grew fainter as they climbed. Cottages were set capriciously on rock ledges, hidden by reeds, or camouflaged in bougainvillaea. The boy stopped before a cottage with a palm-leaf roof.

In front of it was a long tile terrace, with a hemp hammock strung across it. The room inside had whitewashed walls, and contained only a bed, a table, and a chair. Parasoling over the cottage was a giant tree which bore leaves shaped like fans. The encounter of the setting sun and rising moon had combined to paint everything in the changing colors of mercury.

As Lillian opened a bureau drawer, a mouse that had been making a nest of magnolia petals suddenly fled.

She showered and dressed hastily, feeling that perhaps the beauty and velvety softness of the night might not last, that if she delayed it would change to coldness and harshness. She put on the only dress she had that matched the bright flowers, an orange cotton. Then she opened the screen door. The night lay unchanged, serene, filled with tropical whisperings, as if leaves, birds, and sea breezes possessed musicalities unknown to northern countries, as if the richness of the scents kept them all intently alive.

The tiles under her bare feet were warm. The perfume she had sprayed on her self evaporated before the stronger perfumes of carnation and honeysuckle.

She walked back to the wide terrace where people sat on deck chairs waiting for each other and for dinner.

The expanse of sky was like an infinite canvas on which human beings were incapable of projecting images from their human life because they would seem out of scale and absurd.

Lillian felt that nature was so powerful it absorbed her into itself. It was a drug for forgetting. People seemed warmer and nearer, as the stars seemed nearer and the moon warmer.

The sea's orchestration carried away half the spoken words and made talking and laughing seem a mere casual accompaniment, like the sound of birds. Words had no weight. The intensity of the colors made them float in space like balloons, and the velvet texture of the climate gave them a purely decorative quality like other flowers. They had no abstract meaning, being received by the senses which only recognized touch, smell, and vision, so that these people sitting in their chairs became a part of a vivid animated mural. A brown shoulder emerging from a white dress, the limpidity of a smile in a tanned face, the muscular tension of a brown leg, seemed more eloquent than the voices.

This is an exaggerated spectacle, thought Lillian, and it makes me comfortable. I was always an exaggerated character because I was trying to create all by myself a climate which suited me, bigger flowers, warmer words, more fervent relationships, but here nature does it for me, creates the climate I need within myself, and I can be languid and at rest. It is a drug . . . a drug . . .

Why were so many people fearful of the tropics? "All adventurers came to grief." Perhaps they had not been able to make the transition, to alchemize the life of the mind into the life of the senses. They died when their minds were overpowered by nature, yet they did not hesitate to dilute it in alcohol.

Even while Golconda lulled her, she was aware of several mysteries entering her reverie. One she called the sorrows of Doctor Hernandez. The other was why do exiles come to a bad end (if they did, of which she was not sure)? From where she sat, she saw the Doctor arrive with his professional valise. But this burden he deposited at the hotel desk, and then he walked toward Lillian as if he had been seeking her.

"You haven't had dinner yet? Come and have it with me. We'll have it in the Black Pearl, so you will become familiar with the place where you are going to play every night."

The Black Pearl had been built of driftwood. It was a series of terraces overhanging the sea. Red ship lanterns illumined a jazz band playing for a few dancers.

Because the hiss of the sea carried away some of the overtones, the main drum beat seemed more emphatic, like a giant heart pulsing. The more volatile cadences, the ironic notes, the lyrical half-sobs of the trombone rose like sea spray and were lost. As if the instrumentalists knew this, they repeated their climbs up invisible antennae into vast spaces of volatile joys and shrank the sorrows by speed and flight, decanting all the essences, and leaving always at the bottom the blood beat of the drums.

The Doctor was watching her face. "Did I frighten you with all my talk about sickness?"

"No, Doctor Hernandez, illness does not frighten me. Not physical illness. The one that does is unknown in Golconda. And I'm a convalescent. And in any case, it's one which does not inspire sympathy."

Her words had been spoken lightly, but they caused the Doctor's smooth face to wrinkle with anxiety. Anxiety? Fear? She could not read his face. It had the Indian sculptural immobility. Even when the skin wrinkled with some spasm of pain, the eyes revealed nothing, and the mouth was not altered.

She felt compelled to ask: "Are you unhappy? Are you in trouble?"

She knew it was dangerous to question those who were accustomed to doing the questioning, to being depended on (and well did Lillian know that those who were in the position of consolers, guides, healers, felt uncomfortable in any reversal) but she took the risk.

He answered, laughing: "No, I'm not, but if being unhappy would arouse your interest, I'm willing to be. It was tactless of me to speak of illness in this place created for pleasure. I nearly spoiled *your* pleasure. And I can see you are one who has not had too much of it, one of the underprivileged of pleasure! Those who have too much nauseate me. I don't know why. I'm glad when they get dysentery or serious sunburns. It is as if I believed in an even distribution of pleasure. Now you, for instance, have a right to some... not

"I didn't realize it was so apparent."

having had very much."

"It is not so apparent. Permit me to say I am unusually astute. Diagnostic habit. You *appear* free and undamaged, vital and without wounds."

"Diagnostic clairvoyance, then?"

"Yes. But here comes our professional purveyor of pleasure. He may be more beneficent for you."

Hansen sat down beside them, and began to draw on the tablecloth. "I'm going to add another terrace, then I will floodlight the trees and the divers. I will also have a light around the statue of the Virgin so that everyone can see the boys praying before they dive." His glance was cold, managerial. The sea, the night, the divers were all in his eyes, properties of the night club. The ancient custom of praying before diving one hundred feet into a narrow rocky gorge was going to become a part of the entertainment.

Lillian turned her face away from him, and listened to the jazz.

Jazz was the music of the body. The breath came through aluminum and copper tubes, it was the body's breath, and the strings' wails and moans were echoes of the body's music. It was the body's vibrations which rippled from the fingers. And the mystery of the withheld theme known to the musicians alone was like the mystery of our secret life. We give to others only peripheral improvisations. The plots and themes of the music, like the plots and themes of our life, never alchemized into words, existed only in a state of music, stirring or numbing, exalting or despairing, but never named.

When she turned her face unwilling towards Hansen, he was gone, and then she looked at the Doctor and said: "This is a drugging place...."

"There are so many kind of drugs. One for remembering and one for forgetting. Golconda is for forgetting. But it is not a permanent forgetting. We may seem to forget a person, a place, a state of being, a past life, but meanwhile what we are doing is selecting a new cast for the reproduction of the same drama, seeking the closest reproduction to the friend, the lover, or the husband we are striving to forget. And one day we open our eyes, and there we are caught in the same pattern, repeating the same story. How could it be otherwise? The design comes from within us. It is internal."

There were tears in Lillian's eyes, for having made friends immediately not with a new, a beautiful, a drugging place, but with a man intent on penetrating the mysteries of the human labyrinth from which she was a fugitive. She was almost angered by his persistence. A man should respect one's desire to have no past. But even more damaging was his conviction that we live by a series of repetitions until the experience is solved, understood, liquidated. . . .

"You will never rest until you have discovered the familiar within the unfamiliar. You will go around as these tourists do, searching for flavors which remind you of home, begging for Coca-Cola instead of tequila, cereal foods instead of papaya. Then the drug will wear off. You will discover that barring a few divergences in skin tone, or mores, or language, you are still related to the same kind of person because it all comes from within you, you are the one fabricating the web."

Other people were dancing around them, so obedient to the rhythms that they seemed like algae in the water, welded to each other, and swaying, the colored skirts billowing, the white suits like frames to support the flower arrangements made by the women's dresses, their hair, their jewels, their lacquered nails. The wind sought to carry them away from the orchestra, but they remained in its encirclement of sound like Japanese kites moved by strings from the instruments.

Lillian asked for another drink. But as she drank it, she knew that one of the drops of the Doctor's clairvoyance had fallen into her glass, that a part of what he had said was already proved true. The first friend she had made in Golconda, choosing him in preference to the engineer and the night-club manager, resembled, at least in his role, a personage she had known who was nicknamed

"The Lie Detector"; for many months this man had lived among a group of artists extracting complete confessions from them without effort and subtly changing the course of their lives.

Not to yield to the Doctor's challenge, she brusquely turned the spotlight on him: "Are you engaged in such a repetition now, with me? Have you left anyone behind?"

"My wife hates this place," said the Doctor simply. "She comes here rarely. She stays in Mexico City most of the time, on the excuse that the children must go to good schools. She is jealous of my patients, and says they are not really ill, that they pretend to be. And in this she is right. Tourists in strange countries are easily frightened. More frightened of strangeness. They call me to reassure themselves that they will not succumb to the poison of strangeness, to unfamiliar foods, exotic flavors, or the bite of an unfamiliar insect. They do call me for trivial reasons, often out of fear. But is fear trivial? And my native patients do need me desperately . . . I built a beautiful house for my wife. But I cannot keep her here. And I love this place, the people. Everything I have created is here. The hospital is my work. And if I leave, the drug traffic will run wild. I have been able to control it."

Lillian no longer resented the Doctor's probings. He was suffering and it was this which made him so aware of others' difficulties.

"That's a very painful conflict, and not easily solved," she said. She wanted to say more, but she was stopped by a messenger boy with bare feet, who had come to fetch the Doctor on an emergency case.

Lillian and the Doctor sat in a hand-carved canoe. The pressure of the human hand on the knife had made uneven indentations in the scooped-out tree trunk which caught the light like the scallops of the sea shell. The sun on the high rims of these declivities and the shadows within their valleys gave the canoe a stippled surface like that of an impressionist painting, made it seem a multitude of spots moving forward on the water in ripples of changeable colors and textures.

The fisherman was paddling it quietly through the varied colors of the lagoon water, colors that ranged from the dark sepia of the red earth bottom to silver gray when the colors of the bushes triumphed over the earth, to gold when the sun conquered them both, to purple in the shadows.

He paddled with one arm. His other had been blown off when he was a young fisherman of seventeen first learning the use of dynamite sticks for fishing.

The canoe had once been painted in laundry blue. This blue had faded and become like the smoky blue of old Mayan murals, a blue which man could not create, only time.

The lagoon trees showed their naked roots, as though on stilts, an intricate maze of silver roots as fluent below as they were interlaced above, and overhung, casting shadows before the bow of the canoe so dense that Lillian coud scarcely believe they would open and divide to let them through.

Emerald sprays and fronds projected from a mass of wasp nests, of pendant vines and lianas. Above her head the branches formed metallic green parabolas and enameled pennants, while the canoe and her body accomplished the magical feat of cutting smoothly through the roots and dense tangles.

The boat undulated the aquatic plants and the grasses that bore long plumes, and traveled through reflections of the clouds. The absence of visible earth made Lillian feel as if the forest were afloat, an archipelago of green vapors.

The snowy herons, the shell-pink flamingos meditated upon one leg like yogis of the animal world.

Now and then she saw a single habitation by the waterside, an ephemeral hut of palm leaves wading on frail stilts and a canoe tied to a toy-sized jetty. Before each hut, watching Lillian and the Doctor float by would be a smiling woman and several naked children. They stood against a backdrop of impenetrable foliage, as if the jungle allowed them, along with the butterflies, dragonflies, praying mantises, beetles, and parrots, to occupy only its fringe. The exposed giant roots of the trees made the children seem to be standing between the toes of Gulliver's feet.

Once when the earth showed itself on the right bank, Lillian saw on the mud the tracks of a crocodile that had come to quench his thirst. The scaly carapaces of the iguanas were colored so exactly like the ashen roots and tree trunks that she could not spot them until they moved. When they did not move they lay as still as stones in the sun, as if petrified.

The canoe pushed languid water lettuce out of the way, and water orchids, magnolias, and giant clover leaves.

A flowing journey, a contradiction to the persistent dream from which Lillian sought to liberate herself. The dream of a boat, sometimes large and sometimes small, but invariably caught in a waterless place, in a street, in the jungle, in the desert. When it was large it was in city streets, and the deck reached to the upper windows of the houses. She was in this boat and aware that it could not float unless it were pushed, so she would get down from it and seek to push it along so that it might move and finally reach water. The effort of pushing the boat along the street was immense and she never accomplished her aim. Whether she pushed it along cobblestones or over asphalt, it moved very little, and no matter how much she strained she always felt she would never reach the sea. When the boat was small, the pushing was less difficult; nevertheless she never reached the lake or river or the sea in which it could sail. Once the boat was stuck between rocks, another time on a mud bank.

Today she was fully aware that the dream of pushing the boat through waterless streets was ended. In Golconda she had attained a flowing life, a flowing journey. It was not only the presence of water, but the natives' flowing rhythm: they never became caught in the past, or stagnated while awaiting the future. Like children, they lived completely in the present.

She had read that certain Egyptian rulers had believed that after death they would join a celestial caravan in an eternal journey toward the sun. Scientists had found two solar barques, which they recognized from ancient texts and mortuary paintings, in a subterranean chamber of limestone. The chamber was so well sealed that no air, dust, or cobwebs had been found in it. There were always two such barques—one for the night's journey toward the moon, one for the day's journey toward the sun.

In dreams one perpetuated these journeys in solar barques. And in dreams, too, there were always two: one buried in limestone and unable to float on the waterless routes of anxiety, the other flowing continuously with life. The static one made the voyage of memories, and the floating one proceeded into endless discoveries.

This canoe, thought Lillian, as she dipped her hand into the lagoon water, was to be her solar barque, magnetized by sun and water, gyrating and flowing, without strain or effort.

The Doctor's thoughts had also been wandering through other places. Mexico City, where his wife was? His three small children? His past? His medical studies in Paris and in New York? His first book of poems, published when he was twenty years old?

Lillian smiled at him as if saying, you too have taken a secret journey into the past.

Simultaneously they returned to the present.

Lillian said: "There is a quality in this place which does not come altogether from its beauty. What is it? Is it the softness which annihilates all thought and lulls the body for enjoyment? Is it the continuity of music which prevents thoughts from arresting the flow of life? I have seen other trees, other rivers; they did not have the power to intoxicate the senses. Do you feel this? Does everyone feel this? Is this what kept South Seas travelers from ever returning home?"

"It does not affect everyone in the same way," said the Doctor with bitterness in his voice, and Lillian realized he was thinking of his wife.

Was this the mystery in Doctor Hernandez's life? A wife he could not win over to the city he liked, the life he loved?

She waited for him to say more. But he was silent and his face had become placid again.

Her hand, which she had left in the waters of the lagoon to feel the gliding, the uninterrupted gentleness of the flowing, to assure herself of this union with a living current, she now felt she must lift, to prove to the Doctor that she shared his anxiety, and that his sadness affected her. She must surrender the pleasure of touching the flow of water, as if she were touching the flow of life within her, out of sympathy for his anguish.

As she lifted her hand and waited for the drops of water to finish dripping from it, a shot was heard, and water spattered over her. They all three sat still, stunned.

"Hunters?" she asked. She wanted to stand up and shout and wave so the hunters would know they were there.

The Doctor answered quietly: "They were not hunters. It was not a mistake. They intended to shoot me, but they missed."

"But why? Why? You're the most needed, the most loved man here!"

"I refuse to give them drugs. Don't you understand? As a doctor I have access to drugs. They want to force me to give them some. Drugs for forgetting. And I have no right to do this, no right except in cases of great physical pain. That's why when you compared Golconda to a drug I felt bitter. For some people, Golconda is not enough."

The fisherman did not understand their talk in English. He said in Spanish, with a resigned air: "Bad hunters. They missed the crocodile. I could catch him with my bare hands and a knife. I often have. Without guns. What bad hunters!"

The swimming pool was at the lowest level of the hotel and only about ten feet above the sea, so that it was dominated by the roar of the waves hurling themselves against the rocks. The quietness of its surface did not seem like the quietness of a pool but more like that of a miniature bay formed within rocks which miraculously escaped the boiling sea for a few moments. It did not seem an artificial pool dug into cement and fed by water pipes, but rather one of the sea's own moods, one of the sea's moments of response, an intermittent haven.

It was surrounded by heavy, lacquered foliage, and flowers so tenuously held that they fell of their own weight into the pool and floated among the swimmers like children's boats.

It was an island of warm, undangerous water in which one man at least had sought eternal repose by throwing himself out of one of the overhanging hotel windows. Ever since that night the pool had been locked at midnight. Those who knew that the watchman preferred to watch the dancers on the square and that the gate could easily be leaped over, came to sit there in the evenings before going to sleep. The place was barred to any loud frivolity but open for secret assignations after dancing.

It was also Lillian's favorite place before going to sleep. The gentleness of the water, its warmth, was the lulling atmosphere she had missed when she had passed from childhood to womanhood.

She felt an unconfessed need of receiving from some gentle source the reassurance that the world was gentle and warm, and not, as it may have seemed during the day, cold and cruel. This reassurance was never granted to the mature, so that Lillian told no one of the role the pool played in her life today. It was the same role played by another watchman whom she had heard when she was ten years old and living in Mexico while her father built bridges and roads. The town watchman, a figure out of the Middle Ages, walked the streets at night chanting: "All is well, all is calm and peaceful. All is well."

Lillian had always waited for this watchman to pass before going to sleep. No matter how tense she had been during the day, no matter what catastrophes had taken place in school, or in the street, or at home, she knew that this moment would come when the watchman would walk all alone in the darkened streets swinging his lantern and his keys, crying monotonously, "All is well, all is well and calm and peaceful." No sooner had he said this and no sooner had she heard the jangling keys and seen the flash of his lantern on the wall of her room, than she would fall instantly asleep.

Others who came to the pool were of the fraternity who like to break laws, who like to steal their pleasures, who liked the feeling that at anytime the hotel watchman might appear at the top of the long stairs; they knew his voice would not carry above the hissing sea, and that as he was too lazy to walk downstairs he would merely turn off the lights as if this were enough to disperse the transgressors. To be forced to swim in the darkness and slip away from the pool in darkness was not, as the watchman believed, a punishment, but an additional pleasure.

In the darkness one became even more aware of the softness of the night, of pulsating life in the muscles, of the pleasure of motion. The silence that ensued was the silence of conspiracy and at this hour everyone dropped his disguises and spoke from some realm of innocence preserved from the corrosion of convention.

The Doctor would come to the pool, leaving his valise at the hotel desk. He talked as if he wanted to forget that everyone needed him, and that he had little time for pleasure or leisure. But Lillian felt that he never rested from diagnosis. It was as if he did not believe anyone free of pain, and could not rest until he had placed his finger on the core of it.

Lillian now sat in one of the white string chairs that looked like flattened harps, and played abstractedly with the white cords as if she were composing a song.

The Doctor watched her and said: "I can't deceide which of the two drugs you need: the one for forgetting or the one for remembering."

Lillian abandoned the harp chair and slipped into the pool, floating on her back and seeking immobility.

"Golconda is for forgetting, and that's what I need," she said, laughing.

"Some memories are imbedded in the flesh like splinters," said the Doctor, "and you have to operate to get them out."

She swam underwater, not wanting to hear him, and then came up nearer to where he sat on the steps and said: "Do I really seem to you like someone with a splinter in her flesh?"

"You act like a fugitive."

She did not want to be touched by the word. She plunged into the deep water again as if to wash her body of all memories, to wash herself of the past. She returned gleaming, smooth, but not free. The word had penetrated and caused an uneasiness in her breast like that caused by diminished oxygen. The search for truth was like an explorer's deep-sea diving, or his climb into impossible altitudes. In either case it was a problem of oxygen, whether you went too high or too low. Any world but the familiar neutral one caused such difficulty in breathing. It may have been for this reason that the mystics believed in a different kind of training in breathing for each different realm of experience.

The pressure in her chest compelled her to leave the pool and sit beside the Doctor, who was looking out to sea.

In the lightest voice she could find, and with the hope of discouraging the Doctor's seriousness, she said: "I was a woman who was so ashamed of a run in my stocking that it would prevent me from dancing all evening. . . ."

"It wasn't the run in your stocking...."

"You mean... other things... ashamed... just vaguely ashamed...."

"If you had not been ashamed of other things you would not have cared about the run in your stocking...."

"I've never been able to describe or understand what I felt. I've lived so long in an impulsive world, desiring without knowing why, destroying without knowing why, losing without knowing why, being defeated, hurting myself and others.... All this was painful, like a jungle in which I was constantly lost. A chaos."

"Chaos is a convenient hiding place for fugitives. You are a fugitive from truth."

"Why do you want to force me to remember? The beauty of Golconda is that one does not remember...."

"In Eastern religions there was a belief that human beings gathered the sum total of their experiences on earth, to be examined at the border. And according to the findings of the celestial customs officer one would be directed either to a new realm of experience, or back to re-experience the same drama over and over again. The condemnation to repetition would only cease when one had understood and transcended the old experience."

"So you think I am condemned to repetition? You think that I have not liquidated the past?"

"Yes, unless you know what it is you ran away from..."

"I don't believe this, Doctor, I know I can begin anew here."

"So you will plunge back into chaos, and this chaos is like the jungle we saw from the boat. It is also your smoke screen."

"But I do feel new...."

The Doctor's expression at the moment was perplexed, as if he were no longer certain of his diagnosis; or was it that what he had discovered about Lillian was so grave he did not want to alarm her? He very unexpectedly withdrew at the word "new," smiled with indulgence, raised his shoulders as if he had been persuaded by her eloquence, and finally said: "Maybe only the backdrop has changed."

Lillian examined the pool, the sea, the plants, but could not see them as backdrops. They were too charged with essences, with penetrating essences like the newest drugs which altered the chemistry of the body. The softness entered the nerves, the beauty surrounded and enveloped the thoughts. It was impossible that in this place the design of her past life should repeat itself, and the same characters reappear, as the Doctor had implied. Did the self which lived below visibility really choose its characters repetitiously and with only superficial variations, intent on reproducing the same basic drama, like a well-trained actor with a limited repertory?

And exactly at the moment when she felt convinced of the deep power of the tropics to alter a character, certain personages appeared who seemed to bear no resemblance to the ones she had left in that other country, personages whom she received with delight because they were gifts from Golconda itself, intended to heal her of other friendships, other loves, and other places.

The hitchhiker Fred was a student from the University of Chicago who had been given a job in the hotel translating letters from prospective guests. Lillian called him "Christmas," because at everything he saw which delighted him—a coppery sunrise or a flamingo bird, a Mexican girl in her white starched dress or a bougainvillaea bush in full bloom—he would exclaim: "It's like Christmas!"

He was tall and blond but undecided in his movements, as if he were not sure yet that his arms and legs belonged to him. He was at that adolescent age when his body hampered him, as though it were a shell he was seeking to out-grow. He was still concerned with the mechanics of living, unable as yet to enjoy it. For him it was still an initiation, an ordeal. He still belonged to the Nordic midnight sun; the tropical sun could not tan him, only freckle him. Sometimes he had the look of a blond angel who had just come from a Black Mass. He smiled innocently although one felt sure that in his dreams he had undressed the angels and the choir boys and made love to them. He had the small smile of Pan. His eyes conveyed only the wide expanse of desert that lay between human beings, and his mouth expressed the tremors he felt when other human beings approached him. The eyes said do not come too near. But his body glowed with warmth. It was his mouth, compressed and controlled, which revealed his timidity.

At everything new he marveled, but with persistent reference to the days of his childhood which had given him a permanent joy. Every day was Christmas day; the turtle eggs served at lunch were a gift from the Mexicans, the opened coconut spiked with rum was a new brand of candy.

His only anxiety centered around the problem of returning home. He did not have time enough to hitchhike back; it had taken him a full month to get here. He had no money, so he had decided to work his way back on a cargo ship.

Everyone offered to contribute, to perpetuate his Christmas day. But a week after his arrival he was already inquiring about cargo ships which would take him back home in time to finish college, and back to Shelley, the girl he was engaged to.

But about Shelley there was no hurry, he explained. It was because of Shelley that he had decided to spend the summer hitchhiking. He was engaged and he was afraid. Afraid of the girl. He needed time, time to adventure, time to become a man. Yes, to become a man. (He always showed Shelley's photograph and there was nothing in the tilted-up nose, the smile, and her soft hair to frighten anyone.)

Lillian asked him: "Couldn't Shelley have helped you to become a man?"

He had shrugged his shoulders. "A girl can't help a boy to become a man. I have to feel I am one *before I marry*. And I don't know anything about myself . . . or about women . . . or about love. . . . I thought this trip would help me. But I find I am afraid of all girls. It was not only Shelley."

"What is the difference between a girl and a woman?"

"Girls laugh. They laugh at you. That's the one thing I can't bear, to be laughed at."

"They're not laughing at you, Christmas. They're laughing because they wish to hide their own fears, to appear free and light, or they laugh so you won't think they take you too seriously. They may be laughing from pleasure, to encourage you. Think how frightened you would be if they did not laugh, if they looked at you gravely and made you feel that their destiny was in your hands, a matter of life and death. That would frighten you even more, wouldn't it?"

"Yes, much more."

"Do you want me to tell you the truth?"

"Yes, you have a way of saying things which makes me feel you are not laughing at me."

"If . . . you experimented with becoming a man before you married your girl, you might also find that it was *because* you were a boy that she loved you . . . that she loves you for what you are, not for what you will be later. She might love you less if you changed. . . ."

"What makes you think this?"

"Because if you truly wanted to change, you would not be so impatient to leave. Your mind is fixed on the departure times of cargo ships!"

When he arrived at the pool Lillian could almost see him carrying his two separate and contradictory wishes, one in each hand. But at least while he was intent on juggling them without losing his balance, he no longer felt the pain of not living, of a paralysis before living.

His smile at Lillian was charged with gratitude. Lillian was thinking that the primitives were wiser in having definitely established rituals: at a certain moment, determined by the calendar, a boy becomes a man.

Meanwhile Fred was using all his energy in rituals of his own: he had to master water skiing, he had to be the champion swimmer and diver, he must initiate the Mexicans into his knowledge of jazz, he had to outdo everyone in going without sleep, in dancing.

Lillian had said: "Fears cannot bear to be laughed at. If you take all your fears, one by one, make a list of them, face them, decide to challenge them, most of them will vanish. Strange women, strange countries, strange foods, strange illnesses."

While Fred dived many times into the pool conscientiously, Diana arrived.

Diana had first come to Mexico at the age of seventeen, when she had won a painting fellowship. But she had stayed, married, and built a house in Golconda. Most of the time she was alone; her husband worked and traveled.

She no longer painted, but collected textiles, paintings, and jewelry. She spent her entire morning getting dressed. She no longer sat before an easel, but before a dressing table, and made an art of dressing in native textiles and jewels.

When she finally descended the staircase into the hotel, she became an animated painting. Everyone's eyes were drawn to her. All the colors of Diego Rivera and Orozco were draped on her body. Sometimes her dress seemed painted with large brushstrokes, sometimes roughly dyed like the costumes of the poor. Other times she wore what looked like fragments of ancient Mayan murals, bold symmetrical designs in charcoal outlines with the colors dissolved by age. Heavy earrings of Aztec warriors, necklaces and bracelets of shell, gold and silver medallions and carved heads and amulets, animals and bones, all these caught the light as she moved.

It was her extreme liveliness that may have prevented her from working upon a painting, and turned a passion for color and textures upon her own body.

Lillian saw her once, later, at a costume party carrying an empty frame around her neck. It was Diana's head substituted for a canvas, her head with its slender neck, its tousled hair, tanned skin and earth-colored eyes. Her appearance within an empty frame was an exact representation of her history.

With the same care she took in dressing herself, in creating tensions of colors and metals, once she had arrived at the top of the staircase she set out to attract all the glances, exposing the delicately chiseled face belonging to a volatile person and incongruously set upon a luxurious body which one associated with all the voluptuous reclining figures of realistic paintings. When she was satisfied that every eye was on her, she was content, and could devote herself to the second phase of her activity.

First of all she thrust her breasts forward, as if to assert that hers was a breathing, generous body, and not just a painting. But they were in curious antiphony, the quick-turning, sharp-featured head with its untamed hair, and the body with its separate language, the language of the strip teaser; for, after raising her breasts upward and outward as a swimmer might before diving, she continued to undulate, and although one could not trace the passage of her hand over various places on her body, Lillian had the feeling that, like the strip teaser, she had mysteriously called attention to the roundness of her shoulder, to the indent of her waist. And what added to the illusion of provocation was that, having dressed herself with the lavishness of ancient civilizations, she proceeded gradually to strip herself. It was her artistic interpretation of going native.

She would first of all lay her earrings on the table and rub her ear lobes. The rings hurt her ears, which wanted to be free. No eyes could detach themselves from this spectacle. She would remove her light jacket, and appear in a backless sundress. After breakfast, on a chaise longue on the terrace, she would lie making plans for the beach, but on this chaise longue she turned in every ripple or motion which could escape immobility. She took off her bracelets and rubbed the wrist which they had confined. She was too warm for her beach robe. By the time she reached the beach even the bathing suit had ceased to be visible to one's eyes. By an act of prestidigitation, even though she was now dressed as was every other woman on the beach, one could see her as the naked, full brown women of Gauguin's Tahitian scenes.

Whoever had voted that she deserved a year to dedicate herselt to the art of painting had been wise and clairvoyant.

Illogically, with Diana Fred lost his fear of women who laughed. Perhaps because Diana's laughter was continuous, so that it seemed, like the music of the guitars, an accompaniment to their days in Golconda.

Every day Fred wanted Diana and Lillian to accompany him in his visits to the cargo ships which were to sail him home. The one that had accepted him was not ready yet. It was being loaded very slowly with coconuts, and dried fish, with crocodile skins, bananas, and baskets.

They would walk the length of the wharf watching the fishermen catching tropical fish, or watching the giant turtle that had been turned on its back so that it would not escape until it was time to make turtle soup.

Watching the small ships preparing to sail, questioning the captain who wore a brigand's mustache, the mate who wore no shirt, and obtaining no definite sailing date, the anxiety of Christmas reached its culmination.

He had something to prove to himself which he had not yet proved. He was simultaneously enjoying his adventure and constantly planning to put an end to it.

When the captain allowed him to visit the ship, he would stand alone on its deck and watch Diana and Lillian standing on the wharf. They waved good-by in mockery and he waved back. And it was only at this moment that he noticed how alive Lillian's hair was, as if each curl were weaving itself around his fingers, how slender Diana's neck and inviting to the hand, how full of light both their faces were, how their fluttering dresses enveloped and caressed them.

Behind them rose the soft violet mountains of Golconda. He had known intimately neither woman nor city and was already losing them. Then he felt pain and a wild desire not to sail away. He would run down the gangplank, pushing the porters to one side, run back once more to all the trepidations they caused him by their nearness.

Neither Diana nor Lillian was helping him. They both smiled so gaily, without a shadow of regret, and did not force him to stay, or cling to him. And in the deepest part of himself he knew they were helping him to become a man by allowing him to make his own decisions. That was part of the initiation. They would not steal his boyhood; he must abdicate it.

He loved them both, Diana for incarnating the spice, the color, and the fragrance of Golconda, and Lillian because her knowledge of him seemed to incarnate him, and because she was like a powerful current that transmitted life to him.

Just as he climbed the gangplank as a rehearsal for his departure, he felt that he was not ready to leave, so when he returned to them he felt unready to live, painfully poised between crystallizations. He could not follow Diana's invitations into the unknown, unfamiliar life of the senses, and he could not sail either.

An invisible race was taking place between Diana's offer of a reclining nude by a Gauguin and the ship's departure. And as if the ship, the captain, the mate, and the men who loaded it had known he was not ready to leave, one day when he went to the pier at four o'clock as he did every day, the ship was gone!

He could still see it on the horizon line, a small black speck throwing off not quite enough smoke to conceal its departure.

Sabina

The brain of man is filled with passageways like the contours and multiple crossroads of the labyrinth. In its curved folds lie the imprint of thousands of images, recordings of millions of words.

Certain cities of the Orient were designed to baffle the enemy by a tangle of intricate streets. For those concealed within the labyrinth its detours were a measure of safety; for the invaders it presented an image of fearful mystery.

Sabina had chosen the labyrinth for safety.

There existed five or six versions of her birthplace, parents, racial origins. For Jay her first version was: my mother was a Hungarian gypsy. She sang in cafes and told fortunes. My father played the guitar. When they came to America they opened a night club, mostly for Hungarians. It was like a continuation of life in Hungary.

But when Jay asked her: "What did you do as a girl in that environment? Did you sing? Did you tell fortunes? Did you learn to dance? Did you wear long braids and a white blouse? How did you learn to speak such beautiful English?" Sabina did not answer. Jay had taken her to a Hungarian restaurant and waited for her response to the music, the dances, the songs, to the swarthy men whose glances were like a dagger thrust. But Sabina had forgotten this story by then and looked on the scene with detachment. When Jay pressed her she began another: "I was born on the road. My parents

Reprinted from *Chicago Review,* 15:3 (Winter-Spring 1962), pp. 45-60.

were show people. We travelled all the time. My father was a magician in a circus. My mother was a trapezist."

Had she learned there her skill in balancing in space, in time, avoiding all definitions and crystallizations? Had she learned from her father to deal in camouflage, in quick sleight of hand? (This story came before the one in which she asserted her father had been anonymous. Not knowing who he was, he might turn out to be any of the men she admired at the time.)

"But," said Jay, "You told me once your father was a Don Juan, that it was his faithlessness which had affected your childhood, giving you a feeling of impermanency."

"That was true, too," said Sabina, "one can be a faithless magician!"

"And you learned from him, no doubt, to juggle with facts."

From the very first day Jay who had always lived joyously and obviously outside, in daylight, had been drawn into this labyrinth unwittingly by his own curiosity and love of facts. He had believed only in what he saw, in one dimension, like a candid photographer, and he now found himself inside rows of mirrors with endless reflections and counter reflections. Sabina was like those veiled figures glimpsed turning the corner of a Moroccan street, wrapped from head to foot in white cotton, throwing to a stranger a single spark from fathomless eyes. Was she the very woman one had been seeking? There was a compulsion to follow her.

From story to story, from a mobile evanescent childhood, to a kaleidoscopic adolescence, to a tumultuous and smoky womanhood, a figure whom even a passport official would have had difficulty in identifying.

Jay had the primitive urge of the invader. But from the first day he was trapped by what he believed to be a duel between reality and illusion. It was difficult to invade a labyrinth! Sabina felt: once my supply of stories is exhausted, I die. Jay felt: once the stories are exhausted, I will possess Sabina.

Every man she had known had demanded of her, ultimately, an abdication of the Sabina she wanted to conceal. If she answered Jay's questions he would be disillusioned. Only illusion could create a human being one could love with passion.

This was her labyrinth, and her Minotaur wore the open face of Jay asking such direct questions as would a compiler of statistics, a census taker. How old are you? Are you married? Do you have children?

She had used every curvature in the maze to escape his questions. Why had he assumed the role of detective?

When she first met him in the cafe, he seemed so candid. He talked without premeditation. He seemed the incarnation of spontaneity. Such a contrast to herself was a source of fascination at first. He seemed direct, open, naked. He never withheld what he thought or felt. He passed no judgment on others, and expected none to be passed on him.

But Sabina lived in expectation of such a judgment. She could see the danger in his moments of anger, when he painted savagely those who had not given him what he asked of them. But what did he ask? If they offered beauty he was suspicious of it. Beauty was artifice. Truth only lay in people and things stripped of aesthetics. What did he ask of her? Was he the lover who was not content with possessing the body but curious about its essence?

While he talked Sabina remembered reading that the Arabs did not respect the man who unveiled his thoughts. The intelligence of an Arab was measured by his capacity to elude direct questions. The questioner was always suspect. Sabina was of that race. Did she truly originate thousands of years ago from the people who veiled their faces and their thoughts? Where did she come from that she understood so well this racial dedication to mystery?

He had a habit of asking naive questions, of prying. When his curiosity was satisfied, he seemed to be saying: "you see, there was nothing behind that." He would have walked behind the magician's props, he would have exposed Houdini. He hated poetry and he hated illusion. His own savage self-confessions encouraged confessions. This passion for stripping, unveiling, exposing the truth, compelled him to enter Sabina's labyrinth.

At first it seemed like the natural preoccupation of a lover: does she love me? Does she love me alone? Does she love others as she loves me? Does she love anyone?

This was in turn born of her habit of never saying: I loved him, or I loved her, but he loved me, she loved me, thus eluding all responsibility, all commitment. She had made the core of her individuality elusive. Had *she* loved? Had *she* chosen?

The first time Jay had walked into the cafe, softly and casually, with an air of being nobody at all, smiling, relaxed, with a warm mellow voice, slightly thinning hair which gave him the air of a Buddhist monk, roseate, lean, content, in spite of poverty and difficulties, she had distrusted him.

In appearance he could have passed anonymously through a crowd but his laughter was contagious. The mouth was sensual and vulnerable but the eyes were watchful, cool, shadowless, analytical.

He seemed so different from his brutal, violent paintings. Warmed-voiced, joyous, gentle. His mouth, amorous, slightly open, lips very full, seemed eager to eat, to kiss, to savour all that his eyes would later ruthlessly caricature. He treated the whole world as men treated prostitutes, desiring and then discarding, skipping love, knowing only hunger and then indifference. A gentle savage, who lives by moods, effervescence, rhythm, in a self-created glow, euphoria. Not noticing other's moods.

"Ever since Lillian left," he told her, "I have no place to live in. Last night I slept in a movie house. I watched the film three times and then I slipped down into my seat. They never clean the place till morning, and even then the cleaning woman only grunts and lets me sleep on. Did you ever stay in a movie house when it's empty? Films are a dose of opium anyway. Coming out in the street usually shocks one awake. When you stay on you never wake up! The opium goes on working. I would fall asleep for a little while and then see images on the screen which were the images of my dreams and the dream and the film I had seen would become one and the same."

Sabina too had offered to help him so he could get a studio and continue painting: "Do you earn money?" he asked candidly. She did not answer, but began a complicated story of intrigues and bartering, miraculous arrangements which he could not translate. Later, when the rent was overdue she asked to see the landlord. She came back smiling; the landlord had promised to wait again. She reminded him of the gypsies in the South of France who returned to their shacks, lifted up their skirts and exposed a chicken or two they had stolen!

Only Jay felt that Sabina's bargaining powers came not from objects but from herself, her body.

"Why can't you trust me with the truth?" asked Jay.

"Because you always turn around and caricature."

"But Sabina, I only turn around and caricature when I am angry."

"But I'm never sure of what will make you angry."

"Your mysteriousness makes me angry. You mystify me."

"You're like a mythical animal, so innocent about your appetites, your sensual enjoyments." She did not add: but you would not grant me the same innocence.

"Our age has been of violence, it deals in hypocrisies. I feel like a human bomb," said Jay.

Sabina could not explain that it was this she feared, never knowing what would cause him to explode. She was baffled by his contradictions between enthusiasm and sudden destructive rebellion, between passion and hatred, between euphoria and caricature. Was he, as Lillian had thought, a very hurt man? Hurt men were dangerous, like wounded animals in the jungle. He wanted everything blasted away: hypocrisy, fear, falseness.

She feared to see a distorted image of herself in him. As she saw a distorted image of others ın him. She felt like the Arabs, who do not believe in mirrors, or in being painted, or photographed.

While Jay was so concerned to know whether Sabina had other lovers, whether she loved women, or took drugs, he overlooked the true mystery: *why were such secrets necessary?*

Every meeting was then a holiday. Jay would arrive with paint on his workman's suit. One did not know if it was a tree, or body, or a river which had overflown on him. It was as if he had been walking through the greens, yellows, reds, and blacks. He had found a studio in Montmartre, in a workman's quarter. He had already covered the walls with sketches. On one long page he had scrawled in large letters:

Merlans à la Bercy
Coquilles de Cervelles au Gratin
Flamri de Semoule

Galantine de Volaille à la Gelée
Anguilles Pompadour
Selle de Mouton Bouquetière

"These are the dishes I want to eat someday." There were many maps covered with red pencil lines marking the places he wanted to visit. But for the moment he had to show her his Paris.

He was in love with a black sooty angel who guarded the well house, a begrimed angel who ruled a round courtyard no larger than a well and as dark. He was in love with a courtesan Mona Paiva who had reigned a hundred years ago and whose photograph he had found on the Quays. He was making a study of poisons at the Bibliotheque Nationale. He noted fragments of conversations on menus, on toilet paper, on envelopes. He took Sabina to the Mariner's flop house to eat an omelet with the pickpockets. He played chess at the cafe where the old actors met for a game, to the tune of tired classical musicians. At dawn he liked to sit and watch the tired prostitutes walking home.

An eagerness to catch everything without makeup, without embellishments, women before they combed their hair, waiters before they donned artificial smiles with their bow ties. A quest for naturalness which came to a stop before Sabina's painted eyes, a Sabina whom daylight refused to touch. Even in the morning she exuded her own lighting, and it was the enhancing lighting of her life at night.

In Jay's glaring, crude daylight upon externals and in Sabina's preference for the night lay the core of their conflict from the first day.

Until he met Sabina, women confounded themselves in his mind, were interchangeable, and his desire did not become a desire to know them intimately, to understand them.

At first he thought Sabina had fixed his attention because she had a more voluptuous body, a more penetrating voice, a more dazzling smile, more burning eyes than other women. She was a woman painted in more opulent colors.

He had never been too concerned about identity, but because Sabina would not acknowledge any, he began to demand one.

He did not know, and never learned, that she had already told the truth about herself when she had spoken of the need of being loved as her guiding element. Her desire to *be* loved. No passion or desire springing from independent desires of her own, but from the desire to be loved.

Jay suspected that much was being hidden from him; it was hidden not by Sabina, but by his own purely external vision. Among the chaotic confessions, the rambling talks, the flow of fiction, he had not been able to detect the revelatory ones. Sabina escaped direct questions, but offered other clues.

But it was not only that Sabina had the body of the women who climbed every night upon the stage of music halls and gradually undressed, but that it was impossible to situate her in any other atmosphere. The luxuriance of the flesh, its vivid tones, the fevered eyes and the weight of the voice, its huskiness, became instantly conjugated with sensual love. Other women lost this erotic phosphorescence as soon as they abandoned their roles of dance hall hostesses. Sabina's night life was internal, it glowed from within her and it came in part from treating every encounter as either intimate or to be forgotten. It was as if before every man she lighted within herself the lamp lighted by waiting mistresses or wives at the end of day, only they were her eyes, and it was her face which became like a poem's bedchamber, tapestried with twilight and velvet. As it glowed from within her it could appear in totally unexpected places, early in the morning, in a neglected cafe, on a park bench, on a rainy morning in front of a hospital or a morgue, anywhere. It was always the soft light kept through the centuries for the moment of pleasure.

His first letter to her was delirious, and contained a description of Babylon in such goldleaf words that she asked him if he took drugs.

The question startled him. His intoxication came from images, words, colors. It occurred to him that she must have taken drugs if the idea of wild flights of imagination was linked in her mind inevitably with the use of drugs.

"Do you?" he demanded. And was distressed by this speculation as by the idea of madness, because as an artist he held the proud notion that every image came out of his own spontaneous chemistry, not from any synthetic formula. "Do you?"

Sabina eluded the question. She often talked about drugs, but never acknowledged any intimate experience with them. This became one of Jay's obsessional themes of detection.

Up to that moment of his encounter with Sabina, he had been so at ease in his physical, evident world, and now the dimensions she opened were like countless mirrors.

The devastating charade sometimes entered upon by lovers had begun. It was on the theme of truth and nontruth, illusion and reality. The meshing only took place in the interlocking of desire. Sudden, violent desires. No time to turn down coverlets, to close windows, to turn out lights. Against the wall, on the carpet, on a chair, a couch, in taxis, in elevators, in parks, on rivers, on boats, in the woods, on balconies, in doorways at night they grappled body to body, breath to breath, tongue against tongue as if to enclose, enmesh, imprison once and forever essences, odors, flavors which eluded them at other times.

Jay earthy, roseate, lusty, relaxed, Sabina feverish, supple, their voices mingling in the night like the cries heard in tropical forests, words which added weight to the bodies, density to the blood. The full weight of flesh. Crushed grass, tilted boats, creaking beds, wrinkled sheets, fallen pillows, scattered clothes. They were locked at least for an instant in a common pulsation.

They were drawn together by his need to expose illusion, her need to create it. A satanic pact. One must triumph: the realist or the mythmaker. The painter turned detective of what lay behind appearance, and Sabina created mysteries as a natural flowering of her femininity. How else to hold his interest for a thousand nights?

Her symbolic resistance to nakedness of thought and feeling became associated in his mind with the image of the strip tease, women exposing gradually areas of their bodies and vanishing when they were about to be seen completely.

He entered the labyrinth with a notebook! If he annotated enough facts he would finally possess the truth. The black stockings, the overfull handbags, the missing buttons, the hair always about to topple down, a strand always falling over the eye, the hasty dressing, the mobility, the absence of repose.

Her speech, for instance. She had a beautiful speech, half-way between stage English, softly modulated, like that of a mature and skilled actress, but she would not say where she had learned it. She had run away from school. She had not studied with anyone. She would not tell where she had been raised. She had two distinct manners, one, that of a street urchin, brawling, crude (when she lost her temper or was frightened by a taxi), another as "on stage," entrancing, refined. They corresponded to her attitude about clothes: at times she had holes in her stockings, wore unwashed jeans, and used safety pins to hold everything together; at other times she rushed to buy gloves and perfume. But at all times, her eyes were carefully painted like the eyes on Egyptian frescoes.

No mysteries in the rites of the body. Palpable rites, hands full of evidence.

They lay back to back. He was still immersed in her. Her breath was quieting down. He wanted to lie blind in the furls of her flesh. On what wings was she taking flight? As if the sensual act had been but a mouth applied to an opium pipe. And now Sabina was rising in whirls of smoke.

She demanded illusion as other women demanded necklaces. For Jay illusion and lies were synonymous. Art and illusion and lie were one. He had asked: "What color was your hair originally?"

"They do not always match," she answered. And turned her back to him. What did he seek? A Sabina as naked within as without? A soul as softly curved, as accessible to his knowing hands. Gold behind gold.

With the question about her hair he had caused a departure.

How often was he to cry out: "Perhaps there is nothing at all, perhaps the mystery is that there is no mystery at all. She is empty, empty, empty." But how could an empty woman have such a vivid presence, how could an empty woman cause insomnia, and awaken so many dreams? How could an empty woman cause other women to take flight, abdicating instinctively.

"Do you betray me? Do you take drugs? Do you love women?"

She smiled at the questions, as if to say: "And if I answered you, would you know me then?"

He did not ask the correct question of the Sphinx. He did not say to Sabina what Djuna said to her later: "I am not concerned with the secrets, or the lies, or the mysteries. I am concerned with *what made them necessary.*"

"The books she reads," said Jay, "or pretends to read, are summed up for her by others, she echoes their opinions. The childhood she invented, I saw it in a film the other night, she lifted it complete, in every detail."

Sabina brought to his studio a treasure house of curios, paintings, statues, with vague stories as to how they had been acquired. She made use of the soft part of the bread for a napkin. She fell asleep at times with her shoes on, on unmade beds.

When a little money came in, Sabina bought delicacies for the palate or for her skin. Strawberries in winter, and caviar and bath salts.

She read very little. She was impatient at movies, and even at the theatre. She wanted firsthand knowledge of everything intimate experience only. Whatever took place, a crime, the arrival of a new personality, Sabina never listened attentively. She had already known the criminal. Had talked to him for a whole night in a cafe. He had confessed what he intended to do. The new actress who was starring had been her friend in school. She had lived at the home of the painter who had suddenly become celebrated. She was always inside. She had loved a revolutionist, nursed the discarded mistress who later committed suicide, confessed the defrocked literary priest. She was always inside. She did not care for films, newspaper reportages, the radio. She wanted personal knowledge. While others relied on secondhand journalism, she spent a night in a cafe talking with a consulate secretary and knew the contents of some cables before they appeared in print. She was not interested in fiction or news because she only cared to be involved while they were being lived, created, she only cared for the moment at which they happened. People were never "characters" or news items. They were her companions of the moment.

People spoke of Africa. Sabina was silent. She knew the body of Mambo, the flavor of his skin, his dreams, his feelings as no one else did. He was the continent of Africa. Its songs, its vegetation, its spices, its rhythms.

She was restless at the movies, but not restless if they spent an evening with a future star of the movies, or went out after a play with the actors, or to a party with the dancers after a ballet.

She only believed in proximity, in confessions born in the darkness of a bedroom, in the quarrels born of alcohol, in the communion born of exhausting walks through the city. She only believed in those words which came like the confessions of criminals after long exposure to hunger, to intense light, to cross questioning, to violent tearing away of masks. It took hours to descend into these depths where all the treasures lay.

She would not read books on travel, but she sat alert at the cafe to catch the appearance of an Abyssinian, a Greek, an Iranian, a Hindu, who would bear direct news from home, who would be carrying letters and photographs from his family, and would bring to her personally, all the flavors of his country.

Then she would end the evening in the Abyssinian quarter of Paris which few people knew, or in the Greek quarter, in their homes, meeting their relatives, eating their food, learning their language, becoming as familiar with their lives as if she had spent years in the country from which they came.

She refused to be tender and warm in between the storms of passion. She would arise from possession cool and collected, unwilling to remain in intermediate temperate zones. It was the state of friendship she denied.

When Sabina grew anxious she merely changed her disguises. If anyone was about to assert that Sabina could not control her caprices and desires, she presented the image of a Sabina who once lived with a young man who never made love to her.

Jay often attacked her, denigrated, disparaged. He wanted to fix her dispersed attention, to contain her chaos and her fluidity. He hated the multiple changes and transformations which were like so many unknown, foreign Sabinas to be pursued, tracked down, possessed. A distracting harem.

While Sabina said to Djuna: "How can I be faithful to Jay when he does not love all of me, when I see a stranger always in his eyes and in his portraits?"

"Yes," Djuna agreed, "the truly faithless one is the one who makes love to only a fraction of you."

To Djuna Jay confessed that he had a haunting fear that Sabina was a creation of his own brain.

"She is loaded with riches given to her by others. The only difference is that instead of furs and jewels she prefers painters and writers."

"Then she exists in her selections," Djuna said. "Doesn't she exist in her selection of you? Of Lillian? Of me? What certitude do you seek? She is suspicious of words. She lives by her senses. We do not have a language for the senses. Feelings are images."

"For example," said Jay, not hearing, "once she told me that she had been tubercular. But she will not say if she is completely cured, and how long was she ill, and all she concedes is that it taught her to live more intensely."

"Perhaps" said Djuna, "she thinks you may be one of those people who love people better after their death!"

Djuna did not feel she could confide to Jay the night Sabina's talk had spiraled obsessionally around the death of her mother. Sabina repeating: "I didn't love her well enough." Through the turgid, whirling, opaque words Djuna had understood this from Sabina's confession: conceding love and admiration to her mother would have meant an acceptance of traits potential in Sabina and which Sabina considered dangerous to her existence, such as her maternal qualities. Sabina's mother sought to make of Sabina a woman she refused to be, wife and mother, and while her mother was alive she endangered Sabina's aspiration to escape the servitudes of women. She was determined to become the women who enchanted her father and for whom he deserted her mother. Her mother he needed, but the other women gave him euphoria. But when she died, how deeply Sabina had loved her voice which was a balm, her enveloping tenderness, her attentive care. "How well I loved her after her death!"

The traits which were in opposition to Sabina's love of freedom, which threatened to alter her, were forgotten. It was not the loss of her mother which awakened Sabina's love, it was that her mother's disappearance removed the danger of her influence, and left a human being no longer concerned with its own survival but with a recognition of her mother's qualities.

"During her life I fought off her influence. And she fought in me the kind of women who had displaced her."

And when her mother died she was forced to recognize that all the time she had acted out in secret from her mother an aspect of maternity towards the weak and the helpless. She was also a woman who could take care of others on the same level as her mother did; the exception was the lover, with whom she was always engaged in a special duel.

As soon as her mother died her rebellions collapsed. She became "possessed" by the spirit of her mother. It was her only way of maintaining her alive within herself. How wise the primitives were who retained their ritual so they would know *when* this possession took place, and also know how to exorcise it.

Djuna saw the alteration in Sabina's character, which was a need to act out her mother's attitude in life. Sabina told her of how her brother called her to come and help him distribute her belongings. And for the first time she told Djuna a simple and direct story.

"My brother stood far away at the other end of the gleaming airport hall, a small figure in black and white with, even from that distance, a tragic way of standing, like those paintings of St. Sebastian pierced by arrows. I felt I had done right to come, for he was at the end of his strength. When we arrived at the house I was silent. I missed my mother's face at the window, or her standing at the door, smaller each year, and with her hair so white it seemed more like a halo of light. What was more often true lately, she would be asleep already when I arrived and would turn on her light to greet me. It was when I entered her empty bedroom that I broke down. It was only then I realized I would not see her again. I had to help him dispose of her belongings. A box of holy medals, rosaries, prayer books, for the Sisters of St. Vincent de Paul. A box of lace remnants, (the one we carried about all through our lives and travels, from Europe to America, from home to home, my mother saying: some day we will make a whole tablecloth of all these small pieces of lace). I wanted her unfinished bobbin lace, the little pale blue pillow with a pattern pinned to it, and the white thread on bobbins which her hands wove in and out, but my brother knew of a nun who made such lace and would finish it, and I realized suddenly that I would have suffered seeing constantly this last unfinished piece of work. The pain was deeper from the little objects, her bobby pins, her comb, her face powder. I never saw anyone who possessed as little as my mother. A few dresses, and only the gifts we gave her. The stark simplicity of her taste, but a love of momentos. She kept all our letters, our childhood teeth and hair, my first embroidery, our first drawings. We gave all her clothes to the poor, as she would have wanted but we felt like criminals, dispersing parts of her, the coat which had warmed her, her modest handbag. I can now understand those who lock the door upon everything . . . and yet . . . and yet better for these objects to continue to live. The final casting off of an object which belongs to the dead one is full of taboos and full of the pains of the ritual of separation. Separate from my mother, separate from my mother. Some of our decisions were dictated by austere mourning: we cast off the Christmas tree ornaments as if Christmas were no longer possible to celebrate without her, cast off the playing cards with which she played solitaire or other card games with us when she was ill, as if we would never play cards again. Cast off the detective stories she liked to read in those days when I had the feeling that she sat waiting for death. But we kept the black lace fan, the one she waved with a Latin rhythm in church, which seemed irreverent to the American priest. I knew that my brother wanted to go to church, and that he was embarrassed to ask me, knowing my rebelliousness. He was happy when I suggested it. I waited for him, refusing to pray as I had as a child. I watched the little blue lights wavering in their oil glasses, some freshly lit by the penitents, some already burning out. I watched the one which was burning out, and I could not bear it, my mother's life burning out, so I went and lit a new one and my brother thought it was an offering, a renewal of my faith. It was after that I asked him for my mother's gold thimble, and for her sewing machine. And I don't know how to use either of them."

"She is such a comedian," said Jay. "She is always bringing back objects from her adventures. Gifts, antiques, statues, rare books. What do you think she came back with the other day, and which she silently concealed in her closet? A sewing machine! Do you think she wants to play the role of a wife now?"

Sabina came back from the cafes with new friends and her introduction always was: they talked to me, they sought me out. As if she were a passive wax receiving other's imprint. To Jay this always seemed as if she were concealing the motive of her interest. His blue eyes would scrutinize the strangers as if he were trying to look at them through Sabina's eyes.

Djuna said to Jay once, "Perhaps she is telling the truth. Like an actress, she may need to be nourished by a public, by praise, admiration. They may be necessary to her as a proof of her visibility. I know that the idea of Sabina doubting her existence, or her lovableness, may be impossible for you to imagine, Jay. In terms of your palette you never find enough colors to register the heightened range of her moods, of her presence. But to her indifferent father Sabina was invisible. A child's existence is first concretized in the eyes of the parent. If they see him, he exists. Sabina's efforts may be directed not towards experiencing her own existence within herself but obtaining outward proofs of it."

As Sabina matured, this need, Djuna felt, increased like the addict's need of drugs. Sabina increased the dose of friendships, admirers, devotees, lovers.

"What are you seeking, Jay? Are you chafing under your bondage, because she disperses her affections? What will you gain if you discover that Sabina can love more than one? What are you seeking? To disentangle yourself? They say that people who have more than one self are mad, but you yourself, how many Jays are there in you? And you think yourself the sanest of men!"

"I want the key, the key, the key to the lies. I thought that with passion I could break her open, break her elusiveness, find a naked woman who would give all of herself."

"You make it sound like rape. Passion and violence never opened a human being."

"Love, then," said Jay, mockingly.

"Strange irony," Djuna said. "In Spanish, compassion means '*with* passion.' Your passion is without compassion."

Jay laughed again: "Compassion and Sabina are absolutely incompatible. Absolutely absurd. As well have compassion for Venus, for the moon, for a statue, for a Queen, a tigress."

"That is the only key I ever found, which fits everyone..."

"And what would you say aroused your compassion for Sabina?"

"The Don Juan in her."

"You mean faithlessness."

"Oh, no. Don Juan was seeking in passion, in the act of possession, in the welding of bodies, something that has nothing to do with passion and was never born of it."

"A Narcissus pool," Jay said.

"No, he was seeking to be created, to be born, to be warmed into existence, to be imagined, to be known, to be identified, he was seeking a procreative miracle. The first birth is often a failure. He was seeking the love which would try once more. Passion cannot achieve this because it is not concerned with the true identity of the lover. Only love seeks to *know,* and to create or rescue the loved one."

"And why seek that from me," said Jay. "I don't even care to feed a stray cat."

"You're the artist. Sabina thinks of the artist as a creator of life."

"If I were to go about as you say, dispensing compassion, as you do, I'd be followed by a thousand cripples, nothing more. I would attract them as a doctor does. I say, let them die."

"You asked for a key to Sabina, Jay."

"You also think of Sabina as a human being in trouble? The kind of key you offer, Djuna, I would throw into the Seine. I'm a man of passion."

"Sabina knows that."

"She's a woman of passion."

After a while he laughed softly: "You and Lillian. You want to spare a man a season in hell. Do you know what Lillian did before she left? She stoked my closet full of food, because I had said once that the only thing I feared as a result of past experience, was hunger. To be left without food and money to buy it with. Lillian wanted to extend the period of nourishment beyond her stay."

This was the kind of image one must return quickly to the bottle of wine, like an escaped evil genii that can only cause trouble. Drink the wine, empty the bottle, return these images of tenderness into it, recork it, throw it out to sea. Worse luck, it would surely be

Djuna who would spot it as a distress signal, pick it up lovingly, and read into it a request for compassion.

Even though Jay had laughed at Djuna's words, and drowned them in a Pernod, he found when he returned to Sabina that she had lost some of that mythological larger-than-nature proportion which he liked to give to her. What had happened? Sabina seemed less powerful, more vulnerable. Quite obviously Djuna did not believe that the world was peopled with giants.

It happened that this night Sabina had a fever. The fever too he had never believed in, he had considered it symbolic, a quality of voice and eyes and gestures. Tonight it was a fever which rouged her cheeks and dampened her hair. Could a human being diminish in stature?

The figures in his paintings had been outsize, whether tyrant or victim, man or woman. Could people change size according to our vision of them? Jay had always seen his mother immense in the scale of the universe. He was shocked on one of his trips home to find her smaller than he remembered her. He believed it was her aging. If a person continues to see only giants, it means he is still looking at the world through the eyes of a child. Could his vision have been altered by Djuna's words? Certainly it was difficult to feel compassion for giants.

That night for once Jay was considerate of Sabina's fever. He watched her fall asleep.

As if poured from a spout of moonwhite liquid, coiled, a fluid woman carved by the waters, long lulled in its deeps, and the curves not quite the curves of a woman, but the curves of a wave that had for a moment taken the shape of a woman while keeping the rhythmic flow of a wave, its heaving restlessness, its mobility.

from Collages

Vienna was the city of statues. They were as numerous as the people who walked the streets. They stood on the top of the highest towers, lay down on stone tombs, sat on horseback, kneeled, prayed, fought animals and wars, danced, drank wine and read books made of stone. They adorned cornices like the figureheads of old ships. They stood in the heart of fountains glistening with water as if they had just been born. They sat under the trees in the parks summer and winter. Some wore costumes of other periods, and some no clothes at all. Men, women, children, kings, dwarfs, gargoyles, unicorns, lions, clowns, heroes, wise men, prophets, angels, saints and soldiers preserved for Vienna an illusion of eternity.

As a child Renate could see them from her bedroom window. At night, when the white muslin curtains fluttered out like ballooning wedding dresses, she heard them whispering like figures which had been petrified by a spell during the day and came alive only at night. Their silence by day taught her to read their frozen lips as one reads the messages of deaf mutes. On rainy days their granite eye sockets shed tears mixed with soot.

Renate would never allow anyone to tell her the history of the statues, or to identify them. This would have situated them in the past. She was convinced that people did not die, they became statues. They were people under a spell and if she were watchful enough they would tell her who they were and how they lived *now.*

From *Collages* (Swallow, 1964), pp. 7-10, 33-36, 44-47, 59-69, 112-122.

Renate's eyes were sea green and tumultuous like a reduction of the sea itself. When they seemed about to overflow with emotion, her laughter would flutter like windchimes and form a crystal bowl to contain the turquoise waters as if in an aquarium, and then her eyes became scenes of Venice, canals of reflections, and gold specks swam in them like gondolas. Her long black hair was swept away from her face into a knot at the top of her head, then fell over her shoulders.

Renate's father built telescopes and microscopes, so that for a long time Renate did not know the exact size of anything. She had only seen them diminutive or magnified.

Renate's father treated her like a confidante, a friend. He took her with him on trips, to the inauguration of telescopes, or to ski. He discussed her mother with her as if Renate were a woman, and explained that it was her mother's constant depression which drove him away from home.

He relished Renate's laughter, and there were times when Renate wondered whether she was not laughing for two people, laughing for herself but also for her mother who never laughed. She laughed even when she felt like weeping.

When she was sixteen she decided she wanted to become an actress. She informed her father of this while he was playing chess, hoping that his concentration on the game would neutralize his reaction. But he dropped his king and turned pale.

Then he said very coldly and quietly: "But I have watched you in your school plays and I do not think you are a good actress. You only acted an exaggerated version of yourself. And besides, you're a child, not a woman yet. You looked as if you had dressed up in your mother's clothes for a masquerade."

"But, Father, it was you who once said that what you liked about actresses was that they were exaggerated women! And now you use this very phrase against me, to pass judgment on me."

Renate spoke vehemently, and as she spoke her sense of injustice grew magnified. It took the form of a long accusation.

"You have always loved actresses. You spend all your time with them. I saw you one night working on a toy based on an interplay of mirrors. I thought it was for me. I was the one who liked to look through kaleidoscopes. But you gave it to an actress. Once you would not take me to the theater, you said I was too young, yet you took a girl from my school, and she showed me all the flowers and candy you sent her. You just want to keep me a child forever, so I will stay in the house and cheer you up."

She did not talk like a child angry that her father did not believe in her talent, but like a betrayed wife or mistress.

She stormed and grew angrier until she noticed that her father had grown paler, and was clutching at his heart. Frightened, she stopped herself short, ran for the medicine she had seen him take, gave him the drops, and then kneeled beside him and said softly: "Father, Father, don't be upset. *I was only pretending.* I was putting on an act to prove to you that I could be a good actress. You see, you believed me, and it was all pretense."

These words softly spoken revived her father. He smiled feebly and said: "You're a much better actress than I thought you were. You really frightened me."

Out of guilt she buried the actress. It was only much later she discovered that her father had long been ill, that she had not been told, and that it was not this scene which had brought on the first symptoms of a weak heart.

In every relationship, sooner or later, there is a court scene. Accusations, counter-accusations, a trial, a verdict.

In this scene with her father, Renate condemned the actress to death thinking that her guilt came from opposing his will. It was only later that she became aware that this had not been a trial between father and daughter.

She had, for a few moments, taken the place of her mother and voiced accusations her mother had never uttered. Her mother had been content to brood or to weep. But Renate had spoken unconsciously a brief for an unloved wife.

It had not been the rebellion of a daughter against a father's orders she felt guilty of, but her assuming what should have been her mother's role and place in her father's heart.

And her father too, she knew now, had not been hurt by a daughter's rebellion, but by the unmasking of a secret: he had not looked upon Renate as a daughter but as a woman, and his insistence on maintaining her a child was to disguise the companionship he enjoyed.

After this scene, Renate's father searched for a tutor because Renate had at the same time refused to continue to go to school.

He had a brother who had refused to go to school and had locked himself up in his room with many books. He only came out of it to eat and to renew his supply of books. At the end of seven years he came out and passed his examinations brilliantly and became a professor.

He indulged in one gentle form of madness which did not affect his scholarly and philosophical knowledge. He insisted that he had no marrow in his bones.

Renate's father thought that his brother would be a good tutor for Renate. He could teach her music, painting, and languages. It would help to keep her at home, away from the influence of other girls. But he explained the professor's obsession to her, and stressed clearly that she must never refer to bones or marrow as it ignited his irrational obsession.

Renate was naturally strongly tempted to discuss this very mystifying theme, and the marrow madness of her uncle interested her far more than anything else he might teach her.

She spent many days trying to find a tactful way to introduce this theme in their talks together. She did some preparatory research in the library. She discovered that birds have no marrow in their bones. She bought her uncle a canary with a coloratura voice and said: "Did you know that birds do not have marrow in their bones?"

"Yes," said her uncle, "but neither have I."

"How marvelous," said Renate, "that means that you can fly!"

Her uncle was impressed but would not put himself through the test. For fear she might urge him to explore this new concept, he never referred to his handicap again. But before adopting complete silence on this subject he offered her a rational explanation of its cause.

"My mother told me that she became pregnant while still nursing me. Slowly I realized that this other child, my brother, had absorbed all the nourishment away from me, thus leaving me without marrow in my bones."

Renate gathered together all the linen of the house stained with marks of love, dreams, nightmares, tears and kisses and quarrels, the mists that rise from bodies touching, the fogs of breathing, the dried tears, and took it to the laundromat at the foot of the hill.

The man who ran it mystified her. He was tall, dark-skinned, dark-eyed. He wore a red shirt which set off his foreign handsomeness. But it was not this which made his presence there unexpected. It was the pride of his carriage, and his delicate way of handling the laundry. He greeted Renate with colorful modulations of a voice trained to charm. He bowed as he greeted her. His hands were long-fingered, deft.

He folded the dry sheets as if he were handling lace tablecloths. He was aloof, polite, as if laundry were a country gentleman's natural occupation. He took money as if it were a bouquet. He returned change as if it were a glass of champagne.

He never commented on the weather, as if it were a plebeian interest. He piled up the laundry as if he were merely checking the contents of his own home's closets. He was proud and gracious. He pretended not to see the women who came in hair curlers, like a high born valet who overlooks his master's occasional lapse in manners.

For Renate he had a full smile. His teeth were strong and even but for one milk tooth which gave his smile a touch of humor.

Renate also handled her bundle of laundry as if it were pastry from a fashionable shop.

The rhythm of the machines became like the opening notes of an orchestra at a ball. She never mentioned the weather either, as if they both understood weather was a mere background to more important themes. They agreed that if human beings had to attend to soiled laundry, they had been given, at the same time, a faculty for detaching themselves, not noticing, or forgetting certain duties and focusing on how to enhance, heighten, add charm to daily living.

Renate would tell him about each visitor who had come to see her, describe each costume, each character, each conversation, and then hand over the bundle as if it were the discarded costumes which had to be re-glamorized for the next party. While she talked they both handled the guest towels from Woolworth's as if they were lace tablecloths from Brussels.

He looked over the bundles lined up on the shelf and ready to be called for as if he were choosing a painting in an art exhibition and said: "I always recognize yours by its vivid colors."

As his brown, fine-bred hand rested on the blue paper around the package, she noticed for the first time a signet ring on his finger. It was a gold coat-of-arms.

She bent over it to examine the symbols. The ring was divided into four sections. On one was engraved a lion's head, on the second a small castle, on the third a four-leaf clover, and on the fourth a Maltese cross.

"But I have seen this design somewhere," said Renate. "Could it have been on one of the shields on one of the statues in a Vienna park?"

"Yes, it could have been. I have some ancestors there. My family has a castle forty miles from Vienna. My parents still live there. The coat-of-arms is that of Count Osterling."

He brought out his wallet. Instead of photographs of round-faced babies she saw a turreted castle. Two dignified old people stood on the terrace. The man wore a beard. The woman carried an umbrella. One could see lace around her throat. Her hand rested on the head of a small boy.

"That is me."

Renate did not want to ask: and how did you come here, what are you doing here when you could be opening bottles of old vintage wine from your own property, sitting at beautiful dining tables and being waited on?

"After the war we were land poor. I felt our whole life growing static and difficult. Tradition prevented me from working at any job. I came to America. I went to Chicago. I was only seventeen and it was all new and elating. I felt like a pioneer. I liked forgetting the past and being able to work without feeling I was humiliating a whole set of relatives. I did all kinds of jobs. I liked the freedom of it. Then I met the Rhinegold Beauty Queen that year. She was unbelievably beautiful. I married her. I did not even know what her father did. Later I found out he owned a chain of laundromats. He put me to work as an inspector. At first we travelled a lot, but when he died we wanted to stay in one place and raise children. So we came here."

"You never went home again?"

"We did once, but my wife did not like it. She thought the castle was sad. She was cold, and the plumbing was not efficient. She didn't like so much politeness, motheaten brocades, yellowed silks, dust on the wine bottles."

Count Laundromat, she called him, as she watched the gold signet ring with the family coat-of-arms flashing through detergents.

An enormous woman appeared through the back door and called out to him. She was as tall and as wide as Mae West. The beautiful eyes, features and hair were deeply imbedded in cushions of flesh like a jewel in a feather bedspread.

"My wife," he said, to Renate, and to her he said: "This is a neighbor who once lived in Vienna."

Then he took up her bundle of laundry and carried it to the car, opened the door, fitted it in the seat with care that no piece should be caught when the door closed, as if it were the lacy edge of a petticoat.

From the day he told her the story of his title, the smell of kitchen soap, of wet linen, wet wool, detergents, became confused in Renate's nostrils with the smell of an antique cabinet she had once opened in a shop in Vienna.

The inside of the drawers were lined with brocade which was glued to the wood and which retained the smell of sandalwood. The past was like those old-fashioned sachet bags filled with herbs and flowers which penetrate the clothes and cling to them.

Everytime she visited Count Laundromat, the perfumes of the antique cabinet enveloped her, the smell of the rose petals her mother kept in a small music box, the smell of highly polished sandalwood of her sewing table, the vanilla of Viennese pastry, the pungent spices, the tobacco from her father's pipe, all these overpowered the detergents.

◈

While driving along Pacific Palisades, Renate had stopped several times to offer a lift to an old man with his arm in a sling. He was going to get his arm treated nearby and, very slowly, he unravelled his story to her.

He lived in Malibu, the place by the sea which the Indians called the Humped Mountain, and which in French, if you sang it, sounded like Evil Owl—*Mal Hibou,* Malibu.

When he was a young man he became a lifeguard at Will Rogers' beach. He sat on a chair twelve feet high and studied the moods of the sea. He had no need of weather bureaus. He knew by every undulation, every contortion, every flourish and flounce of the waves, the sea's exact mood and whether it would be treacherous for the swimmers, or tender and mocking. He knew the omens of the clouds, read the future in their colors and density. He knew the topography of the sand covered by the sea as if he had mapped its depths. From where he sat the cries of the gulls, of children and bathers all fused together and made a sound he liked, *musique concrète.* He had never been concerned with words.

He knew the entire coast, from Will Rogers' beach to where Malibu became wild and solitary.

He married and had children, but he was restless in the house. The static walls irked him. He did not like the smell of enclosure, of cooking, of wax, nor the sound of the vacuum cleaner. He missed the wind's flurries, and the spicy smells of the seashore. He felt entombed by the stillness of objects, the unchanging landscapes in frames. And the torrent of words spoken by his wife and children did not give him the stinging, whipping sense of aliveness he felt at the beach.

He returned to his old job as a lifeguard. But each evening he stayed longer at the beach. He liked it best when it was deserted, and when he would start walking homeward along the coast. He discovered the treasures of the sea which lay in the rock crevices, either thrown there by storms, or growing there. The humid, never-withering sea-lemon, the sea-lilies which did not close at night, the sea-lentils tied to giant Serpentine string beans, sea-liquor brine, sea-lyme grass, sea-moss, sea-cucumbers. He never knew the sea had such a lavish garden—sea-plumes, sea-grapes, sea-lace, sea-lungs.

In the summer he began to stay on after dark. He learned skin diving and stole crabs and lobsters people trapped. He cooked his dinner on the beach. He came home rarely.

The rocks were continually filled with surprises from ship-wrecks, and the nights with sounds which the regular rhythm of the sea orchestrated. The wind flung itself between the rocks, dishevelled, wrestled with the waves until one of them expired. The sky put on its own evanescent spectacles, a pivoting stage, fugitive curtains, decors for ballets, floating icebergs, unrolled bolts of chiffon, gold and pearl necklaces, marabous of oyster white, scarves of Indian saris, flying feathers, shorn lambs, geometric architecture in snows and cotton. His theater was the clouds, where no spectacle repeated itself.

On land he was a foreigner. Land for him was stasis, and it pulled him into immobility, which was his image of death.

One night he slept in one of the caves. He thought to himself: Now I am a merman.

He passed the time detecting mild sea-quakes, he made friends with the sea-lark, he collected sea-palms and made a rug of them for his cave. But some element was missing. The friendship of the sea-gulls was too ephemeral. Their visits were too short. They were always impatient to be off in space.

One night he walked on to the end of a natural rock jetty and came upon a shoal of seals. They swam, dived, clowned, but always crawled back to the rocks to have their young ones there. They kissed, barked, leaped, danced on their partly fused hind limbs. Their black eyes were like mirrors reflecting sea and sky, but the ogival shape of their eyelids gave them an air of compassion, almost as if they would weep with sympathy. Their tails were of little use except for swimming but they liked to shake their webbed-flipper-like limbs as if they were about to fly. Their fur shone like onyx, with dark blue shadows under the fins.

They greeted the man with cries of joy. By this time he was an old man. The sea had wrinkled his face so intricately, it was a surprise when his smile scattered the lines to shine through, like a beautiful glossy fish darting out of a fishing net.

The old man fed the seals, he settled near them in a cave, cooked his dinner, and rolled over and fell asleep with a new feeling of companionship.

One night several men came. They wanted to catch the seals for a display in a pool in front of their restaurant. A publicity stunt which attracted the children. But the pool was small, it was surrounded by barbed wire and the old man did not want this to happen to his seals. So he warned them by an imitation of their cry and bark, and they dove quickly into the sea. By the time the men reached the end of the jetty the seals were gone. From then on the old man felt he was their guardian. No one could get through at night without walking through his bedroom. In spite of the tap-dancing of the waves and the siren calls of the wind, the old man would hear the dangerous visitors and always had time to warn the seals in their own language.

The old man discovered the seal's names. They answered to Hilarious, Ebenezer, Ambrosius, Eulalee and Adolfo. But there was one seal whose name he did not know, who was too old when they first met. The old man did not have the courage to try out names on him, to see which one he answered to, for the seal could hardly move and it would have humiliated him.

One severe winter the old man's children began to worry about him, as he was growing old and rheumatic. One rainy day they came and forced him into their car, and took him to their home and fixed him up a bedroom.

The first night he slept on a bed, he fell off and broke his arm. As soon as his arm was well again he returned to the cave.

One night when he felt minor quakes were taking place in the area of his heart, he thought he was going to die, so he tried to crawl nearer to the seals, into the crevices where they slept. But they gently, compassionately, nosed him out of the place.

By then he resembled them so much, with his mustache, his rough oval eyebrows, his drooping eyelids, and his barking cough, that he thought they would help him to slide down the rocks and be buried at sea, like a true seal.

Varda lived on a converted ferry boat in Sausalito and sailed the bay in his own sail boat; so it was surprising to see him arrive at Paradise Inn in an old station wagon bringing his newest collages for an exhibition: "Collages are not sea-faring."

He unloaded them at the entrance and stood them up against the rocky banks in the sunlight. They eclipsed the sun, the sea and the plants. The laminated blues dimmed the refractions of the ocean and made it seem ponderous and opaque. His treble greens vibrated and made the plants seem dead and the flowers artificial. His shafts of gold made the sunrays pale.

With small pieces of cotton and silks, scissors and glue and a dash of paint, he dressed his women in irradiations; his colors breathed like flesh and the fine spun lines pulsated like nerves.

In his landscapes of joy, women became staminated flowers, and flowers women. They were as fragrant as if he had painted them with thyme, saffron and curry. They were translucent and airy, carrying their Arabian Night's cities like nebulous scarves around their lucite necks.

Sometimes they were masked like Venetian beauties at masquerades. They wore necklaces of solar meteorites, and earrings which sang like birds. Velvet petals covered their breasts and stared with enticing eyes. Orange tones played like the notes of a flute. Magenta had a sound of bells. The blues throbbed like the night.

After his scissors had touched them, his women became flowers, plants and sea shells.

He cut into all the legendary textiles of the world: damask of the Medicis, oyster white of Greek robes, the mixed gold and blue of Venetian brocades, the midnight blue wools of Peru, the sand colors of the African cottons, the transparent muslins of India, to give birth to women who only appear to men asleep. His women became comets, trailing long nebulous trains, erratic members of the solar system. He gave only the silver scale of their mermaid moods, the sea shell rose of their ear lobes, corollas, pistils, light as wings. He housed them in facades of tent shelters which could be put up for a moment and folded and vanished when desire expired.

"Nothing endures," said Varda, "unless it has first been transposed into a myth, and the great advantage of myths is that they are ladies with portable roots."

He often spoke of paradise. Paradise was a distillation of women panoplied with ephemeral qualities. His collages taught how to remain in a state of grace of love, extract only elixirs, transmute all life into lunisolar fiestas, and all women, by a process of cut-outs, to aphrodisiacs.

He was the alchemist searching only for what he could transmute into gold. He never painted homely women, jealous women, or women with colds. He dipped his brushes in pollen, in muteness, in honeymoons, and his women were interchangeable and mobile.

He allowed space and air in their bodies so they would not become too heavy, nor stay too long. He never depicted the death of a love, fatigue or boredom. Every collage was rich with a new harem, the constancy of illusion, fidelity to euphorias born of woman.

He took no time to weep over fadings or witherings; he was always mixing a new brew, a new woman, and when he sat at his large table, scissors in hand, searching for a new marriage of colors, a variation in triangles, in squares and semicircles, interweaving cupolas and breasts, legs and columns, windows and eyes on beds of pleasure, under tent of rituals of the flesh, each color became a music box.

He canonized his women, they bore the names of new brands of sainthood.

Saint Banality, who reigned over the artists who could take everyday objects and turn them into extraordinary ones, like the postman in France who built a castle out of the stones he found on his route every day; the shoe cleaner in Brooklyn who decorated his shoeshine box with medals, unmatched earrings, broken glass and silver paper to look like a Byzantine crown; the mason in Los Angeles who built towers out of broken cups, tiles, tea pots and washstands.

There was Saint Perfidia who knew how to destroy the monotony of faithfulness, and Saint Parabola who decorated with halos those whose stories no one could understand, and Saint Hyperbole who cured of boredom.

Saint Corona arrived at sunrise to wake him, and Saint Erotica visited him at night.

The women were interchangeable and flowed into one another

as in dreams. He admitted and loved all of them except women in black. "Black is for widows," he said, for the severe women who had raised him in Greece, for women in churches and women in cemeteries. Black was the absence of color.

He saw women as feathers, furs, meteorites, lace, campaniles, filigree; and so he was more amazed than other fathers to find his own daughter made of other substances like a colorless doll lying inside a magician's trunk, with eyes not quite blue, hair not quite gold, as if she had been the only one he had forgotten to paint.

When she was six years old he felt there was yet time, that it was merely because he had never painted children, and that his gift for painting women would become effective on the day of her womanhood. At seven years of age she listened to his stories and believed them, and he felt that with patience, luminosity and plumage would grow.

A tall, very strong woman came to visit Varda, and the gossips whispered that she was a gangster's moll. When she saw Varda's daughter she said: "Varda, would you mind if someday I kidnapped your daughter?"

This frightened her and every evening before going to bed she would ask: "She won't come and kidnap me while I'm asleep, will she?"

"No," said Varda, "she can't take you away without my permission, and I won't let her. She has tried to bribe me. She came this morning in a boat loaded with sacks of sugar and sacks of fruit (and you know how much I love them) to exchange for you and I said, 'No, I love my daughter and you can take back your sugar and your fruit.' "

The next evening at bedtime Varda said: "Today the kidnapper came with a hundred bottles of red wine (and you know how much I love wine) and I told her that I loved my daughter and didn't want any wine."

And the next evening he told her: "She was here with a hundred elephants (and you know how much I love elephants) and I sent her away."

Each day she awaited new proofs of her father's love. One day he turned down a hundred camels left over from a film, and then a hundred sacks of paint (and she knew how much Varda loved paint) and then a hundred sacks of bits of cloth for his collages, beautiful fragments from all over the world (and she knew how much he loved textiles).

And then Varda said one evening: "The kidnapper thought of the most diabolical offer of all. What do you think it was? She had a hundred little girls, just like you, with blue eyes and blond hair and willowy figures, and all fit for a harem and once again (though I was sorely tempted) I said, 'No, I love my own girl best of all.' "

But in spite of the stories, it was as if she had determined to grow contrary to all the women he loved. She let her hair fall as it willed, never brushing it to bring out the gloss. She wore faded jeans and greasy tennis sneakers. She shredded the edge of her jeans so they would look like those of beggars on the stage. She wore Varda's torn shirts and discarded sweaters and went out with boys more sullen and mute than herself.

On her fifteenth birthday when he expected a metamorphosis as spectacular as that of a butterfly, she wrote him a long reproachful letter from school asking him to give up "those women." She said that she would not stay with him anymore while those flashy, glittering women were about.

She doubted his prestidigitations with words, as if he were a stage magician, as if to say: "See, they have no effect on me. I do not believe in fairy tales. I am going to study science."

When she came on holiday Varda told her another story: "There was a woman from Albania who was famous for her beauty. A young man from America came, very handsome, slim and blond, and he paid court to her and said: 'I love you because you remind me of a cousin of mine I loved when I was in school. You also remind me of a movie actress I always adored on the screen. I love you. Will you marry me?' The Albanian girl took a small pistol out of her boot and shot him. When she was brought to trial the old Albanian judge listened with sympathy as she made her own defense. 'Your honor, I have been humiliated several times in my life.' 'How could that be,' said the judge, 'you are such a beautiful woman,' 'Yes, your honor, it has happened. I was humiliated the first time by a man who left me waiting in church when we were to be married. He was in a car accident, it is true, but still in my family there is a tradition of unfailing courtesy about marriage ceremonies. The second time I was told by a Frenchman that I was too fat. The third time I was "clocked" by a policeman on a motorcycle. He said I had been speeding and I contradicted him and he said he had "clocked" me. Imagine that. But, your honor, I never killed before. You know Albanian pride. Until this American came and told me I reminded him of two other women, and that, your honor, was too much. He offended my uniqueness.'"

She shrugged her shoulders. "Women in Albania do not carry pistols in their boots. And who wants to be unique anyway? It's a dated concept."

When she criticized modern painting he tried to explain the state of painting today.

"There was a painter who was asked to send his best painting to an exhibition and he accepted on condition that it would be curtained off until the day of the opening. This condition was accepted. The crowd came, quite a large one. His painting was the only one hidden behind a curtain in a box, and the last to be exposed. When the curtain was finally parted, the painting was a large square canvas, pure blank. Blank! The public was outraged. There were insults: 'Surrealist! Dadaist! Beatnik! Mutant!' Then the painter came forward and explained that he had painted a self-portrait and that his dog had found it such an exact likeness that he had licked it all off. But there had been a portrait, and this was merely the proof of the faithfulness of the likeness. And so, dear daughter, for those who are interested in progress, twenty years ago painting was judged by critics, and today it is judged by a dog. This is the state of painting today."

Varda also had a theory on uncouth manners which he told very often in the presence of his daughter's sulky visitors.

"This is a modernized version of the Princess and the Dragon. Today she would be the Imperial Valley Lettuce Queen and the young man could be anyone of you. The dragon had to be killed before the young man could marry the girl. The dragon had a corrugated skin, bluish and silvery and scaly like a mirror broken into a thousand small pieces. His eyes wept chronically. He spouted fire with the regularity of a lighter. The young man turned off the gas first and then cut off the dragon's head. He took the beauty queen brusquely by the arm and, pushing her ahead of him, said in a Humphrey Bogart style of speech: 'Oh, come on, we've wasted enough time on the old dragon. I've got a motel room waiting.' The queen looked at the expiring dragon weeping at her leaving, and suddenly she put her arms around the beast and said: 'I'll stay with him. I don't like the rough tone of your voice.' And as she encircled the scaly dragon, he turned into a young man handsomer and tenderer than the one she had jilted."

His daughter shrugged her shoulders, blew into her bubble gum of a pink Varda had never in all his life conceded to use, counted her new freckles, and went back to her science homework.

She was chewing the end of her pencil while she studied a chemical which produced visions and hallucinations. She read to her father in a flat-toned voice the effect of consciousness-expanding chemicals.

"Colors breathe and emit light."

"But my colors do that," said Varda.

"Figures dissolve into one another and appear at times transparent."

"As they do in my collages," said Varda.

"Someone saw whirling clouds, suns and moons," she read in the same voice as she might have read: "Imperial Valley produced 20,000 head of lettuce."

"As in the paintings of Van Gogh," said Varda. "What need of chemicals?"

"But when you take a chemical you know it will affect you for only a few hours and then you will return to normality. You can control it, modify it, you can even stop its effects if you wish to, if you don't like what is happening to you."

"In other words, a return ticket," said Varda.

"The next day the world is back again in its proper place, the real colors are back."

"Doesn't that prove that when you remove an inhibiting consciousness and let men dream they all dream like painters or poets?"

"But you dream all the time, whereas a pill is more scientific."

Perhaps science would illumine his cautious child. Perhaps by way of a chemical she might respond, vibrate, shine? He watched the eyelashes pulled down like shades, the ears covered by hair, the lips parsimonious of words.

What had he absorbed through the years which had opened these worlds to him which others sought in mushrooms? Where had he learned the secret of phosphorescence, of illumination, of transfiguration? Where had he learned to take the shabbiest materials and heighten them with paint, alter their shapes with scissors?

"What I wanted to teach you is contained in one page of the dictionary. It is all the words beginning with *trans*: transfigure, transport, transcend, translucent, transgression, transform, transmit, transmute, transpire, all the trans-Siberian voyages."

"You forgot the word transvestite."

"When I was ten years old I made up my first story."

"I'm going to be late for my expanding-consciousness lecture!"

"This is a very short story. It's about a blind old man who had a daughter. This daughter described to him every day the world they lived in, the people who came to see him, the beauty of their house, garden, friends. One day a new doctor came to town and he cured the old man's blindness. When he was able to see, he discovered they had been living in a shack, on an empty lot full of debris, that their friends had been hobos and drunks. His daughter was crying, thinking he would die of shock, but his reaction was quite the opposite. He said to her: 'It is true that the world you described does not exist but as you built that image so carefully in my mind and I can still see it so vividly, we can now set about to build it just as you made me see it.' "

His daughter remained neutral, and as silent as her rubbersoled tennis shoes. She hung her long legs over the edge of the deck and swung them like a boy. She dissected snails.

"Such cruelty," said Varda.

"Not at all," she said with a newborn scientist's arrogance. "They have no nervous system."

Meanwhile Varda continued to make collages as some women light votive candles. With scissors and glue and small pieces of fabrics, he continued to invent women who glittered, charmed, levitated and wore luminous aureoles like saints. But his daughter resisted all her father's potions, as if she had decided from the day she was born never to become one of the women he cut out in the shape of circles, triangles, cubes, to suit the changing forms of his desires.

And the one day after she had been away for a few days she wrote Varda the following letter:

"Before I took the chemical called L.S.D., it was as if light, color, smell and touch could not reach me. It was as if I were outside looking through glass. But that day (I think it was the second time) I was finally *inside.* I looked at the rug on the floor and it was no longer a plain rug but a moving and swaying mass like hair floating on water or like wind over a field of wheat. The door knob ceased to be a plain door knob. It melted and undulated and the door opened and all the walls and windows vanished. There was a tremor of life in everything. The once static objects in the room all flowed into a fluid and mobile and breathing world. The dazzle of the sun was multiplied, every speck of gold and diamond in it magnified. Trees, skies, clouds, lawns began to breathe, heave and waver like a landscape at the bottom of the sea. My body was both swimming and flying. I felt gay and at ease and playful. There was perfect communicability between my body and everything surrounding me. The singing of the mocking-birds was multiplied, became a whole forest of singing birds. My senses were multiplied as if I had a hundred eyes, a hundred ears, a hundred fingertips. On the walls appeared endless murals of designs I made which produced their own music to match. When I drew a long orange line it emitted its own orange tone. The music vibrated through my body as if I were one of the instruments and I felt myself becoming a full percussion orchestra, becoming green, blue, orange, gold. The waves of the sounds ran through my hair like a caress. The music ran down my back and came out my fingertips. I was a cascade of red blue rainfall, a rainbow. I was small, light, mobile. I could use any method of levitation I wished. I could dissolve, melt, float, soar. Wavelets of light touched the rim of my clothes, phosphorescent radiations. I could see a new world with my middle eye, a world I had missed before. I caught images behind images, the walls behind the sky, the sky behind the Infinite. The walls became fountains, the fountains became arches, the arches domes, the domes sky, the sky a flowering carpet, and all dissolved into pure space. I looked at a slender line curving over space which disappeared into infinity. I saw a million zeroes on this line, curving, shrinking in the distance, and I laughed and said 'Excuse me, I am not a mathematician.' How can I measure the infinite? But I understand it. The zeroes vanished. I was standing on the rim of a planet, alone. I could hear the fast rushing rounds of the planets rotating in space. Then I was among them, and I was aware that a certain skill was necessary to handle this new means of transportation. The image of myself standing in space and trying to get my 'sea legs' or my 'space legs' amused me. I *wondered who had been there before me* and whether I could return to earth. The solitude distressed me, so I returned to my starting point. I was standing in front of an ugly garden door. But as I looked closer it was not plain or green but it was a Buddhist temple, a Hindu colonnade, Moroccan mosaic ceiling, gold spires being formed and re-formed as if I were watching the hand of a designer at work. I was designing spirals of red unfurled until they formed a rose window or a *mandala* with edges of radium. When one design was barely born and arranged itself, it dissolved and the next one followed without confusion. Each form, each line emitted its equivalent in music in perfect accord with the design. An undulating line emitted a sustained undulating melody, a circle had a corresponding musical notation, diaphanous colors, diaphanous sounds, a pyramid created a pyramid of ascending notes, and vanishing ones left only an echo. These designs were preparatory sketches for entire Oriental cities. I saw the temples of Java, Kashmir, Nepal, Ceylon, Burma, Cambodia, in all the colors of precious stones illumined from within. Then the outer forms of the temples dissolved to reveal the inner chapel and shrines. The reds and the gold inside the temples created an intricate musical orchestration like Balinese music. Two sensations began to torment me: one that it was happening too quickly and that I would not be able to remember it, another *that I would not be able to tell what I saw,* it was too elusive and too overwhelming. The temples grew taller, the music wilder, it became a tidal wave of sounds with gongs and bells predominating. Gold spires emitted a long flute chant. Every line and color was breathing and constantly mutating. The smoke of my cigarette became gold. The curtain on the window became gold. Then I felt my whole body becoming gold, liquid gold, scintillating warm gold. I *was gold.* It was the most pleasurable sensation I have ever known and I knew it was like passion. It was the secret of life, the alcemist's secret of life.

"When I gradually returned from this dream-like experience I was in your studio. I looked around at your collages and recognized them. It was as if I had been there for the first time. I saw the colors, the luminosity and the floating, mobile, changeable quality. I understood all your stories, and all you had said to me. I could see why you had made your women transparent, and the houses open like lace so that space and freedom could blow through them."

When she came home on vacation, she had emerged from her grey cocoon. She was now sixteen and sending forth her first radiations and vibrations dressed in Varda's own rutilant colors.

The bell rang. It was Doctor Mann with flowers for Lisa and a cigar for Bill.

He was collecting paintings to exhibit in Israel. He wanted to borrow some of Lisa's Mexican paintings.

He had heard about Renate's paintings and said he would be proud to take some back with him.

But he was not a painting fetichist. His particular hobby was quite exceptional.

Once a year Doctor Mann flew from Israel on a mysterious mission. But his leisure time he spent in visiting women writers. One by one he visited them all. He brought them brandy and chocolates from Israel, books to sign for his collection of autographed editions, and kissed them only once on parting.

He boasted of these friendships as other men boast of sexual conquests.

Many of these visits required patience, diplomacy and research work. First of all, to find their addresses, and then someone who might introduce him, and then to obtain an appointment, and, most difficult of all, to gain the privilege of a tête-à-tête.

His hair grew grey. His library of dedicated books was rich in treasures.

Just as Don Juan was always eager to test his charm on frigid women, Doctor Mann finally encountered the most inaccessible of all women writers and felt challenged to woo her.

He heard that Judith Sands was not only difficult to meet but that she avoided everyone related to the literary world. She led a secluded life in the Village, New York, and it was rumored that she preferred obscure village bars and anonymous company.

A few bar addicts vaguely remembered talking with a woman called Judith Sands but they insisted that she talked like a truck driver and could not possibly have written the poetic and stylized mythological novel she was praised for.

Those who lived in Paris before the war remembered a handsome, red-haired amazon in a tailored suit who sat at the Dôme.

A few who lived in the Village knew her, but no one had anything to say, no revelations, no messages, as if those who knew her practiced a sick room secrecy, as if she had sealed their lips. There was an unnatural silence around her, either because she had satirized everyone, which she was known to do, or because those who respected her work did not wish to expose a Judith who did not resemble her parabolic work.

Several of the flat-soled women in tailored suits who walked down Eighth Street could have been Judith Sands. In an age of glaring, crude limelight, she had been able to avoid all familiarity, and her anonymity was preserved by an invisible repellent.

It was as if her novel had been the story of an earthquake by one of its victims; the book once written, and the author with it, seemed to have fallen into a crevice.

This shadowy figure aroused Doctor Mann's love of conquest.

He bought a bottle of champagne and rushed to the address he had been given. There was no name on the bell to the apartment, but he had been told that she lived on the second floor. Doctor Mann climbed the dark stairway and knocked on a dark door. No answer.

He waited and knocked again.

Silence.

He paced the frayed rug. He stared with an ironic smile at the empty niche where the stairway made a turn. When the Village was Italian, the statue of a saint had nestled there. He sat down inside the niche and waited. His ear caught a rustle inside, and it was enough to encourage his verbal gallantry.

He began an interminable monologue like one of the characters in her novel.

Every novelist knows that at one time or another he will be confronted with the incarnation of one of his characters. Whether that character is based on a living person or not, it will draw into its circle those who resemble it. Sooner or later the portrait will attract its twin, by the magnetism of narcissism, and the author will feel this inhabitant of his novel come to life and hear his character speaking as he had imagined.

And so, Doctor Mann, in the same fast liquid monologue she had set down, picked up his own story in Siberia where he had been sent for rebellion against the régime, and where there was nothing to nourish him except books; where his faith in woman's intuitive knowledge had made him translate Judith Sand's book into Hebrew; from there to his American wife and children in a modern apartment in Israel and his work with a newspaper which put him in touch with all the plays and books being written. "You know, my dear Judith Sands, I am not here to frighten you, or violate your privacy. I am not a man visiting a woman. I am a man with profound love of words. In the words of the Talmud: 'Kaka'tuv...It is written.' I know you do not like strangers; but, just as you are no stranger to me, I cannot be a stranger to you because I feel that, in a sense, you gave birth to me. I feel you once described a man who was *me* before I knew who I was, and it was because I recognized him that I was able to be myself. You will recognize me when you see me. I am sure you have already recognized how I think; this mixture in me which makes me feel my way through experience as women do, and yet talk even when I do not wish to talk like an intellectual, a scholar (which is mockery as I do not believe that they know as much as the poet in his delirium). I have grown grey hairs waiting to meet you. I could not find your address or anyone who knew you. Then a taxi driver told me he had just driven uptown a woman who talked as I did, with a man with an English accent, and he said they were going to the opening of his cocktail party; and then I knew you were in New York and had been with T. S. Eliot. Every word you wrote I ate, as if it were manna. Finding one's self in a book is a second birth; and you are the only one who knows that at times men behave like women and women like men, and that all these distinctions are mock distinctions, and that is why your doctor put on a wig when he wanted to talk about his loves, and I don't know why Thomas Mann wrote about Transposed Heads for there are other transpositions of far greater interest, and your story is the most accurate in the world."

No answer.

But there was a creak of a chair and a soft footstep on the floor behind the door.

Doctor Mann added: "I am leaving my gifts to you on the door mat. I hope you like champagne."

"I don't drink," said a low, deep voice behind the closed door.

"Well, you can offer it to your friends. Tomorrow I fly back to Israel at nine in the evening. I will come again at five o'clock. Perhaps you will open your door to a man who is going away. And you will see I am no stranger. Remember this, it is good for a writer to meet with the incarnation of a character he has invented. It gives him an affirmation, a substantial proof of his intuitions, divinations. Here I stand before you, talking as you said I might, and reminding you that what may have seemed a ghost in a dream, in your smoke-filled heart at night, is a man who got his knowledge and his degrees from books in a cell in Siberia, and who translated you by the light of a candle."

"Come back tomorrow. We'll have coffee together," said the voice.

The next day he came. But there was no answer to his knock and so he began his monologue: "When you deny me the presence of a writer, you really deny me a part of myself that has not yet been born, and whose existence I need to believe in. I always wanted to be a writer, but I talk too much, it evaporates, or it may be I have not yet decided whether to write as a man or as a woman. But you have been my writer self writing for me. I could talk wastefully, negligently, only because you were there preserving and containing my spirit. When you deny me your presence, you commit spiritual murder, for if I have been for years talking with your words, spending them lavishly, extravagantly, it was only because I believed I could always renew myself at the source. You may feel this was an imposition. No one should be forced to carry the unfulfilled self of another. But if you are so skilled with works and have already written *me,* in a sense you have stolen *me,* and must return what you stole. You must come out and say: 'I will go on writing for you, I will be your articulateness. I gave birth to you and I must grant you the fullest expansion of speech.' And you need me, Judith Sands. You must not stifle yourself behind closed doors. Solitude may rust your words. Silence is not your element. It will asphyxiate you. We need each other! We are indispensable to each other. I to your work and you to my life. Without me spending your words you may not be incited to mint new ones. I am the spendthrift and you the coiner. We cannot live completely apart. And if I speak your character on perhaps a lower key than you had intended, even perhaps with a few false notes, it is because I have never met a writer with perfect pitch. If you refuse to talk to a plain man like me, your ambiguities will become intolerably tenuous, like the end of your book, which I do not understand."

The door opened halfway. Judith Sands appeared shadowed against the light. Behind her, a chaotic lair, indistinguishable objects in wild disorder. She closed the door upon her cavernous dwelling and gave Doctor Mann her strong, firm hand.

"I am not absolutely certain of the meaning of that end to my book, but I am sure of one thing, that human beings can reach such desperate solitude that they may cross a boundary beyond which words cannot serve, and at such moments there is nothing left for them but to *bark.*"

As they walked together Doctor Mann asked: "Is it true what they say that you have written another book, that you keep it hidden in cartons under your bed, that no one has read it?"

"Yes, it is true."

"Why won't you let it be read, published? It will shatter your solitude."

"No, it will only aggravate it. The more they read of me, the louder they deny my existence, the existence of my characters. They say I have only described unique specimens."

"But I can show you these specimens reproduced themselves. They are scattered over the world. I will take you to the places where I know your book is a perpetual house guest, always sitting in the library, a guest of honor. You will only meet those who nourished themselves on it, the descendants of your characters."

Doctor Mann observed how carefully Judith Sands had sought to efface in herself all traces of having been the woman once so wildly loved in her own novel. She had created a neutral appearance, wearing colors one would not notice nor remember, anonymous clothes, a cape which concealed the lines of her body, a Tyrolian hat with a feather on it. The feather, however, had retained its impertinence, from the days when she won every tournament with her wit.

"Solitude," said Doctor Mann, "is like Spanish moss which finally suffocates the tree it hangs on."

"Don't you think I have thought of that whenever someone slips a piece of paper under my door saying 'I love you Judith Sands'; don't you think I ask myself if this is another come to love me and also destroy me? Another one staying out all night and with each step away from me wearing out the soles of my heart with waiting? Or another come to steal my own image of me and expose it to the world, distorted of course? Or another come to resuscitate parts of me which I have already buried?"

"But you and those you loved have children scattered all over the world. They are descendants in direct line from your creations. Aren't you curious about them?"

"You can fly now and pay later. Jet by Alitalia, Bonanza, Lan Chile, the Comet Service, the Flying Tiger, Slick Airways, El Israel, Futura. You have your choice of names. Oh, I forgot the Pink Cloud Flights. We will visit only those who kept your book on the top shelf hidden from their parents, those who read it in other languages, in Dutch, Italian, German, Japanese, Yugoslavian, Hungarian, Russian, Flemish; those who read it and pretended they never heard of it but proceeded to live their lives oriented by its flow; those who succumbed to its contagion and searched for a similar atmosphere as if it were the only air they could breathe in; those who fell in love with your characters and searched for their counterparts. Those who quoted it to each other as a password to enter a unique and exclusive world. We will only go where your book is a part of the furniture."

"What is going on tonight that we don't have to get on a jet to see?"

"I will take you to see Tinguely's Machine that Destroys Itself."

"I thought only dreamers destroyed themselves."

As they hailed a taxi she raised her head and watched a plane flying above them leaving a trail of smoke which took the shape of words: SEE THE GREATEST STORY EVER TOLD.

The courtyard of the Museum of Modern Art in New York; a winter night; the snow had already fallen; a blue mist came up from the pavement as if it were breathing.

In the courtyard of the museum stood a floodlighted pile of objects one could not at first identify, a pile of objects such as one might find in a junkyard: an old piano, a broken bicycle, a child's carriage with only three wheels, a broken ladder with only half its rungs, punctured tires, soap boxes, old bottles, odd pieces of machinery like those of an automobile cemetery.

The entire pile was painted chalk white; it looked like a mound of debris covered by snow. Hung on the scaffolding were large bottles of colored chemicals. A giant roll of paper hung ready to unroll, like a newspaper going through a printing press. A giant brush hung poised over it to write on it as on a ticker tape.

The entire structure was wired and several men were still testing the connections which would set it in motion. A huge balloon topped the edifice, and a torn umbrella opened over a fire extinguisher.

The public began to wander in, to stumble over the TV wires, to be blinded by flash bulbs.

In the icicle blue night the floodlights looked orange. Smoke came from everyone's mouths as they talked.

There was a tussle between a museum guard and a camera man who had climbed on one of the valuable statues and rested his camera bag on a valuable naked arm. Faces were violently lighted, cameras whirred, the wired structure seemed about to totter, the snow melted.

The fire chief in his uniform looked solemn and concerned.

Tinguely himself was smiling and calm. When he had dragged his machines through the streets of Paris for an exhibition, had he not been arrested as the suspected designer of a new kind of destructive, death-dealing instrument?

There was a rumble as of an advancing earthquake. Clattering, steaming, hiccoughing, vibrating, puffing, hissing, juggling, dislocating, trembling, the entire structure went into a spasm which opened the bottles of chemicals, and they exploded into colored smoke which filled the balloon with air, set the roll of paper unrolling and the brush painting erratically the names of the artists like stock market quotations. But before the list was finished, the roll of paper rolled backwards, perversely, and swallowed the names in desperate inversion.

The child's carriage detached itself from the mass of shaking, sputtering, burning structure, as if it wished to escape destruction. It rolled towards one of the spectators as if looking for a child in the audience. It carried a drum which played automatically. And then it returned, as if hypnotized by electronic umbilical cords, resigned to its fate, unable to escape. It made one more sortie towards the spectator, one more appeal from its drum, an appeal for life, and inevitably rolled back into the pyre.

The piano started to burn slowly, and as it burned the notes played wistfully, out of tune, unreal, like a pianola. The flames consumed the wood but not the notes and not the wires. The notes played like the cry of trapped music, hollow, expiring.

The whole structure rattled erratically, in counter-rhythms, steaming senselessly, all motions in reverse, each interfering with another, negating it, inverted activity, bending and twisting and tearing at itself, introverted activity ending sometimes in a dead-lock so that the fire was allowed to spread more quickly. The ladder trembled, lost a few rungs, fell. The balloon at the very tip of the structure, a huge orange balloon, gasped and burst. The chemicals smoked green, orange and blue.

The paper with the names of artists unrolled again, a few more names were added, and then it swallowed them all again, finally catching fire.

It seemed at times like an infernal factory in which every operation had gone mad, in which the levers and buttons did the opposite of what they were designed to do, all the mechanisms reversed.

The fire devoured one more note of the piano, and only three notes were left playing. Then two. Then one which would not die.

The fire chief stood by, preoccupied, wondering at which moment the suicide of the machine would become an attempt to overthrow the government.

Smoke and winter's breath met in mid-air. The snow melted at the edges, but the white paint did not.

The piano played the last will and testament of a dying piano. The public pressed closer to hear its last melody. The fire chief picked up the fire extinguisher.

At this point the artist protested against the interrupted climax. The public hissed the fire chief. The artist said everything was under control, but the fire chief did not believe him. He began to extinguish the fire.

One more explosion of an orange chemical, one more balloon bursting, one more umbrella closing mournfully, one more piece of wood falling to the ground, one more tire rolling out of the pulsing machine, epilepsy of tin, turmoil, one more gasp, one more twist of metal, one more hiccough.

The fire chief interfered with the drama. He retarded the process. If the ladder had not burned he would have climbed on it to rescue the piano, the baby carriage. Suicide is illegal.

The skeleton of the mischievous dinosaur of the dump heap did not collapse; its suicide was about to fail. The artist gave a quick, discreet kick to the last supporting beam and then it collapsed, and the public moved closer to the smoking remains, picking up fragments for souvenirs, dismantling.

What the photographers caught was the kick.

The crowd dispersed. The newspapermen went off to write their copy. Each person carried a piece of the white debris. Doctor Mann had rescued the roll of paper with the signatures of artists which had not burned. The name of Judith Sands was among them. As they stood in the corner hailing a taxi, Renate and Bruce came out of the revolving door. Renate recognized Doctor Mann. When Doctor Mann introduced Judith Sands, Renate flung her arms around her.

"I love your book so much I have worn it down with readings; it looks like a pack of cards worn out by a gypsy fortune teller."

"We wanted to rescue the piano," said Renate. "I felt it still had a song in it. I didn't want to rescue anything dead."

"Let's sit somewhere and have a drink, and read the roll of artists' names."

Judith Sands said in a slightly rough voice: "Come back to my place. I have something to show you."

They followed her. In the dimly lit apartment they could only see paintings on the walls and many books. The only light came from a desk lamp. Judith Sands without taking her cape off, went to the couch, nudged two cats off who had been sleeping on it, got on her knees, pulled out a carton overflowing with papers, pulled out a bunch which had been clipped together and gave it to Renate to read.

It began:

"Vienna was the city of statues. They were as numerous as the people who walked the streets. They stood on the tip of the highest towers, lay down on stone tombs, sat on horseback, kneeled, prayed, fought animals and wars, danced, drank wine and read books made of stone..."

NON-FICTION

from # *D. H. Lawrence: An Unprofessional Study*

EXPERIENCES

Lawrence approaches his characters not in a state of intellectual lucidity but in one of *intuitional reasoning.* His observation is not *through the eyes but through the central physical vision*—or instinct. His analysis is not one of the mind alone, but of the senses.

In his characters there is usually a double current of life: there is the act of living with corresponding articulateness, and there is also the *articulateness of dreams,* in symbols.

He recognized a deep, subterranean connection between what he called the "dark gods" in us, entirely apart from the sophistries of the intelligence. Lawrence had divined that the intelligence is a juggler, an adroit juggler who can make everything balance and fall right. But the "dark gods" are instinctive, undeceived, undeceivable. They are intent on that flow of blood-life. We have tried to deceive them in our modern life. We have felt mind, the juggler, omnipotent. Lawrence is hostile to the juggler.

> And don't, with the nasty, prying mind, drag it
> (sex) out from its deeps
> and finger it and force it, and shatter the rhythm it keeps
> when it's left alone, as it stirs and rouses and sleeps.
> ["Sex Isn't Sin," *Complete Poems*]

(The deeps are also the "darkness." There is "beauty and dignity in the darkness.")

From *D. H. Lawrence: An Unprofessional Study* (Swallow, 1964), pp. 18-37.

When the realization came to the moderns of the importance of vitality and warmth, they willed the warmth with their minds. But Lawrence, with the terrible flair of the genius, sensed that a mere mental conjuring of the elemental was a perversion.

So here are his people struggling to achieve *complete life* and a sincere understanding of the gods in the *center of our bodies.*

Lawrence believed that the feelings of the body, from its most extreme impulses to its smallest gesture, are the warm root for true vision, and from that warm root can we truly grow. The livingness of the body was natural; the interference of the mind had created divisions, the consciousness of wrong-doing or well-doing.

Imprisoned in our flesh lives the body's own genie, which Lawrence set out to liberate. He found the body had its own dreams, and that by listening attentively to these dreams, by surrendering to them, the genie can be evoked and made apparent and potent.

He well knew that often the body's dreams come out in awkward or ugly forms. Many modern realistic novels showed to what triteness these dreams had dwindled—pitiful, graceless attempts.

Lawrence was patient. He gave his characters time (*The Lost Girl*). They are to find their own way and hour of resurrection. It was very slow, this gaining of confidence in the wisdom of the body. So Lawrence was patient, through a maze of timidities, retractions, blunders, awkwardnesses.

In *Sun* a woman gives herself to the sun, and is "vivified." Her body now *walks* beautifully, and her soul is realized. The life-flow stirred in her is a state of grace. The object to which her realization now urges the woman is unimportant. With the creator's strange indifference to personalities, Lawrence pursues a more important creation. It does not matter that the woman in *Sun* now desires a peasant. It matters that the woman now *desires.* Lawrence raises us to a plane of vital, impersonal creation and recreation.

Why should not an impulse be wise, or wisdom become impulsive? "Real knowledge comes out of the whole corpus..." [*Lady Chatterley's Lover*]

Life is a process of *becoming,* a combination of states we have to go through. Where people fail is that they wish to elect a state and remain in it. This is a kind of death.

Did Lawrence remain in this state of physical consciousness, in the mere efflorescence of his blood-life? No. We shall see later how he progressed from this point in his own way.

Meanwhile he did want to bring us into the plenitude of this physical state so that from there we could go along with him. But at the very first step of his philosophy he encountered opposition. *The Rainbow* was burned by the authorities.

In himself he was utterly convinced of the soundness of his philosophy. No man ever wavered less in his convictions. But he was waiting for the world to catch up with him and so he remained long on this first ground, propounding, pleading, emphasizing and re-emphasizing his ideas. This accounts for much in his work that seems redundant and over-emphatic.

But there was another reason.

Lawrence had been educated a Christian, the neutral, inoffensive (to society), restrained kind. He himself has found it very difficult to express his "primordial flow." In the world about him the mind and the will were supreme, and it required something like a miracle to reestablish confidence in the wisdom of the flesh.

His accents, while those of a man who knew how deeply right he was, exposed the relentless struggle within himself to throw off the mind and the will he was born with and to let the miracle accomplish itself in him.

In *Kangaroo,* where Lawrence himself is most revealed, there are curious pages.

Somers (Lawrence) and Harriet see Jack and Victoria, the next-door neighbors, openly express their feelings for each other:

> Victoria looked up with a brightly-flushed face, entirely unashamed, her eyes glowing like an animal's. Jack relaxed his grip on her but did not rise [to accompany the Somers who are leaving].

And the Somers leave precipitately, and with distaste:

> "Well," said Harriet, "I think they might have waited just two minutes before they started their love making. After all, one doesn't want to be implicated, does one?"

And Somers agrees.

This is a most un-pagan reaction. It is revelation of hypersensitiveness and self-consciousness which is in clear contradiction with Lawrence's philosophy. But it is true to his feelings.

There is another moment when Somers realizes that Victoria is silently offering herself to him. But he refuses:

> Why not follow the flame, the moment sacred to Bacchus? Why not if it was the way of life? He did not know why not. Perhaps only old moral habit. It was Victoria's high moment—; all her high moments would have this Bacchic weapon-like momentaneity: Should not a man know the whole range? *But his heart of hearts was stubbornly puritanical.*

When William Blake was constructing his world he made no attempt to exteriorize his imaginings in his own life; he knew that the time had not come. His life would have been a failure, and unconvincing. His poetry and prose had been flung out beyond his own boundaries, to *future generations.* He was content to live as others did, to go on perfecting his prophecies and his visions.

The very nature of Lawrence's philosophy, on the other hand, forbade any attempt on his part at detachment. His convictions were the emanations of a *life deeply lived* through all its failures and contradictions. He was personally involved. And this personal presence that we feel in Lawrence's world gives it a warmth lacking in other prophets. He gave much of his strength; and over and over again he exposed himself recklessly to bitter criticism and hostility because he would not evade the last test of his sincerity. He gave of his own blood. The denial and detachment of Blake is a sacrifice. But so is the giving of blood.

Lawrence had that quality of genius which makes a man realize experiences unknown to other men.

Middleton Murry tells us in his *Reminiscences of D.H. Lawrence* that Lawrence wanted "men who would understand a bit along with him . . . it was beyond the experience of his friends to go along with him." Murry admits that "somewhere in ourselves we were set against the experiences he wanted us to partake . . . there were realms of experiences, which Lawrence knew, which I had not entered. Even now I cannot pretend that the fearful struggle between Anna Lensky and Will Brangwen in *The Rainbow* is a thing I understand."

Had Lawrence detached himself so much from current human problems that he could not be understood by the intelligent men of his time? Precisely that. He detached himself from the current human problems which current writers could fathom.

There was an unknown world within the known. He had a vision. Will it take us one hundred years to understand Lawrence's vision as it took us one hundred years to understand Blake's?

What were those experiences his friends could not enter with him?

Anna Lensky and Will Brangwen marry. They spend their honeymoon alone in a cottage, absorbed in each other. It is all blissful, and soothing, and complete. He discovers all kinds of little traits in her that he likes; she in him. Her blitheness is a balm to him. He feels that he is born anew:

> He surveyed the rind of the world: houses, factories, trams, the discarded rind; people scurrying about, work going on, all on the discarded surface. An earthquakc (the marriage) had burst it all from the inside. It was a if the surface of the world had been broken away entirely: Ilkeston, streets, church people, work, rule-of-the-day, all intact; and yet peeled away into unreality, leaving here exposed the inside, the reality: one's own being, strange feelings and passions and yearnings and beliefs and aspirations, suddenly become present, revealed to the permanent bedrock, knitted one rock with the woman one loved.

Thus he is dreaming. But Anna is suddenly roused to activity and wants to give a tea party:

> The wonder was going to pass away again. All the love, the magnificent new order was going to be lost, she would forfeit it all for the *outside things.* She would admit the outside world again, she would throw away the living fruit for the ostensible rind. *He began to hate this in her.*

It is not the tea party: Will could not hate her because she wants to give a tea party. But in the light of deeper values, the tea party is a disaster. It reveals to Will that Anna loves the *outside* things. Now this is important. It indicates a whole difference between them. He senses the portentousness of it, senses the division which will take place later. To a mere tea party the reaction is excessive. As a symbol, it is comprehensible. Women have always done their reasoning and drawn inferences from such *trifles*. It has been termed pettiness. Women are intuitive: the trifle is an ominous sign, a direct warning of a greater issue ahead. It is the betraying ripple on the surface. Man's logic is against *a priori* deductions from isolated trifles. But that is the way women "reason" and Lawrence employs the same method.

Now Will is deeply disappointed, and Anna does not understand why.

"His soul grew blacker" and he is hard, recoiled. Now she is hurt in her own sensitiveness, and infers the existence in him of a darkness, recoil, and hardness, which frighten her.

Finally when she cries they kiss and are reconciled, but the struggle has been violent, not in proportion to the event, but in proportion to that conflict beginning in them.

They go to church together.

In church he "wanted a dark, nameless emotion, the emotion of all the great mysteries of passion . . . She could not get out of church the satisfaction that he did . . . Her mind is set against mystic experience." So she is exasperated because he has a power to escape from her into ecstasy. She moves about, drops her glove, knocks him, to annoy and arouse him. And she does not know why she is angry.

Later he is looking over illuminated books of symbolical images. She jeers at his absorption.

"He was partly ashamed of the ecstasy into which he could throw himself with these symbols . . ." But her laughter and indifference to them is agony to him. He hates her again. He leaves her alone. But when he comes back, black and surly, his anger has abated. "She had broken a little of something in him."

Physical love unites them again.

We are far from the tea party, but the tea party was the beginning of the same conflict. And now it is set deeper.

They are enemies, as many men and women in love with each other are enemies. Making use of their love, the blood-connection, to assert their will over each other, or to alter each other's inner world.

"They fought an unknown battle, unconsciously. Still they were in love with each other . . ." Because their love is in danger of death, the struggle is fierce in them:

> She wanted to be happy, to be natural, like the sunlight and the busy daytime . . . And he wanted her to be dark, unnatural.

"Dark" and "unnatural" are Anna's way of describing the thoughtfulness, the deep feelings of her husband.

"She had thought him just the bright reflex of herself."

There is much cruelty, and moments of partial understanding.

"Then he loved her for her childishness and for her strangeness to him, for the wonder of her soul which was different from his soul . . ."

Only a moment. "She begins to combat his deepest feelings." She scoffs at miracles, and he "tastes of death . . . Because his life was formed in these unquestioned precepts."

They irritate, torture each other.

When she begins to bear him children, she is Anna Victrix. He cannot combat her anymore. And she lapses into vague content:

> She was not with him. . . . A pang of insufficiency would go over him as he heard her talking to the baby. . . . He stood near, listening, and his heart surged, surged to rise and submit. *Then it shrank back and stayed aloof.* He could not move, a denial was upon him, as if he could not deny himself. He must, *he must be himself.*

The struggle never ends. The humanness in Anna is also a glowing thing, which attracts him. He wishes he could understand, or at least be wholly satisfied.

All this is easily translated as the projection of the little things of life into their larger significance, as we begin to see below the surface and become altogether conscious.

But there remains unexplained the intensity of Lawrence's description of these experiences. They are important, profound, but must the style be so tense, the expressions so extreme? Do people really swing from one extreme emotion to another in so short a span? We know that poets do.

Lawrence is giving his characters an extreme sensibility, the power of the poets; see how they can fall into mystic trances in church, can flare into demoniac anger, brood, or pass rapidly from despair to bliss. "—Life always a dream, or a frenzy," to the poet.

Lawrence often probes so intensely the significance of persons or events that they are sometimes deformed out of their normal shapes and become abstractions. But this habit of deformation of the normal is merely poetic means to an end, an end which is understanding. Through the intensity of his emotion for the smaller he divines the meaning of the greater. This is a justification for what at first glance may seem exaggerated or even obsessional.

For the same reason Lawrence does not create what we generally understand by a "character," that is, a definitely outlined being who bears a resemblance to those we know. He does not give such a clear outline because the personages in his books are symbolical; he is more preoccupied with the states of consciousness and with subconscious acts, moods, and reactions. His characters act by deeper and more chaotic motives than those in ordinary novels: they are experiments—subjected to all the shiftings of experimental living. They are more sensitive to the laws of subconscious actions than to the formulas by which ordinary people live down their subconscious And as Lawrence's delving is new, in the sense that delving into chaos is a characteristic of our epoch, and none other, he himself was aware of the imperfections and difficulties, and that is why he afterwards elucidated and analyzed his ideas in books of essays and psychology.

The key to his characters, then, or the simplest way of understanding them, is to think of them as artists. There is another example of this in *The Rainbow.* In this book the violent union of Anton and Ursula is devastating, and at first sight, incomprehensible. They seek violently in each other a satisfaction they do not find. Yet the experience is not a purely animal one — its meaning is not confined to a sexual struggle — it expresses at the same time another struggle, another craving. It is no mere sexual phenomenon, but more truly *the creator's craving for a climax far bigger than the climaxes life has to offer*. It is symbolical of the creative voraciousness which is, as a general instinct, unsatisfiable, because it is out of proportion with the universe, with the realities surrounding him. It is the allegory of the urge which was never meant to be answered but merely to exist, like the urge to live in spite of, and even because of the certain knowledge of death, to live in the largest possible "circuitous way towards death," in Freud's words.

Now when the creator submits to that urge for livingness it almost destroys him because his emotional receptivity is in proportion to the extreme of his desire and his hunger. That Lawrence did not mean this as a merely sexual struggle is clear for another reason. (Lawrence never means what is literally apparent.) It symbolizes also the search for balance in physical love. Lawrence realized the tragedy of inequality in love as no one else ever realized it. And with it he realized the tragedy not alone of physical but of spiritual and mental love which is the cause of torment in human relationships. It is inequality of sexual power which causes disintegration in sexual relationships. Each man and each woman must find his own level. If Lawrence had not meant that, the union of Lady Chatterley and Mellors would not have been a fulfillment, while that of Anton and Ursula proved destructive. It was a fulfillment because the former were balanced forces, while Anton and Ursula were not. Ursula was too strong for Anton.

It is this struggle for balance which is at the basis of Lawrence's descriptions of love and hate, destruction and creation, between men and women. He was aware of the see-saw rhythm in relationships.

Rebecca West has given us a beautiful interpretation of Lawrence's intensity in her "Elegy":

> When he cried out at Douglas for shaking hands with the innkeeper because the North and South were enemies, and when he saw the old crones who had come to cheat him out of an odd lira or two over the honey as Maenads too venomous even to be flamboyant, I thought he was seeing lurid colours that were in his eyes and not in the

> universe he looked on. Now I think *he was doing justice to the seriousness of life, and had been rewarded with a deeper insight into its nature than most of us have.*

* * *

The intensity of *The Nightmare* in *Kangaroo* is easier to understand just because Lawrence has called it a nightmare. He has in a way drawn a boundary line. We are entering a nightmare, but it is *reality,* heightened by a terrific effort at comprehension. It is the story of the individual's fearful struggle to remain sane in spite of the madness of the mob when it accepts war.

The whole meaning of the war for Lawrence is in the Nightmare.

> It was the whole spirit of the war, the vast mob-spirit which he could never acquiesce in. The terrible, terrible war, made so fearful because in every country practically every man lost his head, and lost his own centrality, his own manly isolation in his own integrity, which alone keeps life real.
>
> Plenty of superb courage to face death. But no courage in any man to face his isolated soul and abide by its decisions. Easier to sacrifice one's self.

Because many, many men thought and felt as Lawrence did. But many preferred death to isolation. Many preferred death rather than denying a dead ideal—for war was one of the dead ideals.

"It is not death that matters, but the loss of the integral soul." And: *"I won't have popular lies."* That is Lawrence's frequent cry: "I won't have popular lies." But popular lies are immense, and powerful, and they would have none of Lawrence.

And there is a moving example here of Lawrence's peculiar loyalty to his own body: Somers has been found unfit, as Lawrence had been:

> Somers did not care. "Let them label me unfit," he said to himself. "I know my own body is fragile, in its way, but also it is very strong, and it's the *only body that would carry my own particular self."*

Surely individuality was never so absolute in any man.

Somers "had nothing to do but hang on to his own soul. So he hung on to it, tried to keep his wits... the plank was his own individual soul."

But why should this attitude be accompanied by such intensity of feeling? The egoist holds on emotionlessly to his own plank. The fundamental reason for Lawrence's emotional condition is that he is sensitive, fearfully and profoundly so: he suffers, he suffers much from pity, tenderness, horror—he participates with feeling. What drives him to despair is his very conviction of the sacredness of the body—and war is a monstrous holocaust of innumerable bodies.

There is always in Lawrence, on the one hand, the individualist struggling for isolation, on the other the man tormented with pity, with his feeling of kinship, with a desire for understanding with his fellow-men. And this tenderness it is, as well as the rejection of his tenderness, which makes him violent. Fighting the world he fights his own tenderness. That is the reason for his intensity. Mere egoists are not intense in this way. Their withdrawal is self-preservation. Fruit sweetened, preserved, in complacent peace.

And as for the *Englishness* of Lawrence it is in Somers: "One of the most intensely English little men England ever produced, with a passion for his country, even if it were often a passion of hatred."

* * *

If the reality of the war is compared to a nightmare, dreams are often realities. To the poet the experience of a dream is no different from the experience of reality: "Life always a dream or a frenzy." There is no boundary line. Through other books Lawrence had dreamed, and had fancies, had improvised, and people could only say: *This* is chaos, *this* is nonsense.

The boundary line exists only for those who always want to return to the first peace and security. They carefully mark the way of their wandering for recognition on the way back: *This* is a dream, *this* is a fantasy; I only have to deny that they have any connection with myself, only to say that they are accidents, fragments, fluid, for them to disappear like ghosts. And I will be with my real self again.

But in Lawrence's books, dreams and reality are often interwoven just as they are in our own natures.

In *St. Mawr*, in *The Rainbow*, in *Women in Love* the boundaries are undetectable. Where the allegory begins, where the symbolism, where the images, where the drama, it is impossible to say.

In *The Rainbow* Ursula goes for a walk on a stormy afternoon. She has just resolved that "woman was a giver of life," and that she would return to her husband, and bear him children, and give up all the intricate desires and aspirations of her secret inner world.

The rain and storm are a "fluctuation." After a long while she wants to "beat her way back through all this fluctuation, back to stability and security." The instability is not in the storm, but in her own mental conflict, and she is going back to a decision, to shelter.

> Suddenly . . . some horses were looming in the rain, not near yet. *But they were going to be near*. She continued her path inevitably. There were horses in the lee of a clump of trees beyond, above her. She pursued her way with bent head. *She did not want to lift her face to them*. She did not want to know they were there. She went on in the wild track. *She knew the heaviness on her heart*. It was the weight of the horses. But she would circumvent them. She would bear the weight steadily, and so escape . . . Suddenly the weight deepened and her heart grew tense to bear it. *Her breathing was laboured*. But this weight also she could bear . . . She was aware of the great flash of hoofs . . . the horses thundered upon her . . .

She is broken by the struggle to escape. She lies faint and still on the roadside.

Ursula's decision to return to Skrebensky, to bear his children, has extended into the whole world. The world, woods, and storm are to become *images* of the feelings which torment her. Nature is to re-enact her fluctuations and her fears. The horses are symbols of maternity and the sexual experience of marriage. Now the whole page reads differently: "There were horses in the lee of a clump of trees beyond, above her . . . *She did not want to lift her face to see them*."

She did not want to face the full consequences of her decision. But: "she knew the heaviness of her heart."

Her heart is over-full of aspirations, dreams, and desires for another kind of life.

"It was the weight of the horses."

It was the weight of maternity and purely physical existence.

"But she would bear the weight steadily and so escape."

Perhaps through living as a wife and mother, through denial, she can still preserve her inner life intact.

"Her breathing was laboured."

As it would be in child-bearing.

"The great flash of hoofs" is the sexual pounding in her womb.

* * *

Such entanglements in relations between men and women, between reality and unreality, fantasies and life, are denied by most people.

The first analysis of an event or a person yields a certain aspect. If we look at it again, it has another face. *The further we progress in our reinterpretation, the more prismatic are the moods and the imaginings coordinating the facts differently each time.* People who want a sane, static, measurable world take the first aspect of an event or person and stick to it, with an almost self-protective obstinacy, or by a natural limitation of their imaginations. They do not indulge in either deepening or magnifying.

But others know that the imagination is a constant deformer. It needs to be, it must be, in order to be capable of extending from comparatively small happenings, in a comparatively short span of life. Otherwise to understand one thought, one feeling, we would have to go through a thousand experiences. But one experience can be multiplied by our imagination. And it is this power to multiply and to expand which creates at the same time intricacies and entanglements. Entanglements are the other face of the same activity.

In the conflict of Anna and Will, the death of Gerald, the nightmare, and the horse fantasy, we are given the clues to more than one kind of conflict, one kind of obsession, one kind of nightmare. And this is simply the *fundamental basis of poetic creation* with which Lawrence has animated his characters.

The love and hate alternating in men and women, as in *Women in Love* is due to the same profound sense of oscillation, of flux and reflux (Herakleitos), revulsions and convulsions, *mobility. The becoming always seething and fluctuating.*

There can never be, according to Lawrence, a perfect relationship between people. We are doomed to solitariness.

> This individuality which each one of us has got and which makes him a wayward, wilful, dangerous, untrustworthy quantity to every other individual, because every individuality is bound to react at some time against every other individuality, without exception—or else lose its own integrity; because of the inevitable necessity of each individual to react away from any other individual, at certain times, human love is truly a relative thing, not an *absolute*.

Lawrence's descriptions of the undercurrents of body and mind were but means of bringing to the surface many feelings that we do not sincerely acknowledge in ourselves. Freud and Jung have also done this, but they are essentially scientists and they are read with the detachment and objectivity of scientific research. Lawrence's characters, whether in poetry, allegory, or prophecy, are actors who speak with the very accents of our emotions; and, before we are aware, our feelings become identified and involved with theirs. Some have recoiled from such an awakening, often unpleasant; many have dreaded having to acknowledge this power of their physical sensations, as well as to face in plain words, the real meaning of their fantasies.

Lawrence was reviled for going so far. *There are always those who fear for that integral kernel in themselves, for that divine integrity which can be preserved by ignorance* (before psychology) *or by religion* (before and after psychology) *or by the cessation of thought* (by the modern paroxysm of activity).

So it was not the truth, but the stirring, live quality in Lawrence's truth which upset people. Besides the scientists there were novelists like André Gide and Aldous Huxley who had left nothing unexplored. But Huxley and Gide travelled with the intellect and with that upper-strata in the head, and therefore as they went along we were *hit in our heads,* and the experience took on a scientific aspect, became pure abstract knowledge.

Huxley was his Philip: "*. . . loyal only to the cool indifferent flux of intellectual curiosity.*" There is nothing more devastating to ordinary standards of value than pages of Gide's *L'Immoraliste* and pages of Huxley's *Point Counterpoint.*

But Lawrence went at the reversal of values, not with indifference, but with poetry, with religious fervor, and he *hit lower* than either Huxley or Gide. He hit the center, the vulnerable center of our bodies with his *physical language,* his *physical vision.* He hit us vitally.

And the self-protective, integrity-preserving instincts of society rose bitterly against him.

Lawrence had been unforgivably persuasive.

He had not only thought about everything but he had felt everything, and he greatly cared, and so we were forced to care, and his voice had strange, potent accents.

And as no one would go along with him, he went alone, through hell. And the more experiences he went through, the more he understood. The more you know about hell, the more you know about heaven. The more you know of decadence, the more virile the reaction back to livingness.

* * *

Love between men. His mind deliberated here, long enough to give more qualms to his self-preserving friends.

More oscillations.

There was an equation in the love between men and women. Was it the only creative one? Lawrence doubted pat equations. There was a suspicious dignity, decorum, and facility about them. Perhaps oscillation was the right permanent state of being, and perhaps a creative and natural one too.

The assumption of what is natural may rise out of a wrong premise. Many errors had slipped down unnoticed through the centuries. The family was a unit which was eminently useful to society. Society had a genius for making everything that was useful appear to issue from religious decrees, divine dictates. Society was very intelligent in the care of itself. The family taught kindness, self-sacrifice, and fecundity. Fecundity was useful in war time.

Love between men and women might not be the only basis of life. The fact that they were biological complements did not mean that they were always mental complements.

So Lawrence speculates on the value of the association of man with man. Wherever there is an undercurrent attachment and flow, there is life. Here he seeks more keenly than ever the truth concealed under appearances. The apparent physical completeness of the love of man and woman may not be the only completeness. Everything was possible in a state of livingness which transcends human laws, or in a nature which contradicts itself and is constantly feeling its way, blunderingly, contradictorily. There was the possibility that feelings might run in two streams.

If you go very far all values shift. It will not do to stay on the same ground forever. If you are terribly truthful, the ground will always move from under you, and you will have to shift with the constantly shifting truth. (System of mobility.)

After all, if we let the whole universe flow through us, then our experiences become fluid, run into new shapes.

There are things Lawrence likes to do, and to talk over with men, and it is with men that man works at the building of his world. There is an association and community of interest.

In *Kangaroo,* Somers:

> . . . loved working with John Thomas . . . picking, or resting, talking in the intervals with John Thomas, who loved a half-philosophical, mystical talking about the sun, and the moon, the mysterious powers of the moon at night, and the mysterious change in man with the change of season, and the mysterious effects of sex on a man . . .
>
> Poor Harriet spent many lonely days in the cottage. Somers was not interested in her now . . . Then would come John Thomas with the wain, and the two men would linger putting up the sheaves, lingering, talking, till the dark, talking of the half-mystical things with which they were both filled.

The same is true with Gerald and Birkin in *Women in Love.*

But it is in *Aaron's Rod* that Lawrence went through hell. Here the matter of connection and flow between men reaches a peak of anxiety. There is a desire for connection, but how is it to be answered?

The fact that he concludes that between men there must be a relationship not based on sex is important:

> He dreamed a new human relationship. A stark, stripped human relationship of two men, deeper than the deeps of sex. Deeper than property, deeper than fatherhood, deeper than marriage, deeper than love. So deep that it is loveless. The stark, loveless, wordless unison of two men who have come to the bottom of themselves.

But even more important is that he *understood*—understood the subterranean flowing of men as part of a state of being.

With this understanding he will continue the creation of his world —a more complete world because of the understanding. A world closed to no true state of body or soul.

He is "liberated from the laws of idealism." Of ordinary idealism. Ordinary idealism is composed mainly of dead ideals.

> But evening is also the time for revelry, for drink, for passion. Alcohol enters the blood and acts as the sun's rays. It inflames into life, it liberates into energy and consciousness. But by a process of combustion. That life of the day which we *have not lived,* by means of sun-born alcohol we can now flare into sensation, consciousness, energy and passion, and live it out. It is a liberation from the laws of idealism, a release from the restrictions of control and fear. It is the blood bursting into consciousness. But naturally the course of the liberated consciousness may be in either direction: sharper mental action, greater fervor of spiritual emotion, or deeper sensuality.
>
> [*Fantasia of the Unconscious*]

Alcohol and sun are symbols. Fearless experience, passionate experience accomplish the same thing. Lawrence's world is liberated not from idealism but from dead-ideals. He is constantly making lists of dead ideals (as the ideal of war in *Kangaroo*). For ideals also have a fundamental mobility: they are born and they die. And to stick to dead ideals is to die.

Lawrence had completed his cycle. There has been a progression, but not a strictly philosophic progression, since Lawrence has stated the whole of his philosophy before in other books. Philosophically, then, *Lady Chatterley's Lover* is not a climax.

He has said this before:

> When a man and woman truly come together, when there is a marriage, then an unconscious vital connection is established between them like a throbbing blood-circuit. A man may forget a woman entirely with his head, and fling himself with energy and fervor into whatever job he is tackling, and all is well... if he does not break that inner vital connection which is the mystery of marriage... *The immediate union is woman, the wife.*

What then has been the real climax of progression in Lawrence? There has been a *progression in perfection,* and the climax is in the *perfection.* (It is unnecessary to dwell on the occasional retrogression—the imperfections and technical weaknesses, since they are quite unimportant in an ultimate valuation of his work.)

Lady Chatterly's Lover is, as we shall see, a more perfect expression of his mystical attitude towards the flesh than any other book he wrote.

But:

> ...does all life work up to the one consummating act of coition? In one direction it does... But we are not confined to one direction only, or to one exclusive consummation. Was the building of cathedrals a working towards the act of coition? Was the dynamic impulse sexual? No... there was something else, of even higher importance and greater dynamic power.
>
> And what is this other greater impulse? It is the desire of the human male to build a world, to build a world out of his own self and his very own belief and his own effort, something wonderful. Not merely useful. Something wonderful.
>
> [*Fantasia of the Unconscious*]

Mellors, Lady Chatterly's lover, at the end of the book, turns to the building of a world.

Preface to Tropic of Cancer

Here is a book which, if such a thing were possible, might restore our appetite for the fundamental realities. The predominant note will seem one of bitterness, and bitterness there is, to the full. But there is also a wild extravagance, a mad gaiety, a verve, a gusto, at times almost a delirium. A continual oscillation between extremes, with bare stretches that taste like brass and leave the full flavor of emptiness. It is beyond optimism or pessimism. The author has given us the last *frisson*. Pain has no more secret recesses.

In a world grown paralyzed with introspection and constipated by delicate mental meals, this brutal exposure of the substantial body comes as a vitalizing current of blood. The violence and obscenity are left unadulterated, as manifestation of the mystery and pain which ever accompanies the act of creation.

The restorative value of experience, prime source of wisdom and creation, is reasserted. There remain waste areas of unfinished thought and action, a bundle of shreds and fibers with which the overcritical may strangle themselves. Referring to his *Wilhelm Meister*, Goethe once said: "People seek a central point: that is hard, and not even right. I should think a rich, manifold life, brought close to our eyes, would be enough without any express tendency; which, after all, is only for the intellect."

The book is sustained on its own axis by the pure flux and rotation of events. Just as there is no central point, so also there is no

From Henry Miller's *Tropic of Cancer* (Obelisk Press, 1934).

question of heroism or of struggle since there is no question of will, but only an obedience to flow.

The gross caricatures are perhaps more vital, "more true to life," than the full portraits of the conventional novel for the reason that the individual today has no centrality and produces not the slightest illusion of wholeness. The characters are integrated to the false, cultural void in which we are drowning; thus is produced the illusion of chaos, to face which requires the ultimate courage.

The humiliations and defeats, given with a primitive honesty, end not in frustration, despair, or futility, but in hunger, an ecstatic, devouring hunger—*for more life.* The poetic is discovered by stripping away the vestiture of art; by descending to what might be styled "a pre-artistic level," the durable skeleton of form which is hidden in the phenomena of disintegration reappears to be transfigured again in the ever-changing flesh of emotion. The scars are burned away—the scars left by the obstetricians of culture. Here is an artist who re-establishes the potency of illusion by gaping at the open wounds, by courting the stern, psychological reality which man seeks to avoid through recourse to the oblique symbolism of art. Here the symbols are laid bare, presented almost as naively and unblushingly by this over-civilized individual as by the well-rooted savage.

It is no false primitivism which gives rise to this savage lyricism. It is not a retrogressive tendency, but a swing forward into unbeaten areas. To regard a naked book such as this with the same critical eye that is turned upon even such diverse types as Lawrence, Breton, Joyce and Céline is a mistake. Rather let us try to look at it with the eyes of a Patagonian for whom all that is sacred and taboo in our world is meaningless. For the adventure which has brought the author to the spiritual ends of the earth is the history of every artist who, in order to express himself, must traverse the intangible gridirons of his imaginary world. The air, pockets, the alkali wastes, the crumbling monuments, the putrescent cadavers, the crazy jig and maggot dance, all this forms a grand fresco of our epoch, done with shattering phrases and loud, strident, hammer strokes.

If there is here revealed a capacity to shock, to startle the lifeless ones from their profound slumber, let us congratulate ourselves; for the tragedy of our world is precisely that nothing any longer is capable of rousing it from its lethargy. No more violent dreams, no refreshment, no awakening. In the anaesthesia produce by self-knowledge, life is passing, art is passing, slipping from us: we are drifting with time and our fight is with shadows. We need a blood transfusion.

And it is blood and flesh which are here given us. Drink, food, laughter, desire, passion, curiosity, the simple realities which nourish the roots of our highest and vaguest creations. The superstructure is lopped away. This book brings with it a wind that blows down the dead and hollow trees whose roots are withered and lost in the barren soil of our times. This book goes to the roots and digs under, digs for subterranean springs.

Rank's Art and Artist

a review

To fully recognize the relevance and contemporary quality of *Art and Artist,* a work written in the thirties and reprinted by Agathon Press, it is important to know the three vital impulses which directed thought towards the future through which Rank can be best understood today. First of all it was the work of a rebel, of a man who stood in a symbolic father-and-son relation to Freud, and who dared to diverge from his theories. Such a challenge of an already established and crystallized dogma is usually punished by repression, which is exactly what happened to Otto Rank. The disciples of Freud pursued a relentless excommunication which is only dying today with the man who practiced it. He was erased from the history of psychoanalysis and from public evaluation of psychoanalytical movements. But his influence was strong, and expressed most directly through the Philadelphia School of Social Work.

The second vital factor was that Otto Rank was a poet, a novelist, a playwright, in short a literary man, so that when he examined the creative personality it was not only as a psychologist, but as an artist, and *Art and Artist* can be read both as an interpretation of the creative processes and an interpretation of art itself. These two aspects alone would suffice to gain him the appreciation of modern thinkers, but there was a third even more important to America's primary interest: Otto Rank was preoccupied with social problems,

Reprinted from *Journal of the Otto Rank Association* (December 1968), pp. 94-97.

and felt individual therapy was not enough to solve its problems. He wanted it more widely and more generally applied and concentrated on its effectiveness through education and through the psychological training of social workers. He contributed to both. The Philadelphia School of Social Work pioneered in this realm. Today The Otto Rank Association is responsible for disseminating his work actively and intelligently, and bringing about the reprinting of his books.

In *Art and Artist* Otto Rank treats of the relation between the artist and art. He states that "For the human urge to create does not find expression in works of art alone: it also produces religion and mythology and the social institutions corresponding to these." He defines the purpose of his book as one "going beyond the limits of the scientific absolutism that characterizes our modern psychology." In 1905 Rank had written as a very young man, a short study of *The Artist* in which he tried to describe the psychology of a creative personality as psychologically intermediate between dreamer and neurotic. According to Rank, the two extremes of creativity, personal and collective, have been studied as separate rather than interrelated activities and it is his contention in *Art and Artist* that, when examined more deeply, the artist's work is related to the collective even if during his lifetime he seems to be running contrary to its course. In the chapter "Creative Urge and Personality" he underlines this distinction: "Religion springs from the collective belief in immortality; art from the personal consciousness of the individual."

He separates the artist from the neurotic: "The neurotic suffers fundamentally from the fact that he cannot or will not accept himself. The artist not only accepts his personality but goes far beyond it." Later on in the book he demonstrates how important this independence of the artist is for he has to remain separate and lucid in regard to the collective if he is to lead it, or illumine the way. Entering the intricate, subtle and complex art from the ideology conflicts, Rank brings us closer to present day problems. When the artist seems to be expressing a collective ideology he then makes the collective community feel its own immortality, he asserts the continuity of its life. If he seems to depart from this he is in a sense ostracized. Rank sees no such conflict between collective and individual art, only in those who do not grasp their interrelation: the critic. Rank demonstrates how art is born of a fear of loss and change. The problem lies in how to distinguish between the perishable, ephemeral forms meaningful only to the present and the eternal values. One of the most beautiful passages is in the opening of "Microcosm and Macrocosm":

> The art work presents a unity, alike in its effect and in its creation, and this implies a spiritual unity between the artist and the recipient. Although temporary and symbolic only, this produces a satisfaction which suggests that it is more than a matter of passing identification of two individuals, that it is the potential restoration of a union with the cosmos which once existedand was then lost. The individual psychological root of this sense of unity I discovered (at the time of writing *The Trauma of Birth*) in the prenatal condition, which the individual in his yearning for immortality strives to restore. Already in that earliest stage of individualization, the child is not only factually one with the mother but, beyond all that, one with the world, with a cosmos, floating in mystic vapours in which present, past and future are dissolved. The individual urge to restore this lost unity is an essential factor in the production of human cultural values.

The last chapter of *Art and Artist* is devoted to "Success and Fame." In it Rank states:

> There is always a distinct reaction of the artist not only against every kind of collectivization, but against the change of his own person, his work, and his ideology into an eternalization-symbol for a particular epoch. This resistance of the artist to his absorption into the community will show itself in more than his objection to success and fame; it will also influence his further activity so far as the assertion of his own individuality is concerned, and become a strong stimulus to further activity in general. Certainly this will be the case with the great artist who always tried to escape this collectivizing influence by deliberate new creations, whereas the weaker talent succumbs to a conscious conces-

> sion to the masses or becomes mere raw material for the collective perpetuation instinct. These diverse outcomes of the struggle of the artist against success and fame, explain, too, how many of the greatest geniuses only attained fame after their own time, and, on the other hand, why mediocre gifts enjoy seemingly undeserved success.

This concept may be applied to Rank's own work and contribution, which were not in harmony with prevalent ideas of his time, which were original and a departure from dogmatism. This is the time for a just evaluation of his interpretation.

The Id of Dostoevsky

a review

Available to the public for the first time in English, these notebooks, translated by Edward Wasiolek [*The Notebooks for "Crime and Punishment"*] from the Soviet edition published in 1931, contain, he explains, schematic plans of major portions of *Crime and Punishment*; "long variants of scenes; characterizations that differ in important points from those in the novel as published; plans, actions and scenes that were never used; ruminations about technical problems; queries, judgments, opinions; and reflections on philosophical and religious ideas." But it is not only the notebooks themselves which make this a unique and valuable contribution; it is also the insight that Wasiolek, a professor of Russian and Comparative Literature at the University of Chicago, has brought to the organization of the material, his comments, his analysis and interpretations, his ability to relate them to the novel in a manner that answers our contemporary need to integrate conscious and unconscious, the work of art and the artist.

Focusing upon the role played in the writer's creation by his personal ambivalences, evasions, and transpositions uncovers layers of dramas behind dramas. Besides watching a novel being born, we are watching a human being cope with revelations flowing from his unconscious, revelations that his complexes make him resist, obscure, transform, or erase altogether.

Reprinted from *Saturday Review* (June 10, 1967 © 1967 Saturday Review, Inc.), pp. 35, 110.

We share Dostoevsky's "intentions, trials, mistakes, uncertainties." But Wasiolek indicates that these are more than considerations of craftsmanship, more than a work in progress. He treats them as keys to Dostoevsky's unconscious and its part in creation, keys to the mystery of a writer's struggle against repressive impulses, his personal need to disguise certain over-explicit formulations from his own vision. Dostoevsky's "dialogue with his novel" discloses his way of creating, his way of being. His individual psychology emerges in relation to the psychology of his characters. They interact, and a different aspect of truth appears.

Fragments rejected from the novel often reveal the secrets that Dostoevsky kept in shadow. Although they have attracted endless study, for the deepest interpretation it was important to decipher these ambiguities as one would the meaning of dream. And this Edward Wasiolek has done. "The novel offers us what Dostoevsky finally chose to say, but the notebooks offer us what he considered and what he discarded.... What do wrong turns, mistakes, blind alleys, and unmined possibilities tell us?"

> They remind us, first of all, that the marvelous coherence of *Crime and Punishment*, the creative logic that takes us with what seems to be inevitable movement from the beginning to end, was once uncertain, halting, and far from clear. They tell us something about the way Dostoevsky's imagination works: its habits, mannerisms, logic; something about his concern for technique; and something about what was recurrent in his thinking about the novel. The notebooks tell us much more about the content of the novel itself; what was left out, what was different, what was undeveloped, and what was at some point fully developed. At times they may help us clear up what is obscured in the novel, and resolve what has been critically disputable.

We know that genius understood everything before Freud, but we also know with our own adoption of psychological interpretation that the genius remains a human being capable of intensely personal blind spots, distorted psychic vision, uncontrollable taboos of which he himself may be entirely unaware. Therefore, to attain the whole truth we have to become adept at interpreting the interrelation between the work of art and the writer. To make our own synthesis from overtones we have to read into them both invisible messages and oblique implications. What the writer finally tells us may be an unconscious selection, and this selection may be made to camouflage a concept unbearable to him. Therefore, the work of art has to be read symbolically as merely a point of departure for infinite adumbrations, and the missing dimensions must be reconstructed.

Wasiolek makes a subtle fusion of these elements, the stated and the implied, the conscious and the unconscious. He analyzes the meaning of the contradictions, the cause for the shadows, the motivations for the reticences.

> . . . it would seem that the motive of sacrificing one's self to humanity or sacrificing humanity for one's self are contradictory. But the real relationship between them, I am convinced, is one of appearance and reality, of evasion and truth. The "pretty" humanitarian motive is flattering to Raskolnikov's ego, evasively presented to the conscious mind as rationalization of an ugly truth.

Dostoevsky, who was the greatest dramatizer of man's dualities and ambivalences, at times subdued them to obtain a clearer image. He would ultimately erase from his characters many of the multiple contradictions—at times too many: Sonya became consistent, idealized to the point of losing some of her human imperfections.

In every generation, the only novelty is the change of emphasis and balances that permit us to perceive new truths about human character. Too many critics have never gone beyond Freud. Wasiolek, who obviously has, shows that he possesses a much wider range of interpretation, one entirely contemporary. "Freud has reminded us of the unbounded compassion Dostoevsky felt for the criminal and explained it by similar criminal tendencies in Dostoevsky. But there was more than neuroticism in this view: Dostoevsky saw the criminal as one who has justifiably defied the judgment of other men and placed himself into contest with the true judge, God." When Wasiolek integrates the personal and the creative, the objective and the subjective in their constant interrelation, he leads us into a deeper awareness of the fecund multiple dimensions of Dostoevsky's work.

"Dostoevsky himself intended Svidrigaylov to embody a 'terrifying amorality.' In the novel his crimes are suggested, but frankly admitted in the notebooks."

This book stresses that the great writer is no different from the ordinary human being who seeks to understand himself and others and yet at the same time conceals from his own eyes as well as from the eyes of the world some part of his true nature which he would be forced to judge and condemn. Such disguises are not dishonest; they merely prove that we cannot bear our guilt, our weaknesses, our obsessions, or our aggressions. Thus we continue to mask the unconscious from the conscious, continue to dream in symbols because we cannot endure explicitness, and continue to transform truth into fiction so that we may engage in our duels with the truth on a level far enough removed from the familiar to become apparently objective and detached from us.

In the collision between these dualities of man's nature, we find sparks of illumination. In the effect at consistency, at crystallization, at clarification of a theme (the novel in its final state) we sometimes lose the valuable drama of the relativity of truth that may occasionally emerge from chaos itself, from instinctive unorganized experience, from the heart of ambivalence and contradiction. Our most precious studies of human nature may not be derived from finite forms, from conclusions, from resolutions, but may often lie in these oscillations, wavering lines, fissures, splits. By uniting *Crime and Punishment* with the notebooks, Wasiolek has given us a remarkable study of interaction, of a psychological reality caught inadvertently in the very moment of conflict, chaos, and paradox, just before experience becomes transformed into fiction.

from *The Novel of the Future*

Jung said: "Proceed from the dream outward . . ."

It is interesting to return to the original definition of a word we use too often and too carelessly. The definition of a dream is: ideas and images in the mind *not under the command of reason.* It is not necessarily an image or an idea that we have during sleep. It is merely an idea or image which escapes the control of reasoning or logical or rational mind. So that dream may include reverie, imagination, daydreaming, the vision and hallucinations under the influence of drugs—any experience which emerges from the realm of the subconscious. These various classifications are merely ways to describe different states or levels of consciousness. The important thing to learn, from art and from literature in particular, is the easy passageway and relationship between them. Neurosis makes a division and sets up defensive boundaries. But the writer can learn to walk easily between one realm and the other without fear, interrelate them, and ultimately fuse them.

Psychoanalysis proved that dreams were the only key to our subconscious life. What the psychoanalysts stress, the relation between dream and our conscious acts, is what the poets already know. The poets walk this bridge with ease, from conscious to unconscious, physical reality to psychological reality. Their profession is to fuse them so that they may function harmoniously. The function of the symbol is to unite and synthesize various forms of reality. Most fiction writers use dreams decoratively, without relating them to daily life, but the contemporary writer is becoming more expert at detecting the influence of one upon the other.

When I was eleven years old I wrote a play which prefigured my life philosophy. It was a melodrama with an unexpected climax. A blind father and his devoted daughter live in extreme poverty in a shack. But the daughter always describes their life, their home, their garden, their friends in terms of beauty and comfort, creating an illusion for her blind father to lull him. Then a doctor comes to the village and operates on the father's eyes. He can now see again. Tragedy? No, when he opens his eyes to the shabby reality, he does not collapse or feel betrayed. He tells his daughter: "It is true you described something which was not there, but you describe it so vividly that now I can set about to construct our life as you had dreamed it." The dream has to be translated into reality.

The dream, scrutinized by scientists in various experiments, has been found to be an absolute necessity to man. It keeps our psychic life alive, in its own proper climate. It sustains a life not corruptible and not susceptible to the pressures of society. When we ceased to believe in this spiritual underground, to nourish ourselves on feelings, our lives became empty shells, automatic, mechanical. We only believed in it when it showed symptoms of neurosis. Literature and the poets continued to assert its presence as the source of creation.

Neurosis was caused by our attempt to separate physical and metaphysical levels, to set them up in opposition to each other, thus engaging in an internecine war. If it is true that we do live on several levels simultaneously—drama and action, past and present, personal and collective—we were given ways to unify them: one by religion, the other by art. Separating such levels is only necessary when they conflict, and separation is a result of conflict. Seeing how these levels can work together in harmony is the task of our contemporary writers.

For this the writer has to learn the passageways. Those passageways are like the locks of canals, feeding each other while controlling levels to prevent flooding. The discipline and form of an artist's work are set in the same system to prevent flooding. The amateur drowns. The writer has to remain open, fluid, pursue and obey images which his conscious structure tends to break or erase. The same writing which is employed by science or the intellect will not carry these images back and forth through the channels of the senses, where they are effective. We categorize and catalogue and file, not so much out of a sense of organization but out of fear. The psychologist, while using dreams as a kind of electronic echo sounder to chart the depths of the unconscious, is often, according to Dr. R. D. Laing, too anxious to draw boundary lines according to definitions of normalcy which really do not exist as finite truths but fluctuate and vary and are altered by new researches.

For the neurotic, the merging of the subconscious and the conscious may be risky, just as it is for the users of drugs. But for the writer who is aware of the way in which this connection exists in reality and nourishes creativity, the sooner he can achieve a synthesis among intellect, intuition, emotion, and instinct, the sooner his work will be integrated.

When one learns the passageways, one discovers a rigorous form and pattern to the unconscious, but one which is not apparent until all the elements are gathered together. One learns the plots of the unconscious from psychoanalysis. It is a detective story of the emotions. This concept was popularized in Eric Berne's *Games People Play*. Any artificial imitation of the unconscious can be easily detected. It is absurd and meaningless, it is chaotic and grotesque. The images are unrelated. They do not lead anywhere.

What the psychoanalyst does is what the novelist also has to do—probe deep enough until he finds where the chain broke. Traumatic experiences cause such breaks. The psychoanalyst repairs the broken links and allows the unconscious, which has its inception in the personal experience, to merge into a life beyond the personal.

The important thing is to learn from the writer the ways and byways of such passageways between conscious and unconscious. The unconscious can become destructive if it is disregarded and thwarted. Neurosis, based on fear, creates solitary cells to protect itself from invasion. Many of today's writers have assimilated the findings of psychoanalysis and are more expert in linking the subconscious with the conscious. We are beginning to see the influence of dream upon reality and reality upon dream. Art is revealing to us the variety of levels on which we live. This may be what we seek to express in what we now call "multimedia."

Almost all of Kafka's work takes place in a waking dream region, and Proust wrote a classical description of the state between sleep and waking reverie in *Remembrance of Things Past*.

In *Winter of Artifice* (pp. 170-75) I sought to examine the different layers of the dream:

> When I entered the dream I stepped on a stage. The lights cast on it changed hue and intensity like stage lights. The violent scenes happened in the spotlight and were enveloped by a thick curtain of blackness. The scenes were cut, interrupted, or broken with entr'actes. The mise en scene was stylized, and only what has meaning was represented. And very often I was at once the victim and the observer.
>
> The dream was composed like a tower of layers without end, rising upward and losing itself in the infinite, or layers coiling downward, losing themselves in the bowels of the earth. When it swooped me into its undulations, the spiralling began, and this spiral was a labyrinth. There was no vault and no bottom, no walls and no return. But there were themes repeating themselves with exactitude. If the walls of the dream seemed lined with moist silk, and the contours of the labyrinth lined with silence, still the steps of the dream were a series of explosions in which all the condemned fragments of myself burst into a mysterious and violent life, with the heavy maternal solicitude of the night ever attentive to their flowering.
>
> *On the first layer of the spiral there was awareness. I could still see the daylight between the fringes of eyelashes. I could still see the interstices of the world.* This was the penumbra, where the thoughts were inlaid in filaments of lightning. It was the place where the images were delicately filtered and separated, and their silhouettes thrown against space. It was the place where footsteps left no trace, where laughter had no echo, but where hunger and fear were immense. It was the place where the sails of reverie could swell while no wind was felt. . . . *The dream was a filter.* The entire world was never admitted. . . . *But with the night came*

> *openness. . . . With the night came space. . . .* The dream was never crowded. It was *filtered through the prism of creation. . . . Time was ordained by feeling. . . . By day I followed the dream step by step. I felt lost and bewildered if the day did not bring its replica. . . . The dream was always running ahead of one. To catch up, to live for a moment in unison with it, that was the miracle. The life on the stage, the life of the legend dovetailed with the daylight, and out of this marriage sparked the great birds of divinity, the eternal moments.*

As a prose poet becoming fascinated with a rich source of images, I concentrated on describing the dream world, perhaps tempted by the difficulties involved. Obviously the physical world is easier to describe. The first misunderstanding about my work which arose and has continued to the present was that I was writing dreamlike and unreal stories.

My emphasis was on the relation between dream and reality, their interdependence.

The novelist today works parallel to the psychologist, recognizes the duality and multiplicity of the human personality. It should not be any more difficult to orient, to navigate, to chart all these different elements than to guide a missile. Dream, waking dream, reverie, fantasy, all interlock and interrelate simultaneously but on different levels. These two ways of describing the unconscious through the symbol and surrealism paralleled exactly the development of the psychological study of dreams. Symbolism was unfortunately associated with romanticism, but we are obliged to reinstate it as the *most important form of expression* of the unconscious.

The genesis of *Children of the Albatross* was again based on a real character, a young man of seventeen who became for me a representation of adolescent fear. He was inarticulate. I used the wordless language of the ballet to be able to render his timidities, his swift exits, his evasions, his pirouettes. The ballet served as an image of adolescent timorousness, light-footedness, disappearances. Paul had tremendous fears, of life, love, art, everything. It made him oscillate, be ambivalent, elusive. Starting from the ballet, I followed many images which seemed to express adolescence, or at least Paul's. The luminosity of youth, the phosphorescence one sees in children and young people, suggested the albatross. I had been reading about the albatross in a scientific journal. The sailors hesitated to kill them and only did so when utterly starving. The albatross followed ships. The legend of their metaphysical quality may have sprung from the fact that the sailors, after killing them, found their entrails phosphorescent. Phosphorescence and flight. All this grew into equivalents for Paul, means of describing a most elusive state of mind. I had observed that children seemed to lose this luminousness. In Paul it was quite striking. He had a glow and a tendency to take flight in the face of life, of emotion, and of his own dreams.

Another inspiration taken from science was information about birds. "Birds live their lives with an intensity as extreme as their brilliant colors and their vivid songs. The reserve air tanks provide fuel for the bird's intensive life and at the same time add to its buoyancy in flight." This I used for the theme of adolescence.

A scientific image can trigger off metaphors, as well as dreams. Part of the novelist's richness comes from how much he assimilates, observes, registers from all the sources. A new word, a new bit of information—all is nourishment. Anything I see, hear. Science could enrich our symbolism but requires technical knowledge and is partly inaccessible to the layman. Science is full of concrete images which could serve to represent an abstract psychological truth. For example, when film-makers talk of superimposition of images, everyone understands. One film exposed over another. Double exposure. When I speak of this happening constantly in our unconscious, it sounds abstract and mysterious (we may fall in love with a face simply because it bears some resemblance to another face we once did love). I like images from science because they are very concrete. I have often spoken of the mathematics of emotion. For example, the fragmentation of the personality (which always existed but which we have become more aware of in an analytic culture) can be analogous to the fission of energy. Proust's fragmentation might have been compared to the microscope, the effect of intense examination of an act causing this magnification of events.

It was a misunderstanding to stress the dreamlike quality of the novels. What I meant to stress was the interrelation between dream and life, between dream and action.

One thing is very clear—that both diary and fiction tended towards the same goal: intimacy with people, with experience, with life itself. One, in the diary, was achieved by daily writing, daily recording, and continuous interest in the development of people around me and in my own growth. Secrecy seemed to be a condition for spontaneity in my case. The personal interest seemed to be a necessary condition to intimacy. An early intuition that *everyone* had areas of subjective or personal or emotional reactions was confirmed by study of psychology. The more I went into the revelations of psychology, the more I realized that spontaneous writing in the present came closer to the truth than impressions remembered, because memory rearranged its collection anew each day with changes in the personality. Stories were altered and fictionalized with time. As the teller changed, so did the versions of the past.

The necessity for fiction was probably born of the problem of taboo on certain revelations. It was not only a need of the imagination but an answer to the limitations placed on portrayal of others.

Not only conventions dictated the secrecy of journals, but personal censorship. Fiction was liberating in that sense. But when it became fixed in a mold, it withered. Until a new form revivified it. The total death of the novel was always being announced, when what should have been observed was the death of certain forms of the novel. People cling to dead forms.

Otto Rank once said that man was more of an artist than woman because he gave freedom to his imagination. Henry Miller was never concerned with the *faithfulness* of his descriptions. He was not concerned with resemblance at all. He invented a world of his own, personages of his own, including himself.

At one time I was very concerned with my faithfulness to the truth. I thought it might be due to uprootings in childhood, loss of country and roots and father, and that I was trying to create relationships based on a true understanding of the other person, in the diary as well as in life and in the novels, too. A world of genuine authentic relationships. Now I can see that what I sought was psychological reality and that this reality has a logic, a pattern, a consistency of its own which cannot be invented. Narrative, or a Joycean symphony, can be invented. Not the subtle plots created by the unconscious. They are marvels of a kind of logic never known before which cannot be imitated or substituted, for every link is essential, every detail. Later I will show how difficult this was to achieve in fiction.

So, the first incentive is to understand not to invent.

This was really the antinovel, antifiction which the French explored recently.

I am still speaking of the time when I separated the two activities as antagonistic and could not see the interrelation between them. Faithful to the notebook and to the human beings I loved, portraying them truthfully, I was wary of invention, and I blamed Henry Miller's inventions for his not understanding people around him. I separated insight from narrative picaresque storytelling. When Henry Miller told a caricatural story about Moricand in *Devil in Paradise,* I felt: this is not Moricand. I only wish he would not call him by his family name. It was *another* story he told. These two drives had to come to terms one day, or I had to choose between them. There is a great deal of conflict and questioning about this in the first two diaries. Finally, I made no choice, I lived out both, and ultimately (thanks to psychoanalysis) they nourished each other and coexisted.

To maintain faith in my vision of people, to be able to say I do understand Moricand, see Moricand, I had to make sure that my vision was clear of all the elements which R. D. Laing enumerated as obstacles to clear insight. In other words, one has to know which areas in one's self are not to be trusted. Acknowledgment of irrational areas.

The diary served a useful purpose in exploring, defining, and then containing these unreliable areas in order to achieve some true objectivity. The idea of total objectivity is erroneous.

The diary, then, was where I checked my realities and illusions, made my experiments, noted progress or its opposite. It was the laboratory! I could venture into the novel with a sense of psychological authenticity and fictionalize only externals, situations, places. Composites, which can do much to enrich, correspond to condensation in the poem and to abstraction in painting.

The necessity for fiction, in my case, also helped to symbolize and add dimensions. The portrait of Henry Miller in the diary is a portrait of Henry Miller, but a composite may become something more than one artist, writer, painter, more than one person—a unit. A composite is no longer the original. It is something else.

How much is lost by retranslating such composites and redistributing each trait where it belongs is exemplified in the biography of Proust by George D. Painter. By replacing all the "types" into the classified box they sprang from, Painter destroyed a magical component.

Only an uncreative person would spend ten years on such reclassification of the alchemist's elements out of which Proust made a world of infinite depth. Why did we read it? Because the personality of Proust himself inspired us with love and a desire for intimacy. We recognized the greatness of the novels, but we were in love with Proust, as well as with his novels, but I do not think it is love of the novelist which drives critics to play sleuth to the personal lives and personal genesis of their art. It is merely the exercise of the art of sleuthing, and as this continues to be a favored sport among the academicians, it might be well for the novelists to make their own confessions for the sake of greater accuracy.

Thus fictionalizing had two motives: one, protection of the personalities; the other symbolization, the creation of the myth. We have no richer example of mythmaking, of enlarging, developing, magnifying, in our time than Marguerite Young's *Miss MacIntosh, My Darling.* Folk characters, ordinary and familiar, become expanded by her talent for poetry, metaphysics, surrealism, and achieve universality, become symphonic. It is the heights and the depths of her measurements, the infinity of her word arches and bridges which make of them containers of the dimensions not calculable to science but to the poet.

If at first diary and fiction did not coexist harmoniously, it was because I could not see their mutual influence upon each other (as we cannot see the influences which two countries at war, like America and Japan, exert upon each other). I was writing better in the notebooks because I was writing outside, in the formal work, and I was writing more authentically in the novels because I sustained the informal, improvised living contact with my relationships, cities, the present.

In the diary I documented a visit to the ragpickers. In the story I showed how it became more than that.

In the diary the preoccupation with the art of expression began more and more to work in harmony with the fiction. It is in the diary I observe that dreams in themselves are boring but dreams related to life are dynamic. It is in the diary that I am first baffled by the intricate way Moricand tells his stories (as I was later by the free-form way Varda told his stories) and make a conscious effort to find a simile for it, a sequence of images which would resemble his talk. In both cases they practiced in talk the free association of the surrealists. It was difficult to capture images and ideas which did not hang together in the usual way but were born spontaneously one from the other.

I used the symbol of the ferris wheel to indicate how Moricand kept people at a distance from the core of the wheel, took them for a voyage and deposited them as far from intimate knowledge of him as they were at the beginning. In the story I refined and expanded upon this.

This intricate interplay could have been disastrous to one form or another. They survived because the same duality existed between my formal art and my love of direct, human contact.

I was always writing fiction as well as the diary. At ten I wrote adventure stories. Completely invented. Unrelated to the reality of my life.

This might be studied as the way the artist finds to walk a tight-rope between the two sides of his duality (a duality experienced in some form or other by almost everyone.)

The difference between symbolic truth (expressing the inner life, the subconscious) and the here-and-now verifiable truth continued to trouble me. But they continued to run in parallel lines. The diary, creating a vaster tapestry, a web, exposing constantly the relation between the past and the present, weaving meticulously the invisible interaction, noting the repetition of themes, developed the sense of continuum of the personality instead of *conclusions or resolutions* which were invalidated by any recognition of the relativity of truth. This tale without beginning or end which encloses all things, and relates all things was a strong antidote to the incoherence and disintegration of modern man. I could follow the real patterns and gain insights obscured in most of the fragmentary or superficial novels with their artificial climaxes and resolutions.

An immediate, emotional reaction to experience reveals that the power to *re-create* lies in the sensibilities rather *than intellectual memory or observation.* This personal reaction I found to be the core of individuality, or originality and personality. A deep personal relation to all things reaches far beyond the personal into the general.

The diary also teaches that it is in the moments of emotional crisis that human beings reveal themselves most accurately. I learned to choose these heightened moments in fiction because they are the moments of revelation. It is the moment when the real self rises to the surface, shatters its false roles, erupts, and assumes reality and identity. The fiery moments of passionate experience are the moments of wholeness and totality of the personality. By this emphasis on the fiery moments, the explosions, I reached a greater reality of feeling and the senses. The preoccupation of the novelist: how to capture the living moments, was answered by the diary. You write while they are *alive.* You do not preserve them in alcohol until the moment you are ready to write about them. I discovered through the diary several basic elements essential to the vitality of writing. Of these the most important are naturalness and spontaneity. These, in turn, sprang from my freedom of selection. Because I was not forced to write about something, I could write about anything which interested me genuinely, what I felt most strongly about at the moment. This enthusiasm produced a vividness which often withered in the formal work. Improvisation, free association of images and ideas, obedience to mood, impulses, brought forth countless riches. The diary, dealing only with the immediate, the warm, the near, being written at white heat, developed a love of the living moment.

There are negative forces which oppress the novelist, which do not affect diary writing. One learns resistance and defiance of them. One of the negative forces is the taboo imposed on certain themes, another is the artificial chronological sequence, a third is the untrained reviewer. Such forces do not oppress research in science. In literature they are preestablished. I am not speaking of the fourth which is commercialism.

Free of all these oppressions, diary writing maintains impetus and the exhilaration born of freedom.

I was discovering the dual aspect of truth: one stemming from the immediate and personal, and one which could be achieved later with an *objectivity not born of detachment* but of the recognition of one's subjectivity and the sifting of it to keep the vital elements intact. The personal involvement is the origin of the life-giving emotion.

Another lesson I learned from diary writing was the actual continuity of the act of writing, not waiting for inspiration, favorable climate, astrologic constellations, the mood, but the discipline of sitting at the typewriter to write so many hours a day. Then when the magnificent moment comes, the ripened moment, the writing itself is nimble, already tuned, warmed.

Why did I not remain merely a diarist? Because there was a world beyond the personal which could be handled through the art form, through fiction.

Why did I not stay within *House of Incest* and write only prose poems, dreamed material, such as *Les chants de Maldoror?*

Because my drive was stated by Jung: *proceed from the dream outward.* I took this as relating dream and life, internal and external worlds, the secrets and persona of the self. Appearance and reality, illusion and reality.

Without the diary, the prose poem, and fiction I could not have achieved the *relation* between them. It is the *relation* which interested me, the *connection,* the *bridges,* the *interaction,* the *dynamics of relation* among human beings as well as among the ways of expression human beings use.

LIMITATIONS OF FICTION

The limitation of the novel sent me back to the diary. For example, when I finished the novel *Winter of Artifice,* I did not feel that I had finished with the relationship of father and daughter, because in the diary I had an example of a continuum which did not come to an end but which changed. Perhaps a novelist is through with a character when he is finished with his novel. I was not. The continuity of relationship and its alterations, as in Proust, made me feel there was always another truth around the corner, there would always be another revelation, another discovery about my father. The concept that this theme was completed would never even have occurred to me, because I could see its continuation in the endless diary. The diary made me aware of organic and perpetual motion, perpetual change in character. When you write a novel or a short story, you are arresting motion for a period of that story, a span of time. There is something static about that. Proust seemed to me the only writer who had flow and infinite continuum. Other novels did not revolve enough. Even in Durrell's *Alexandria Quartet* the promise that we would look at each character from a totally different point of view, and which was achieved externally by a kaleidoscopic view, a changing focus, nevertheless did not succeed in depth. When Durrell tried to give that by creating journals and notebooks, they did not seem to be revelations or to belong to the different characters but to be written by the novelist. The diary cannot be imitated. And so in many cases, reading novels, I had the feeling of still life rather than a perpetual motion.

I enjoyed writing the diary more than I did the novels because it was unplanned, spontaneous. And even if I did not plan the fiction, and tried to be free of a structure or design except the one which would emerge organically from a selection of material, I was not as free.

I may be free in my first version of a novel, but the editing is a discipline, it is an art. Even if it consists mostly of cutting, taking out what had not "happened" (for I did not believe very much in rewriting). For me the act of rewriting was tampering with the freshness and aliveness. I preferred to cut. There is an element of conscious editing after the spontaneous writing. There is an element of selection, passing judgment. It takes a great deal of the pleasure out of it. The pleasure seems to lie in freedom of choice.

Part of the pleasure comes from not being aware of having to construct something that won't fall apart. In the novels, I am aware of being a craftsman. Not in the diary.

The spontaneous writing in the novel has to achieve, ultimately, a form; its theme and mood create a form. You are not sure if the pieces will fit together, if it will form a design (I am talking about an organic form born of the contents, not an imposed plot or structure). There is a tension. Sabina caused me a great deal of trouble because I wanted to describe fragmentation without the disintegration which usually accompanies it. Each fragment had a life of its own. They had to be held together by some tension other than the unity we are familiar with. I was depicting fissions of the atoms of personality, but I did not want to fabricate a bomb. I was in danger of that every moment in the book. If she had no center to hold on to, she could be destroyed as Blanche DuBois was by those who did not understand her fantasy. In Marguerite Duras' *The Ravishing of Lol Stein,* in describing Lol's schizoid state, she caused it to happen to such a degree that Lol was no longer understandable. All communication was broken.

Madness to me, in a novel, was like murder. It was an easy and not quite honorable solution! For it was no solution. It was a curtain. A drama to me was the conflict between sanity and insanity, conflict and serenity, the individual and society, tensions, but the beauty consisted in the *endurance* of the effort to integrate, to reach another rung of awareness. I felt the novel had to take the adventurer all the way in his journey, to the top of the mountain, or the undiscovered river in the jungle, and somehow the substitution of an end cheated one of a complete spectacle, complete experience. I killed my heroes and heroines off when I was fourteen. I thought it was because I did not know then what else to do.

I do not know how the concept grew that objectivity could only come from one's absence, that erasing one's self, not being in the room, would give a description far closer to objective truth. For I believe the opposite. Deena Metzger felt she was seeing Henry Miller in *The Diary* through *my* eyes, but I maintain that the only way to become truly intimate with a person's character is to view him precisely in relation to others. A thousand objective facts would not reveal as much as watching Miller at a heightened moment of personal relationship, in relation to someone, at a moment of crisis. I remember a playwright's saying he would have preferred me absent in the *Mouse* story. That was an absurd statement, for the story was of the Mouse in relation to someone to whom she finally confessed, opened herself, who was caught in sharing her drama. Without me in the story, the Mouse would remain mute and secretive, undecipherable and unknown. There has to be a presence, a register, a recorder, an eye, an ear, a presence which arouses revelation. I do not believe in reportage. I believe in the capacity of certain people to obtain information, secrets, and confessions.

The active conflict between diary and novel gradually ceased. By 1966 it was the experience of the novelist which helped me to edit the diary. It was the fiction writer who knew when the tempo lagged, when details were trivial, when a description was a repetition. I changed nothing essential, I only cut the extraneous material, the overload.

The final lesson a writer learns is that everything can nourish the writer. The dictionary, a new word, a voyage, an encounter, a talk in the street, a book, a phrase heard. He is a computer set to receive and utilize all things. An exhibit of painting, a concert, a voice, a letter, a play, a landscape, a skyscape, a telephone conversation, a nap, a dream, a sleepless night, a storm, an animal's greeting, an aquarium, a photograph, a newspaper story.

I am a fervent believer in the enriching influence of one art upon another, a believer in cross-pollination between the arts, which is now expressing itself in the integration of the arts, in the use of lights, sounds, happenings, theater, sculpture on the stage (such as Noguchi's sets for Martha Graham).

Bergson said there are two kinds of clarities. "The perception of the artist, of the intuitive mind will always seem obscure to those who prefer clear Cartesian perception."

He spoke of "the fringe of nebulosity which surrounds the luminous core of intelligence, affirming by its presence that part of our existence so clearly perceived by our intelligence is not the essential or the most profound part. This penumbra is what must be penetrated if we would seek reality. An orientation inward implies an enlargement of our mental horizon." He denied that "reality could be attained by the intelligence, by conscious thought."

I think that natural truths will cease to be spat at us like insults, that aesthetics will once more be linked with ethics, and that people will become aware that in casting out aesthetics they also cast out a respect for human life, a respect for creation, a respect for spiritual values. Aesthetics was an expression of man's need to be in love with his world. The cult of ugliness is a regression. It destroys our appetite, our love for our world.

The cult of ugliness so apparent in our novels is another misinterpretation of reality. Because so many of our writers were born in ugly environments, in monstrous poverty and humiliation, they continue to assert that this is the natural environment, reality, and that beauty is artifice. Why should the natural state be ugliness? Natural to whom? We may be born in ugliness, but the natural consequences should be a thirst for its opposite. To mistake ugliness for reality is one of the frauds of the realistic school. A hunger for the unknown and an aspiration toward beauty were inseparable from civilization. In America the word art was distorted to mean artificial.

We are born with the power to alter what we are given at birth.

When the Japanese paint flowers or the sea on a kimono, they mean to establish a link with nature. But they select only what is beautiful in nature to maintain their love of life.

The creative personality never remains fixed on the first world it discovers. It never resigns itself to anything. That is the deepest meaning of rebellion, not the wearing of different clothes, haircuts or adopting other cultures.

Those who stay in their hostile and hated environment are the neurotics who are traumatized and paralyzed, or the criminal who takes his revenge for whatever befalls him or others. The criminal destroys the innocent instead of destroying the world he hates in himself. He destroys because he cannot create.

The cult of ugliness has destructive effects. Cocteau in *La belle et la bête* shows the beauty of laundry drying on a line, like flagpoles on a feast day in Venice. His camera made beauty. The true creative impulse chooses life rather than death, and love rather than hatred. What I find predominant in so many novels today is born of hatred. When the writer loses his power to alchemize (turning the laundry into an image of beauty), he is giving a catalogue of detritus. What follows is the loss of appetite for life, produced by such books as Burroughs' *Naked Lunch*.

The concept that symbolism vanished with romanticism is false. Psychology and the study of dreams established once and for all that it is a part of man's being. A scientist once asked me if we would ever dream in direct language. I can only say it has not happened yet. Even when the surface of our culture seems predominantly conscious, its actions continue to be symbolic.

An angry student who considered symbolism part of a decadent culture refused to shake hands with me because she disagreed with me, so I said to her: "In not wanting to shake hands with me you are still practicing symbolism, aren't you?"

The symbol is rich and effective precisely because it does not limit meaning and allows for its expansion according to varied lights played upon it. It teaches flexibility. Alfred North Whitehead called this "further qualifications which at present remain undiscovered." He gave a simple illustration: "Galileo said that the earth moves and that the sun is fixed; the Inquisition said that the earth is fixed and the sun moved; and Newtonian astronomers, adopting an absolute theory of space, said that both the sun and the earth moved. But now we say that anyone of these statements is equally true, provided that you have fixed your sense of rest and motion in the way required by the statement adopted. At that time the modern concepts of relative motion were in nobody's mind: so that the statements were made in ignorance of the qualifications required for their more perfect truth."

The sexual revolution, by itself and alone, is not going to put an end to loneliness or alienation. We must find intimacy and relationship by a greater understanding of the complexities of human beings.

We have other frigidities to overthrow. Frigidities toward the unfamiliar, the unknown, the unexplored, a prejudice toward experiment and research in the art of writing. To say that introspection is a trap in which only the self is caught is like saying that we must not practice deep-sea diving because we may get trapped in some cave, or get the bends. The self is merely the lens through which we see others and the world, and if this lens is not clear of distortions, we cannot perceive others. Our novels are full of deaf-mutes.

The danger of photographic realism is that it discounts all possibility of change, of transformations, and therefore does not show the way out of situations which trap human beings. The naturalists never teach one the possibility of overcoming the life situation given us. The expectation of a change from the outside becomes as dangerous as the old religious teachings of resignation to the will of God. It creates a passive man. The reporter who reports a story literally, the documentary which merely informs us of an existing situation are far from the poet-novelist concerned with creating new patterns, discarding the old, finding life inacceptable and seeking to transform it, to keep our dynamism alive by breaking down uniformity, regimentation. The poet reveals the differences which can rescue man from automatism.

The active, fecundating role of the novelist has been forgotten. We have the supine tape-recorder novelist who registers everything and illumines nothing. Passivity and inertia are the opposite of creation. Poetry is the alchemy which teaches us to convert ordinary materials into gold. Poetry, which is our relation to the senses, enables us to retain a living relationship to all things. It is the quickest means of transportation to reach dimensions above or beyond the traps set by the so-called realists. It is a way to learn levitation and travel in liberated continents, to travel by moonlight as well as sunlight.

from *The Diary of Anaïs Nin*

April 1936

A trip to Morocco. A short but vivid one. I fell in love with Fez. Peace. Dignity. Humility. I have just left the balcony where I stood listening to the evening prayer rising over the white city. A religious emotion roused by the Arabs' lives, by the simplicity of it, the fundamental beauty. Stepping into the labyrinth of their streets, streets like intestines, two yards wide, into the abyss of their dark eyes, into peace. The rhythm affects one first of all. The slowness. Many people on the streets. You touch elbows. They breathe into your face, but with a silence, a gravity, dreaminess. Only the children cry and laugh and run. The Arabs are silent. The little square room open on the street in which they sit on the ground, on the mud, with their merchandise around them. They are weaving, they are sewing, baking bread, chiseling jewels, repairing knives, making guns for the Berbers in the mountains. They are dying wool in vast cauldrons, big cauldrons full of dye in which they dip their bunches of silk and wool. Their hands are emerald green, violet, Orient blue. They are making sienna earth pottery, weaving rugs, shaving, shampooing and writing legal documents right there, under your eyes. One Arab is asleep over his bag of saffron. Another is praying with his beads while selling herbs. Further, a big tintamarre, the street of copperwork. Little boys are beating copper trays with small hammers, beating a design into them, beating copper lamps, Aladdin's lamps. Little boys and old men do the work. They hold the tray between their legs. The younger men walk down the street in their burnouses, going I know not where, some so beautiful one thinks they are women. The women are veiled. They are going to the mosque, probably. At a certain hour all selling, all work ceases and they all go to the mosque. But first of all they wash their faces, their feet, their sore eyes, their leprous noses, their pockmarked skins at the fountain. They shed their sandals. Some of the old men and old women never leave the mosque. They squat there forever until death overtakes them. Women have their own entrance. They kiss the wall of the mosque as they pass. To make way for a donkey loaded with kindling wood, I step into a dark doorway. A choking stench overwhelms me. This stench is everywhere. It takes a day to get used to it. It makes you feel nauseated at first. It is the smell of excrement, saffron, leather being cured, sandalwood, olive oil being used for frying, nut oil on the bodies, incense, muskrat, so strong that at first you cannot swallow food. There is mud on the white burnous, on the Arab legs. Children's heads shaved, with one tuft of hair left. The women with faces uncovered and tattooed are the primitive Berbers from the mountains, wives of warriors, not civilized. I saw the wives of one Arab, five of them sitting on a divan, like mountains of flesh, enormous, with several chins and several stomachs, and diamonds set in their foreheads.

The streets and houses are inextricably woven, intricately interwoven, by bridges from one house to another, passageways covered with lattice, creating shadows on the ground. They seem to be crossing within a house, you never know when you are out in a street or in a patio, or a passageway, as half of the houses are open on the street, you get lost immediately. Mosques run into a merchant's home, shops into mosques, now you are under a trellised roof covered with rose vines, now walking in utter darkness through a tunnel, behind a donkey raw and bleeding from being beaten, and now you are on a bridge built by the Portuguese. Now admire lacy trelliswork done by the Andalusians, and now look at the square next to the mosque where the poor are allowed to sleep on mats.

Everywhere the Arab squats and waits. Anywhere. An old Arab is teaching a young one a religious chant. Another is defecating carefully, conscientiously. Another is begging, showing all his open sores, standing near the baker baking bread in ovens built in the earth.

The atmosphere is so clear, so white and blue, you feel you can see the whole world as clearly as you see Fez. The birds do not chatter as they do in Paris, they chant, trill with operatic and tropical fervor. The poor are dressed in sackcloths, the semi-poor in sheets and bathtowels, the well-to-do women in silks and muslins. The Jews wear a black burnous. In the streets and in the houses of the poor the floor is of stamped earth. Houses are built of sienna-red earth, sometimes whitewashed. The olive oil is pressed out in the street too, under large wooden wheels.

I had letters of introduction. First I visited Si Boubekertazi. He sat in his patio, on pillows. A beautiful Negro woman, a concubine, brought a copper tray full of delicacies. And tea served in tiny cups without handles.

At the house of Driss Mokri Montasseb I was allowed to visit the harem. Seven wives of various ages, but all of them fat, sat around a low table eating candy and dates. We discussed nail polish. They wanted some of mine, which was pearly.They told me how they made up their eyes. They bought kohl dust at the market, filled their eyes with it. The eyes smart and cry, and so the black kohl marks the edges and gives that heavily accented effect.

Pasha El Glaoui de Marrakesh offered me a military escort to visit the city. He said it was absolutely necessary. He signaled to a soldier standing at his door, who never left me from then on except when I went to my hotel room to sleep.

De Sidi Hassan Benanai received me under the fine spun-gold colonnades. But he had just begun a forty-day fast and prayer, so he sat in silence, counting his beads, and tea was served in silence, and he continued to pray, occasionally smiling at me, and bowing his head, until I left.

From outside, the houses are uniformly plain, with high walls covered with flowers. One cannot tell when one is entering a luxurious abode. The door may be of beautiful ironwork. There may be two, or four, or six guards at the door. But inside, the walls are all mosaics, or painted, and the stucco worked like lace, the ceilings painted in gold. The pillows are of silk. The Negro women are simply dressed but always beautiful. One does not see the children or the wives.

The white burnous is called a *jelabba.*

Mystery and labyrinth. Complex streets. Anonymous walls. Secret luxury. Secrecy of these houses without windows on the streets. The windows and door open on the patio. The patio has a fountain and lovely plants. There is a labyrinth design in the arrangement of the gardens. Bushes are placed to form a puzzle so you might get lost. They love the feeling of being lost. It has been interpreted as a desire to reproduce the infinite.

Fez. One always, sooner or later, comes upon a city which is an image of one's inner cities. Fez is an image of my inner self. This may explain my fascination for it. Wearing a veil, full and inexhaustible, labyrinthian, so rich and variable I myself get lost. Passion for mystery, the unknown, and for the infinite, the uncharted.

With my guide I visited the *Quartier Réservé.* It lay within medieval walls, guarded at each gate by a French soldier. The houses were full of prostitutes. Only the poor Arabs go there because the others have enough wives to satisfy their need of variety. Dark, dramatic, tortuous streets. Bare cellars which have become cafés. Arabs slinking in and out. Negroes. Beggars. Arab music heard now and then. The walls, ceilings covered with shabby rugs and potteries. *Thé à la menthe* served, or beer. No wine drinking but much drug traffic. Bare, cellarlike rooms. Doors covered by muslin curtains, or beaded curtains. Front room is the bar or café where the men sit and the musicians play. Back room is for the prostitutes. The muslin curtain was parted and I found myself before Fatima, the queen of the prostitutes.

Fatima had a beautiful face, straight patrician nose, enormous black velvet eyes, tawney smooth skin, full but firm, and the usual Arabian attributes of several folds of stomach, several chins. She could only move with difficulty on her enormous legs. She was both queenly and magnificent, opulent, and voluptuous. She was dressed in a wedding costume, a pink chiffon dress embroidered with gold sequins laid over several layers of other chiffon petticoats. Heavy gold belt, bracelets, rings, a gold band across her forehead, enormous dangling gold earrings. Over her glistening black hair she wore a colored silk turban placed on the back of her head exposing the black curls. She had four gold teeth, considered beautiful by Arab women. The coal-black rim around her eyes exaggerated their size, as in Egyptian paintings.

She sat among pillows in a room shaped like many bedrooms in Fez, long and narrow. At each end of the room she had a brass bed, a sign of luxury and success. They are not used as beds, they are only a symbol of wealth. In between the two brass beds lay all the pillows, rugs, and low divans. (In rich homes the floors are tiled but the brass beds are displayed there too.) Fatima not only collected brass beds but also cuckoo clocks from Switzerland. One wall was covered with them, each one telling a different time. The other walls were covered with flowered cretonne. The atmosphere was heavy with perfume, enclosed and voluptuous, the womb itself. A young girl came in with an atomizer and lifting up my skirt gently atomized my underclothes with rose water. She came once more to throw rose petals around my feet. Then she came carrying a tray with glass tea containers, sheathed in copper holders with handles. We sat cross-legged on vast pillow, Fatima in the center. She never made a vulgar gesture. Two blind, crippled musicians were invited in and played monotonously, but with such a beat that my excitement grew as if I had taken wine. Fatima began to prepare tea on the tray. Then she passed around a bottle of rose water and we perfumed our hands. Then she lit a sandalwood brazier and placed it at my feet. I was duly and thoroughly perfumed and the air grew heavier and richer. The Arab soldier lay back on the pillows. The handsome bodyguard in his white burnous, white turban and blue military costume conversed with Fatima, who could not speak French. He translated my compliments on her beauty. She asked him to translate a question about my nail polish. I promised to send her some. While we sat there dreaming between each phrase, there was a fight outside. A young Arab burst in, his face bleeding: "Aii, Aii, Aiii," he cried. Fatima sent her maid to see what could be done for the young Arab. She never lost her composure. The musicians played louder and faster so I would not notice the commotion and my pleasure would not be spoiled. I spent two hours with Fatima, as it is impolite to hurry here. It is a mortal insult to leave too soon or to seem hurried. It offends them deeply. Relationship does not depend so much on conversation or exchange as in the creation of a propitious, dreamy, meditative, contemplative atmosphere, a mood. Finally, when I was ready to leave, my escort made a parting speech.

It was after midnight. The city, so crowded during the day that I could hardly move in it, was silent and empty. The night watchman sleeps on the doorsteps. There are gates between different quarters. Six gates had to be opened for us with enormous keys. You are not allowed to circulate at night except by special permission and with a pass which the soldier showed to each watchman.

The frogs were croaking in the garden pools behind the walls, the crickets were announcing tomorrow's heat. The smell of roses won the battle of smells. A window was suddenly opened above me, an old woman stuck her head out and threw out a big rat she had just caught, with many curses. It fell at my feet.

Fez is a drug. It enmeshes you. The life of the senses, of poetry (even the poor Arabs who visit a prostitute will find a woman dressed in a wedding dress like a virgin), of illusion and dream. It made me passionate, just to sit there on pillows, with music, the birds, the fountains, the infinite beauty of the mosaic designs, the teakettle singing, the many copper trays shining, the twelve bottles of rose perfume and the sandalwood smoking in the brazier, and the cockoo clocks chiming in disunion, as they pleased.

The layers of the city of Fez are like the layers and secrecies of the inner life. One needs a guide.

I loved the racial nobility of the Arabs, the pride, the love of sweets instead of alcohol, the gentleness, the peace, the hospitality, the reserve, pride, love of turquoise and coral colors, dignity of bearing, their silences. I love the way the men embrace in the street, proudly and nobly. I love the expression in their eyes, brooding, or fiery, but deep.

The river under the bridge was foul. Men held hands while talking on the street. A dead Arab was carried on a stretcher, covered with narrow white bandages like an Egyptian mummy. Over his feet they had thrown a red rug. Silence and quietism. Contemplation and chanting. Music. Tea served on copper trays with a samovar kettle.

Glasses have colored tops. On another tray a big silver box with big rough pieces of rock sugar. Trays with perfume bottles. Trays with almond cakes covered by a silk handkerchief or copper painted lids.

I met the Arab women walking to their baths. They went there always in groups, and carrying a change of clothes in a basket over their heads. They walked veiled and laughing, showing only their eyes and the hennaed tips of their hands holding their veils. Their full white skirts and heavily embroidered belts made them heavy and full-looking, like the pillows they liked to sit on. It was heavy flesh moving in white robes, nourished on sweets and inertia, on passive watches behind grilled windows. This was one of their few moments of liberty, one of the few times they appeared in the street. They walked in groups with their servants, children, and bundles of fresh clothes, laughing and talking, and dragging their feet in embroidered mules.

I followed them. When they entered at the mosaic-covered building near the mosque, I entered with them. The first room was very large and square, all of stone, with stone benches, and rugs on the floor. Here the women laid down their bundles and began undressing. This was a long ceremony, for they wore so many skirts, and several blouses, and belts which looked like bandages, so much white muslin, linen, cotton to unroll, unfold, and fold again on the bench. Then there were bracelets to take off, earrings, anklets, and then the long black hair to unwind from the ribbons tressed into the hair. So much white cotton fallen on the floor, a field of white petals, leaves, lace, shed by the full-fleshed women, and as I looked at them I felt they could never be really naked, that all this they wore must cling to them forever, grow with their bodies. I was already undressed and waiting, standing, as I would not sit naked on the stone bench. They were waiting for the children to be undressed by the African maids, waiting for the maids to get undressed.

An old woman was waiting for us, completely shriveled old woman with only one eye. Her breasts were two long empty gourds hanging almost to the middle of her stomach. She wore a sackcloth around her waist. She gave me a little approving tap on the shoulder and smiled. She pointed to my finger nails and talked but I could not understand, and I smiled.

She opened the door to the steam room, another very large square room all of grey stone. But here there were no benches. All the women were sitting on the floor. The old woman filled pails of water from one of the fountains and occasionally poured one over their heads, after they had finished soaping themselves. The steam filled the room. The women sat on the floor, took their children between their knees and scrubbed them. Then the old woman threw a pail of water over them. This water flowed all around us, and it was dirty. We sat in rivulets of soapy, dirty water. The women did not hurry. They used the soap, then a piece of pumice stone, and then they began to use depilatories with great care and concentration. All of them were enormous. The flesh billowed, curved, folded in tremendous heavy waves. They seemed to be sitting on pillows of flesh of all colors, from the pale Northern Arab skin to the African. I was amazed that they could lift such heavy arms to comb their long hair. I had come to look at them, because the beauty of their faces was legendary, and proved not at all exaggerated. They had absolutely beautiful faces, enormous, jeweled eyes, straight noble noses with wide spaces between the eyes, full and voluptuous mouths, flawless skins, and always a royal bearing. The faces had a quality of statuary rather than painting, because the lines were so pure and clear. I sat in admiration of their faces, and then I noticed that they looked at me. They sat in groups, looking at me and smiling. They mimicked that I should wash my hair and face. I could not explain that I was hurrying through the ritual because I did not like sitting in the darkening waters. They offered me the pumice stone after using it thoroughly all over their ponderous bodies. I tried it but it scratched my face. The Arab women's skin was tougher. The women chatted in circles while washing themselves and their children. I could not bring myself to wash my face with the soap they all used for their feet and armpits. They laughed at what they must have thought was a European woman who did not know the rules of cleanliness.

They wanted me also to pull out superfluous eyebrows, hair under the arms, and to shave my pubic hair. I finally slipped away to the next room where pails of cooler water were thrown over me.

I wanted to see the Arab women clothed again, concealed in

yards of white cotton. Such beautiful heads had risen out of these mountains of flesh, heads of incredible perfection, dazzling eyes heavily fringed, sensual features. Sometimes moss-green eyes in dark sienna skins, sometimes coal-black eyes in pale moonlit skins, and always the long heavy black hair, the undulating tresses. But these heads rose from formless masses of flesh, heaving like plants in the sea, swelling, swaying, falling, the breasts like sea anemones, floating, the stomachs of perpetually pregnant women, the legs like pillows, the backs like cushions, the hips with furrows like a mattress.

They were all watching me, with friendly nodding of their heads, commenting on my figure. By counting on their fingers they asked was I adolescent? I had no fat on me. I must be a girl. They came around me and we compared skin colors. They seemed amazed by my waist. They could enclose it in their two hands. They wanted to wash my hair. They soaped my face with tenderness. They touched me and talked with volubility. The old woman came with two pails and threw them over me. I was ready to leave, but the Arab women transmitted messages of all kinds with their eyes, smiles, talk. The old woman led me to the third room, which was cooler, and threw cold water over me, and then led me back to the dressing room.

On the way back, landing at Cádiz, I saw the same meager palm trees I had carefully observed when I was eleven years old, on my way to America. I saw the cathedral I had described minutely in my child-diary. I saw the city in which women did not go out very much, the city, I said, where I would never live because I liked independence.

When I landed in Cádiz I found the palm trees, the cathedral, but not the child I was. The last vestiges of my past were lost in the ancient city of Fez, which was built so much like my own life, with its tortuous streets, its silences, secrecies, its labyrinths and its covered faces. In the city of Fez I became aware that the little demon which had devoured me for twenty years, the little demon of depression which I had fought for twenty years, had ceased eating me. I was at peace, walking through the streets of Fez, absorbed in a world outside of myself, a past which was not my past, by sickness one could touch and name, leprosy and syphilis.

I walked with the Arabs, sang and prayed with them to a god who ordained acceptance. With the Arabs I crouched in stillness. Streets without issues, such as the streets of my desires. Forget the issue and lie under the mud-colored walls, listen to the copper being beaten, watch the dyers dipping their silks in orange buckets. Through the streets of my labyrinth, I walked in peace at last, with an acceptance of myself, of my strength, of my weakness. The blunders I made lay like garbage in the doorsteps and nourished the flies. The places I did not reach were forgotten because the Arab on his donkey, or on his mule, or on his naked feet, walked forever between the walls of Fez. The failures were the inscriptions on the walls half effaced, and those books eaten by the mice, the childhood was rotting away in the museums, the crazy men were tied in chains and I walked free because I let the ashes fall, the old flesh die, I let death efface, I let the inscriptions crumble, I let the cypresses watch the tombs. I did not fight for completeness, against the fragments devoured by the past or today's detritus under my feet. What the river did not carry away nourished the flies. I could go with the Arabs to the cemetery with colored rugs and bird cages for a little feast of talk, so little did death matter, or disease, or tomorrow. Night watchman sleeping on the stone steps, or mud, in soiled burnous, I too can sleep anywhere. There were in Fez, as in my life, streets which led nowhere, impasses which remained a mystery. There must also be walls. The tips of minarets can only rise as high because of the walls.

It was in Cádiz that I lay down in a hotel room and fell into a dolorous, obsessional reverie, a continuous secret melody of jealousy, fear, doubt, and it was in Cádiz that I stood up and broke the evil curse, as if by a magical act of will, I broke the net, the evil curse of obsession. I learned how to break it. It was symbolized by my going into the street. From that day on, suffering became intermittent, subject to interruptions, distractions, not a perpetual condition. I was able to distract myself. I could live for hours without the malady of doubt. There were silences in my head, periods of peace and enjoyment. I could abandon myself completely to the pleasure of multiple relationships, to the beauty of the day, to the joys of the day. It was as if the cancer in me had ceased gnawing me. The cancer of introspection.

It seemed to have happened suddenly, like a miracle, but it was the result of years of struggle, of analysis, of passionate living. Introspection is a devouring monster. You have to feed it with much material, much experience, many people, many places, many loves, many creations, and then it ceases feeding on you.

From that moment on, what I experienced were emotional dramas which passed like storms, and left peace behind them.